T0322708

THIS IS WHAT
HELL LOOKS
LIKE

THIS IS WHAT HELL LOOKS LIKE

LIFE AS A BOMB DISPOSAL SPECIALIST
DURING THE VIETNAM WAR

STUART ALLAN STEINBERG

FONTHILL

Fonthill Media Language Policy

Fonthill Media publishes in the international English language market. One language edition is published worldwide. As there are minor differences in spelling and presentation, especially with regard to American English and British English, a policy is necessary to define which form of English to use. The Fonthill Policy is to use the form of English native to the author. Stuart Allan Steinberg was born and educated in the United States; therefore, American English has been adopted in this publication.

Fonthill Media Limited
Fonthill Media LLC
www.fonthillmedia.com
office@fonthillmedia.com

First published in the United Kingdom and the United States of America 2018

British Library Cataloguing in Publication Data:
A catalogue record for this book is available from the British Library

Copyright © Stuart Allan Steinberg 2018

ISBN 978-1-62545-065-4

Typeset in 10.5pt on 13pt MinionPro
Printed and bound in England

Acknowledgments

I could not have written this book without the assistance, kindness, and encouragement of my wife, Mona, who told me not to give up and to tell my story.

My son, Jonas, listened as I talked about my experiences as an Explosive Ordnance Disposal (EOD) specialist; he asked the right questions, said the right things. I think he understands now what this means to me. I apologize to him and his mom, Jane, for my excesses in earlier times.

My good friend and fellow combat veteran, Greg Walker—author and twenty-six-year Green Beret and special operations expert—gave sage advice. His encouragement gave me the strength to finish this, and his friendship led me back to Vietnam in early 2012.

It was Greg, after reading one particular chapter, who said the original title was too general and suggested *This Is What Hells Looks Like*, a phrase in the book. I knew he was right when deleting the original title page; I typed those words in their place and looked at them for the first time. His friendship and dedication to his country and family have been inspiring.

Then there are the Vietnam veterans whom I did not know before writing this. I met them on the internet, researching aspects of my eighteen months in Vietnam. Google led me to their websites. We had a shared experience in that each of us was profoundly affected by Vietnam or other places as traumatic.

These men had served with units that saw heavy, sustained combat, who read parts of the book and encouraged me to keep writing.

Bob Griffin's site, www.326ScreamingEagles.com, provided extensive information about the 101st Airborne Division (Airmobile) and the area of operations where one of my EOD teams supported them. This includes the infamous A Shau Valley, and shitholes like Fire Support Base Davis, and Fire Support Base Rifle. When I needed information about a particular event at Davis, Bob sent an email to more than 1,500 other former members of the 101st and other units asking if anyone could help.

Ray Smith, who served with the 1st Battalion, 69th Armor, runs the web site, "Ray's Map Room," located at www.rjsmith.com. He helped locate grid coordinates in my unit's records, recovered from the National Archives and Records Administration. When I wanted to learn how to read Vietnam military maps, something I used to know, he led me through the process. Ray's site helped more than any other in recalling places, and his pop-up windows reminded me of things long forgotten. I would recommend this site to any Vietnam veteran looking to reconstruct their life and experiences during the War.

Ray Blackman of Delta Company ("Delta Raiders"), 2nd Battalion, 501st Parachute Infantry Regiment, 101st Airborne Division, provided pictures of several of the LZs we flew in and out of in Northern "I" Corps, as well as a great picture showing the hugeness of the Phu Bai Combat Base. His site is www.blackied2501.com/.

Randy White, whose site is www.lcompanyranger.com, helped with locations in Northern "I" Corps, especially those in and around the A Shau Valley. His unit, "L" Company, 75th Infantry Regiment (Ranger), 101st Airborne Division (Airmobile), was the 101st's long-range recon unit. We did a number of jobs for them, mostly identifying and destroying dud bombs dropped during air strikes. They performed one of the most dangerous jobs in the War; their heroic actions are described in Gary Linderer's great book, *Black Berets and Painted Faces*.

I met Ken Knowlton researching the Dugway Proving Grounds chapter when I stumbled across his website, www.dugway.net. The information there tells a story most Americans are ignorant of and have little desire to learn. I say this because there has been no outcry about what goes on there still, and what occurred there on March 13, 1968. Only a handful of Dugway "survivors," like Ken and me, have tried to explain what a deadly place it is. The U.S. government continues to deny what some of us know from firsthand experience.

Ed Vogels and Danny Malone were with the 101st Airborne Division at a place called Fire Support Base Rifle. What happened at Rifle on February 11,

1970, altered my life, and I describe it in detail. Ed helped with pictures. Both he and Danny encouraged me to write what happened there. I have never met either in person, but I know them. We were there and we made it back alive.

My good friends from other EOD teams in Vietnam offered great support and encouragement to tell the story of Explosive Ordnance Disposal during the War. Joe Jimenez, whom I replaced at Phu Bai in the 287th Ordnance Detachment (Explosive Ordnance Disposal) near the DMZ when he went to the 170th in Saigon, offered advice, stories, and pictures of the Phu Bai team.

"Big John" Claffy, who served with the EOD Section at the 3rd Ordnance Battalion in Long Bình, helped me and my teammates in Qui Nhon during the cleanup after the ammo dump explosions there in February and March 1969. John was wounded several weeks before I was. He read parts of the book and told me to keep writing. I am sad to report that John took his own life in 2015 due to the many demons he fought after Vietnam. Doug Rhodes and Roger McCormack, with whom I served in Qui Nhon while with the EOD Section of the 184th Ordnance Battalion, helped me with the chapters from my time in Qui Nhon and encouraged me to keep at it. They both provided photos.

Rod Wilkinson came to the 287th near the end of my time in Vietnam, but recognized that, though he was twenty years older and had been in EOD for many years, after eighteen months in country, I was the man the first time he went to the bush. He never pulled rank, and I always respected him for that.

When we reconnected, along with eight other team members in 2004, he encouraged me to stay actively involved with veterans, helping those less fortunate get the benefits they had earned. I am grateful for that. He told my wife I had taken "good care" of him during his first weeks in country. That meant as much as anything anyone has ever said regarding my service in Vietnam. Rod passed away in November 2009, largely due to complications caused by herbicide exposure in Vietnam. I miss him every day.

Then, there is one of my best friends from the War, Paul J. Duffey, with whom I spent only 119 days at the Phu Bai team, but who shared my worst experience in eighteen months in Vietnam. We became brothers through that and other near-death situations and I have loved him ever since. When we saw each other at the 2004 reunion for the first time since 1988, it was like we had just been together the day before. At Fire Support Base Rifle, we saw it raining dead—images that have haunted us both since February 11, 1970.

Paul survived the siege at Fire Support Base Ripcord, along with Chuck Watson, Bobby Lynch, Rod Wilkinson, and our CO, Andy Breland, for which

I am forever grateful. I thank Paul for being my friend all these years. Chuck Watson, with whom I reestablished contact in 2004, has become as close as Paul. I still consider him my little brother, much as when he arrived in Vietnam, nineteen and skinny as a rail. I have similar feelings for the other men in the 287th—Del Randles, our first sergeant, Tom Miller, Dave Becker, Jim Qualls, Rick Lanham, Don Urquhart, and Dan Reese. Even men who served before and after me, like Mike Tavano, the commanding officer who brought the team to Vietnam, and Ron Knight, who was the CO after Andy Breland, are important to me. I am sad to report that Andy Breland passed away in 2016.

On February 26, 2007, I entered a substance abuse rehabilitation and recovery program at a Washington VA Medical Center. I withdrew from prescribed morphine on January 8, after being on prescription narcotics for many years. I used painkillers for the damage to my right knee, caused by an exploding mortar round, and my left knee, caused by another Vietnam incident. Many people helped while I was in rehab, having decided I could not spend the rest of my life as an addict—not just the staff, but also the veterans in this program.

Dave Silva was my primary addictions counselor; his kindness and concern were inspiring. He showed me that I could get through this, and finally put— as I will say many times—that fucking war behind me. He, too, is a PTSD survivor, so he knew what I was talking about and how hard it has been to get beyond all this.

Fred Widman, another addictions counselor, was a total maniac—one of the best motivational speakers I have ever heard—and he taught me things that I knew on some level, but had not been able to express or understand. Both Dave and Fred taught me that I did not have to save everybody, and that it was time to save myself. That helped me understand what Ron Fisher, my first social worker at the VA Clinic in Bend, Oregon, meant when I went for help in August 2002. He asked, "When the fuck are you going to get off mission?" Dr. Ron Kokes, clinical psychologist, and Drs. Bud Carnahan, Jim Tiffany, and Don Anderson, psychiatrists, are, or were, all with the VA Community Based Outpatient Clinic in Bend, Oregon, near my home at Crooked River Ranch. All four helped me understand that my life is worth living, that there are many things to feel good about, despite the sometimes near terminal nature of PTSD.

Sad to say, Ron Kokes passed away from pancreatic cancer. He helped many of my friends, and even though he could have traveled the world, or done something less stressful, he continued to treat combat veterans suffering from PTSD almost until the end.

Recent inspiration comes from the reunion of almost eighty EOD men who served in Vietnam. This happened in August 2007, and came about because of my tracking down most of the members of the team that Paul Duffey, Chuck Watson, Tom Miller, Rick Lanham, Andy Breland, Dave Becker, Rod Wilkinson, and I were on in 1969–70. That team got together in 2004, along with team members from other years, and the reunion came about through that meeting, and a second one in October 2004, at Chuck Watson's house in Valparaiso, Indiana.

Over four days in St. Louis in August 2007, those of us who knew each other found that we were as close as ever. Those who we had not met during our tours, became as close as if we had, and as if we had served on the same team. We organized a national association—Vietnam EOD Veterans Association (VEVA)—and met again in Huntsville, Alabama in October 2008, at the National EOD Association (NATEODA) convention. We are now a subgroup in the national organization, and in 2011, I was elected the commander of the Vietnam group, a wonderful and humbling expression of recognition by my peers. I now serve on the NATEODA board as the Veterans Benefits Coordinator.

Jim Morris is a medically retired Green Beret who served for two years in Vietnam. He has four Purple Hearts and four Bronze Stars. He is the author of the critically acclaimed *War Story*. Jim helped edit my book and gave positive support when I needed it most.

Then there is Fred Reed, a Marine Vietnam vet who was almost completely blinded by glass when a bullet shattered the windshield of his AMTRAC. He is medically retired. We have become great friends since he got in touch with me several years ago, to help him with his VA claims. He lives in Mexico, like a number of Vietnam vets, and was up here in Oregon attending the NATEODA convention in September 2011. He is a great writer, and his web site is just funnier than shit. He also assisted me with editing.

Finally, in terms of editing, my sister, Rebecca, did a complete review after I had self- published and helped get this thing into its final format. I did not realize just how little I actually knew about punctuation and syntax until I got back her copy with the little red markings.

On February 14, 2012, I returned from eighteen days in Vietnam. My friend, Greg Walker, made that happen for me. He was a counselor with the Special Operations Command Wounded Warrior Program and two of his mentors,

Ed Tick and Kate Dahlstadt, run a program called, "Soldier's Heart." Among other things, they take guided healing journeys to Vietnam and made it possible, especially financially, for me to go. Ed has written a wonderful book called *War and the Soul*, and every combat veteran and their significant others should read it, as should their therapists if the veterans are in treatment.

I probably failed to mention others, and I apologize to them. Thanks to the rest of you, who helped shape my life and aided me in finishing this story.

Contents

Prologue

One of the things I write about in several places is how much the men I served with in Vietnam mean to me. I have tried to describe my feelings for these wonderful men and I thought I had done a pretty good job of it. Then, during the last week of April 2013, my friend Ron Morgan, a fellow Vietnam veteran and retired First Sergeant who served his country for 30 years, put the following piece in a veterans' newsletter he publishes for Disabled American Veterans and Vietnam Veterans of America, both organizations of which I am proud to be a member.

"These Good Men"

I now know why men who have been to war yearn to reunite.
Not to tell stories or look at old pictures. Not to laugh
or weep. Comrades gather because they long to be with the
men who once acted their best, men who suffered and
sacrificed, who were stripped raw, right down to their humanity.

I did not pick these men. They were delivered by fate and
the U.S. Marine Corps. But I know them in a way I know no
other men. I have never given anyone such trust. They were
willing to guard something more precious than my life.
They would have carried my reputation, the memory of me.

It was part of the bargain we all made, the reason we were
so willing to die for one another.

I cannot say where we are headed. Ours are not perfect
friendships; those are the province of legend and myth.
A few of my comrades drift far from me now, sending back
only occasional word. I know that one day even these
could fall to silence. Some of the men will stay close,
a couple, perhaps, always at hand.

As long as I have memory, I will think of them all,
every day. I am sure that when I leave this world, my
last thought will be of my family and my comrades.
....such good men.

Michael Norman, USMC (Crown, 1990)

That really says it all. I love you guys.

Introduction

I am writing this for all those men and women who served in Vietnam, and who still wonder what it meant—not the politics, but the personal meaning it has for each of us. Why did it affect the entirety of our lives, even while we were getting educated and succeeding professionally? I am not alone in these feelings; most of my male friends are Vietnam veterans, and we still talk about it.

We in the West have known, at least since the Civil War (when it was called "Soldier's Heart") that combat trauma has a measurable, significant effect on many soldiers, sometimes for many years after the events occurred. The Civil War surgeon who first wrote about these problems thought that the cause of the anxiety symptoms he observed was some kind of heart problem. I suppose, in a sad way, you could say that was true.

For many—myself included—young as we were, our experiences broke our hearts in some psychic way. Mending that break has been difficult. I have recently learned that what happened to us in Vietnam that was traumatic did not injure our brains and is not a problem that all of the psychotherapy in the world is ever going to cure. What happened to us, there, the things too horrible to describe sometimes, wounded our souls and our spirits. Psychotropic drugs will not help with those things.

Some historians believe that Herodotus first described symptoms of combat trauma in 440 BC in his account of the Battle of Marathon, when he wrote about a soldier who went blind after seeing his fellow soldier brutally killed beside him. Other early writers, like Hippocrates in the Peloponnesian

Wars, and the poet Lucretius described combat trauma. Lucretius, who lived from 99–55 BC, wrote about sleep disturbances in combat veterans.

Sometimes, PTSD does not appear until twenty—even thirty or more—years after the fact. I am now assisting veterans with combat experiences that happened more than forty years ago, with claims for veterans benefits. I have also done PTSD claims for WWII and Korean War veterans. It does not affect all of us, but it does affect a significant number who experienced multiple combat traumas. I am one of them. I do not think it makes me, or any of us, less of a person. Those who choose to deal with it are doing something positive and life affirming.

Some, myself included, have been in therapy, used psychotropic drugs, and tried any number of resources to help us get on with our lives. We find these things will only get us so far, and many of us find other ways to relieve the stress. Some never do. For me, writing this book has been good therapy. It has really helped in getting many of these issues out of my head. My trip back to Vietnam in January 2012 helped get a lot more of it out, and I feel better than I have since before "The War."

You may have noted that I am calling it, "The War," and not "The Vietnam War." Here is why: I learned on my trip back to Vietnam that, as you would expect if you thought about it, the Vietnamese call it, "The American War." Before that it was, "The French War" and before that the "Japanese War," and so on. So, now, for me, it is just, "The War."

What I write, here, is not an indictment of the War, or war itself, nor is it meant to be a discourse on the effects of combat trauma, other than my own. It is simply my memory of certain events.

From discussions with former teammates, I know that many have struggled with the same issues I have, despite the fact that each of us has been professionally successful, and appear, outwardly at least, to be living a "normal" life.

We had a job that exposed us to violence and extreme danger on a daily basis. Although most of what we did was not extraordinarily life-threatening, each of us was involved in events that made survival for the next few minutes, sometimes seconds—even the blink of an eye—questionable.

You should know going in that I do not always say things in a polite manner. I drop the "F-Bomb" and the "S-Bomb," so if you find that offensive, you should probably read something else. Some situations cannot be described in polite terms. These events were not pleasant or right when they occurred, and I have no intention of acting as if they were.

I was fortunate to recover substantial documentation from the Internet and the National Archives about the EOD teams I served with in Vietnam, and before that, at Dugway Proving Grounds in the Utah desert. These records helped reconstruct events I could recall, as well as those I had forgotten. Other records and photographs came from fellow Vietnam EOD veterans, including my wonderful teammates, Paul Duffey, Chuck Watson, Roger McCormack, and Doug Rhodes; retired Sergeant Major Mike Vining, Colonel Bob Leiendecker, Major John Claffy, and Lieutenant Colonel Joe Jimenez also contributed. John and Joe were enlisted men when we served in Vietnam.

Why I remember some things and not others is something I am still trying to figure out, though exposure to multiple combat traumas is probably a factor.

I do not think that I experienced things in Vietnam and Utah that were worse than events experienced by other soldiers, including the men with whom I served, nor do I believe these things affected me on a larger scale.

My responses and actions over the forty-seven years since leaving Vietnam have had a profound, often dangerous, impact on every aspect of my life during that time. How have I managed to make it this far? I grapple with this question a lot.

Learning to be glad that I am alive is a new concept. I have spent a lot of time since leaving Vietnam trying to figure out why I am not dead. This also applies to something that happened before Vietnam when I was stationed in Utah. Writing this book, and looking back at events in a clinical way, has helped me begin to move past that old way of thinking and focus on how I am going to live the rest of my life. Getting it down on paper—something that has solidity to it—has helped clear the spaces in my brain where a lot of this stuff had been piling up. Again, my 2012 trip to Vietnam has also helped me leave many things behind me that I never thought I would be able to do, and to realize that they no longer matter.

Due to wounds and chronic pain since, I became addicted to prescription painkillers. Until nine years ago, I thought I was taking these things because of physical problems caused by injuries. What I learned is that I was taking these drugs as much for psychic injuries as anything else, in addition to the alcohol and illegal drugs I used for many years.

Although I knew about "psychic numbing" and "self-medication," I managed to ignore those issues in my own life until January 2007, when I realized I could not live the rest of my life in a pharmaceutical haze—not if I expected to live for the time I am supposed to have left. I decided to end the cycle of prescription remedies.

Writing this book has been part of my recovery: an ongoing process. It may not be helpful to anyone but my family, who have put up with a lot of bullshit over the years. Even so, it will have been worth it. I am hoping, however, that others who read this might find it useful in coming to grips with their own memories, move past them, and live in the here and now. This is not just about the war in Vietnam; it is about the war within, and trying to exorcise it.

1

Fire Support Base Rifle:
The Day It Was Raining Dead

I am opening with this because I want people to understand just what it was we did in Vietnam. Some of you may have watched the show *Bomb Patrol: Afghanistan* on the G4 satellite channel. It was about a Navy EOD team. My wife asked me one night if it was like the work we did in Vietnam, and I had to laugh, as I explain elsewhere, since we had absolutely no high-tech gear of any sort—no robots, no bomb suits, and no assigned security team.

It was two guys, a jeep, our personal weapons, and bags with explosives, electric and non-electric blasting caps, time fuse, plastic explosives, shape-charge containers of different sizes and shapes, detonating cord—referred to as det. cord—and a hand-cranked blasting machine. To be honest, because of the EOD gear we carried, in addition to combat loads when we were in the bush, we did not even wear flak vests or steel helmets. It would have been too much extra weight, and they would have just gotten in the way of our work.

Paul Duffey and I flew into a shithole in the Song Nong Valley called Fire Support Base Rifle early in the morning of February 11, 1970. It was about 25 km south-southeast of Hue and almost due south of the Phu Bai Combat Base, our base camp, at about 3,800-feet elevation. The area was heavily forested and a chopper was the only practical way in and out. There was a road, but it was one of those trips we tried to avoid if possible.

This area was in what was called "I" Corps, in the northernmost part of South Vietnam and about 40 km from the DMZ. During the attack on Rifle, it was obliterated by enemy mortar and rocket fire; the hill's defenders' ammunition dump of M101A1 howitzer, 105-mm high-explosive rounds, and 4.2-inch high-explosive mortar rounds were hit by incoming enemy fire, mostly destroying the dump and throwing damaged rounds all over the place.

My original intention was not to describe the battle at Rifle because Paul and I were not there when it happened. Nevertheless, this was one of those life and death events for the men who defended this place, and their story deserves telling. It was not Khe Sanh or the Battle of the Ia Drang Valley, so it never made the papers and no one saw it on TV. There was a two-paragraph article in the *Stars and Stripes* of February 13, 1970, and what they reported was largely incorrect, which really does not matter. This is what actually happened.

During the early morning hours of February 11, 1970, elements of the 2nd Battalion, 502nd Parachute Infantry Regiment, 101st Airborne Division (Airmobile), the 320th Artillery Regiment, and the 4th Battalion, 54th ARVN Infantry Regiment were overrun by units of the 5th North Vietnamese Army Division. The NVA were supported with mortars, rocket-propelled grenade (RPG) teams, and multiple sapper squads from the 5th Sapper Company.

The situation report of the Battle of FSB Rifle stated:

At approximately 0115 hours, FSB Rifle was hit with a heavy mortar and rocket attack that lasted for approximately 30 minutes. At the end of the rocket and mortar attack, an estimated 12-15 Sappers penetrated the perimeter through the sector occupied by the 4th [Battalion,] 54th ARVN [Infantry] Reg[imen]t soldiers. After placing their charges, the Sappers attempted to exit through the sector occupied by the ... Recon Platoon and [Command Post] personnel which resulted in the killing of 12 of the Sappers. The main attack of mortars, rockets and Sappers was directed against the US sector of defense and the Tactical Operations Center.

As the attack started, the NVA fired 60-mm mortar rounds into the base interior, dropping fifty to sixty rounds inside the perimeter. Then, the NVA fired RPG-2 and RPG-7 rockets at the defenders' bunkers. As the rockets came in, at least two squads of sappers breached the perimeter, some of whom immediately headed for the Tactical Operations Center. How they were able to penetrate the base defenses was no fluke; it was the result of a well-planned advance operation.

When the enemy entered the base, the sappers began throwing satchel charges, and NVA ground troops opened up with AK-47 fire. At this point, a pitched battle was underway inside the perimeter of the firebase as the two sides fired at each other in extremely close quarters. Inside the wire, the base was no more than 100 yards in diameter; much of the fighting was hand-to-hand combat.

By 1.45 a.m., gunships from the 101st arrived on station and began firing 2.75-inch rockets at enemy positions, both inside and outside the wire. Miniguns, as we found when we examined the perimeter for duds and booby traps, had torn up most of the vegetation outside the wire; it looked like a tornado had gone through. Splintered tree debris and shredded plants covered the ground ankle-deep.

As the battle continued to rage, at 2.15 a.m., a flare ship arrived and began to light up the skies so the defenders could see the enemy and pour artillery, M-16, machine gun, and grenade fire into their locations, inside and outside the perimeter. At 3 a.m., the NVA broke off the attack and disappeared back into the heavily forested hills surrounding Rifle. They left their dead behind.

No one ever heard about the battle at FSB Rifle because it was just a small event in the overall context of this sick, demented war. However, on every day in Vietnam, there were events like Rifle. No one except the survivors and the families of the dead ever cared about what happened in these hundreds, maybe thousands, of stinking rat-holes on a daily basis for nineteen years.

Although the official dates of the Vietnam War are 1961–1975, we all know it really started after the French were run out by the Viet Minh in 1954. The first American officially killed there was Air Force Tech Sergeant Richard B. Fitzgibbon, who died on June 8, 1956. He was actually murdered by another airman.

These are the names of the men who died at Rifle, except for the ARVN soldiers. I did not know any of them then, but I feel like I do now:

BURNS	JOHN	JAMES	BUFFALO	NY
CAHOON	MORGAN	LANE	FAIRFIELD	NC
DAVIS	ROBERT	ROY	MASON CITY	IA
FARRELL	TIMOTHY	CHARLES	OMAHA	NE
LAROCCA	VINCENT	MICHAEL	PETERSBURG	MI
MOON	RAYMOND	ROSS	SALT LAKE	UT
PETERSON	MARLIN	TRENT	WILLIAMS	MN
SHULER	HAROLD	WILLIAM	MURRAYVILLE	GA
KELLER	KENNETH	LAVERN	OMAHA	NE
KNECHT	PAUL	HERBERT	SPRINGFIELD	IL

Two days later, on February 13, 1970, Staff Sergeant Ronald L. Haug, wounded in the head and chest by shrapnel during the attack, also died.

We got the call to go into Rifle about 7 a.m. on February 11. It was located west of Route 545—a very dangerous piece of road—and it was a part-time firebase. The 101st used it when they conducted operations close to Phu Bai. That is what they were doing during Operation Randolph Glen when the enemy struck. Previous inhabitants had included the 1st Cavalry Division (Airmobile) and the South Vietnamese Army.

The 101st sent a chopper to our pad and we flew into Camp Eagle, the main forward base camp of the 101st Airborne Division. There, we joined a heliborne combat assault of 101st reinforcements, along with Chinooks and "Flying Cranes" loaded down with artillery pieces and large amounts of ammunition to replace what the NVA had destroyed at Rifle during their assault.

We arrived at Rifle at about 8 a.m. and overflew the LZ. The devastation and carnage were obvious. Most bunker lines along the perimeter, as well as the Tactical Operations Center (TOC), were blown to pieces. Two 105-mm artillery pieces and a 4.2-inch mortar pit were destroyed by incoming fire and the mass-detonation of the ammo dump. At that point, we did not know if it was mortars, rockets, artillery, or satchel charges. It turned out to be a little— okay, a lot—of all of those.

We later determined that the 4.2-inch mortar pit had taken a direct hit from a barrage of 60-mm mortars, and when their ammo exploded, it destroyed the mortar tube and killed one of the crew. There were large holes where artillery and mortar ammunition had exploded when hit by incoming rounds and satchel charges. The same was true for the two 105-mm howitzers.

Their ammunition was hit, destroying the artillery pieces and leaving only one functional gun, which actually ended up saving the day by stopping the attack dead in its tracks. By and large, and luckily, a lot of the artillery ammunition had not been destroyed, or even damaged, as far as we could tell. We eventually told someone to make sure it was all sent back to the rear for destruction.

There were bodies everywhere—inside the compound, in the wire, and outside of the perimeter, both American and NVA soldiers. Many of the NVA had been blown to pieces; some were burned to a cinder. Artillery, mortar, and rocket rounds lay everywhere, and many of the bunkers and the TOC still smoldered. As our chopper made its descent, Paul and I looked at each other. I said, "This is bad. This is what hell looks like."

Think of the visions of that dark, horrible place in Dante's *Inferno*, and you have a sense of the violence, destruction, and bloodshed at FSB Rifle. Being there was a signature moment in the War for me, one that defines who I am. The futility of trying to stop an invisible enemy, one that comes and goes as it pleases, is starkly similar to the Iraq War and what is still happening in Afghanistan. I know that, firsthand, because I went to Afghanistan in 2009–10 to do counternarcotics work for the UN Office on Drugs and Crime.

When I think of that moment, now, I see myself in the chopper doorway looking down at an angle. Then, the Huey came in nose up, and I felt the back of the skids touch down, the chopper rolling forward and settling squarely on the LZ—that "thunk, thunk" sound in the background, the scene rolling by in slow motion.

Paul and I have talked about Rifle many times since coming home and he feels as I do. We get a little choked up. We realize how lucky we were to make it out alive.

There was carnage all around, including three nearby firefights while we were there, and massive gunship fire, yet we managed to accomplish our mission as if nothing was happening around us. We ignored these things in the moment, but they are with us always.

As we landed, a patrol left the perimeter and entered the woods about 100 feet from the chopper pad as we were unloading our gear. Almost immediately, they came under heavy automatic weapons and rocket fire from an NVA ambush just inside the tree line, and up a small, heavily forested hill. The NVA could just as easily have opened up on our chopper as we were landing. We could see the enemy firing positions on the top of a ridge where they were shooting down at the American patrol, and we started pouring fire at the ridge. Infantrymen on the perimeter returned fire. The roar of automatic weapons fire was deafening.

The firefight only lasted a few minutes. By the time another patrol reached the site, two of the first patrol's members were dead and another wounded. Paul and I stood by our chopper when the bodies and the wounded soldier were brought to the LZ. We watched as they zipped the dead soldiers into body bags and placed them on the LZ to be lifted out.

The patrol was from the 3rd Platoon, "B" Company, 2nd Battalion, 502nd Infantry. The official report states that the patrol, which had headed south, "was moving up a high feature on [the] trail." They had picked up that feature at the perimeter wire where the tree line began. As they reached the ridgeline above the firebase, they saw six-to-ten "enemy [soldiers] … digging up stumps on [the] hill top," no doubt to use the holes to launch an attack on any U.S. soldiers happening by on patrol.

When they saw the 101st troopers, the NVA "engaged [the patrol] with … RPG and AK-47 fire. [The patrol] returned fire … [The] enemy [had] engaged" the patrol "at 30 meters and fled south" after breaking contact. U.S. casualties "were 2 [killed by hostile action] and 1 [wounded by hostile action]." By 10 a.m., the wounded soldier had been medevacked to the 85th Evac Hospital at Phu Bai.

Almost as soon as this incident was over, a second patrol—a "Combat Tracker Team" led by a dog and his handler—that had gone out to the northeast of the firebase, "followed [a] trail" and found "[e]vidence of 3 enemy soldiers, one wounded being dragged by two others." As the patrol started to follow the enemy trail, they were "called back due to [Aerial Rocket Artillery] working [the] area."

After the gunships fired up the hillside, the patrol went back in to recon and found "one AK-47 with [a] full magazine, 4 satchel charges, 4 RPG rounds, [and] one NVA canteen." It was clear the NVA were planning another attack. They brought the satchel charges and the RPGs into the firebase. Paul and I disarmed them, and then removed them back to Phu Bai, with the rest of the ordnance we took out of there.

Aerial Rocket Artillery ("ARA") was something that only existed in two units—the 101st and the 1st Cavalry Division, the Army's two airmobile divisions. These infantry units were often choppered into remote areas—like Fire Support Base Rifle—and it was often impossible to get the big guns—8-inch and 175-mm howitzers—into these sites due to their size and weight and the fact that most of the remote firebases like Rifle were very small. So, they invented flying mayhem with massive firepower and called it Aerial Rocket Artillery.

The 4th Battalion, 77th Artillery (ARA) was the 101st's answer to the lack of big guns deep in the bush. By 1970, ARA consisted of heavily armed Huey and Cobra gunships that carried as much firepower as you could ever want. Unlike big guns firing from 10–15 miles away, the ARA pilots could see the enemy, almost face-to-face, and put the fire exactly where they wanted. We did not worry about friendly fire when these pilots were on the scene.

These were close combat aircraft and pilots; their birds were equipped with as many as seventy-six 2.75-inch high-explosive and white phosphorus rockets, 7.62-mm machine guns or miniguns, 40-mm grenade launchers and, in the later version, the Cobras even had 20-mm cannons and Gatling guns. When they fired up that hillside at Rifle, it was another one of those things that happened as we were doing our job. On a conscious level, we paid little attention. It was kind of like background noise while we were stripping ordnance from bodies after clearing them for booby traps.

One of the first things that hit me as we walked around the hill was the overwhelming stench of dead bodies—the foulest, most nauseating smell imaginable, even after only seven hours. We had no eucalyptus to put under our nostrils like the graves registration people; I made a mental note to get some when we got back to Phu Bai.

You cannot wash the smell of death and rotting flesh out of your clothes; it gets in your hair and under your fingernails. You never forget it. When we got back to Phu Bai that night, my clothes went in the burn barrel. When I showered that night, I almost scrubbed myself bloody, making sure that no smell of death lingered. Even then, I would swear that I could still smell it.

The bodies lay everywhere. Many NVA were burned beyond recognition. Most dead Americans lay where they fell because they might have been booby-trapped during the firefight and all had unexploded ordnance still attached to their web gear. Our job was to check every dead body—American and NVA—for booby traps, locate and destroy damaged ordnance, and unexploded satchel charges, as well as dud RPG rounds, stick grenades, and Chinese 60-mm mortar rounds. We also removed ordnance and ammunition still strapped to NVA bodies in their web gear or hanging from bandoliers around their necks and waists.

During our sweep of the perimeter inside the wire, while checking the dead NVA bodies, we determined how the NVA were able to penetrate the base without detection. Throughout the perimeter wire, there were dozens of unexploded claymore mines, which mystified Paul and me. I pulled the electric cap from the first claymore and saw that it had fired. I picked up the claymore and immediately realized that it was empty. When I pried it open, I discovered that the C-4 charge was missing.

The NVA had penetrated the wire on a previous night, undetected, opened all the claymores and removed the C-4, using it to make some of the dozens of satchel charges they threw at the 101st and ARVN soldiers during the attack. The GIs did not know what hit them until it was too late. Without the claymores to stop the attack, sappers came through the wire, throwing satchel charges into bunkers, the TOC, and the artillery and mortar positions.

The situation report from Rifle after the attack informed all commands to check their claymores "daily … to insure [the] C-4 has not been removed or blasting caps have not been tampered with." I would have thought this a standing order from the first time claymores were deployed, but apparently not. Maybe if it had been, the Rifle attack would not have happened, or the defenders could have caught the enemy in the wire before they got inside the perimeter.

Some men were killed and wounded in and around the TOC trying to defend it during the sapper attack, as was at least one member of the recon platoon, and one man from the 4.2 mortar crew. One of the 105-mm artillery pieces took a direct hit from a barrage of 60-mm mortars and turned two of the three artillery pieces into a pile of scrap metal. The explosion killed two artillerymen, and there was not much left after the 105-mm ammo exploded.

While the sappers threw their charges into bunkers and the TOC, RPG teams opened up from all sides and devastated the bunker lines. Simultaneously, sappers tried to get back out after setting and detonating their charges—at least, those that went off—and a pitched battle between them and the surviving 101st and ARVN soldiers lasted for an hour before gunship support could get in due to bad weather. Much of the fighting inside Rifle was hand-to-hand combat.

There were two reasons why every American and ARVN on Rifle were not killed. First, when a second group of NVA started into the wire, a number of dug-in firing positions detonated their fougasse containers. These are 55-gallon drums packed with napalm and tilted outward on an angle of about 45-degrees, with C-4 plastic explosives strapped to the bottom, set off by an electric blasting cap in an M4 burster placed inside the 55-gallon drum. The C-4 blew the gasoline mixture outward, resulting in flaming jellied gasoline raining death down on everything and everyone in its path. Some of the NVA soldiers were burned to death in the inferno.

Second, as another flank of the second wave of NVA penetrated the wire, the remaining 105-mm howitzer loaded flechette— "Beehive"—rounds with a variable time fuse and cranked the time to zero. A flechette round contains tiny steel darts that fly in an ever-widening, cone-shaped pattern when the projectile blows apart. Because the VT fuse was set at zero, the round functioned as it left the barrel, and the NVA were instantly killed.

There were NVA bodies that seemed almost untouched, as the flechettes pierced them, leaving hundreds of small holes. When we first examined these bodies, it was hard to tell why they were dead. At each place where a dart had pierced the body, there was a small drop or two of blood, as though a pimple had popped.

It took us fourteen hours to clear the American and NVA bodies, and destroy most of the dud and unexploded ordnance. We packed 1-pound TNT blocks and disarmed RPGs in ammo boxes for removal back to Phu Bai for destruction in our demolition area. After that, Paul and I just sat on the ground in a daze, waiting for extraction. This was the worst carnage I ever saw—and I had seen a lot by then. There is no way to adequately describe it. The dead were in grotesque poses.

One dead NVA soldier still haunts me. He hung on the second perimeter wire, arms thrown behind him over the wire, supporting him on his knees. His head was gone, blown off, probably by a 40-mm grenade, and three inches of his spine pointed at the sky. He had been in the direct path of a fougasse explosion; what was left of him looked like beef jerky.

His body was a blackened crisp from the burning jellied gasoline, but the piece of his spine pointing heavenward was starkly white. I was mesmerized by how this was possible. In war, however, all things are possible and, often, they are impossible at the same time. I almost took a picture, but I kept my camera in my rucksack. This scene would never be far from my thoughts and would always be in that Technicolor haze that seems to describe Vietnam.

While we were on the perimeter disarming satchel charges and Bangalore torpedoes—think of a pole from the pole vault event packed with explosives; good for breaching a perimeter's wire—another firefight broke out 100 m from our position when a patrol from the 2nd of the 502nd went into the trees and was ambushed. There was heavy automatic weapons fire. We heard the distinctive sound of a flying RPG and a deafening explosion. From our position, all we saw was smoke, so we could not return fire. Two more paratroopers died in that incident.

We disarmed 200 satchel charges loaded with Russian TNT. We disarmed fifteen unfired RPG-2s and one dud RPG-7. We also rendered safe three Bangalore torpedoes, each holding twenty blocks of Russian TNT. The sappers who carried them were dead, killed by the storm of flechettes.

Our clerk, who took the initial call about Rifle, wrote that the 101st reported "2 [Rocket Propelled Grenade] rounds" at "FSB Rifle." Wow—talk about misreported.

The unusual incident report from Fire Support Base Rifle described things that I had completely forgotten. The S-2 of the 101st, the division intelligence officer, flew into the LZ while Paul and I were in the perimeter wire checking NVA bodies for booby traps and stripping them of all the unexploded ordnance they carried—grenades, ammunition, RPG-2s, and satchel charges.

For some reason, the S-2 decided to follow us around as we did our job—not a great idea but, he was a colonel.

Then, another chopper landed with the commanding general—Major General John M. Wright, Jr. of the 101st. There was another general, Hennessey, with him, but I have no idea who he was. They came to survey the damage and give a morale boost—as if that were possible—to the survivors of this bloody battle.

By now, Paul and I were bringing the items we intended to destroy to a large crater near what was left of the Tactical Operation Center. The S-2 colonel, with General Wright looking on, started to tell me that we could not blow all this shit at that location.

I said, "With all due respect, sir, when we're on the job, we make these decisions. You can take it up with our control unit, MACV, whomever you want. They will tell you this is how it is." Paul had put the last of the Russian DK-2 fuses, Chinese blasting caps, and the RPG fuses in the crater. General Wright stood there, watching, and did not say a word, even after I defied his colonel.

I cut some time fuse, maybe two minutes, capped it up, and stuck it in a half-pound of C-4, laying it on top of the pile of fuses and blasting caps. Paul and I got several dozen sandbags and covered the whole mess up. I pulled the fuse lighter and gave that famous EOD call, "Fire in the hole!" Everyone ducked behind something, except General Wright. I do not know why he just stood there but, hey, he was a general, and it was his hill. My report stated:

> After some argument with the S-2 officer, it was decided that EOD would blow the fuses and caps in a firing pit approximately [10 feet] from the entrance to the TOC. The shot was primed and heavily sandbagged and went without a flaw, except for throwing a little sand on [Gen. Wright] who didn't think it necessary to move out of the way.

I got some flak from our control unit for the way I wrote up the Unusual Incident Report on Rifle. Apparently, it was because I put in some zingers, like the way I described my run-in with the Colonel—whom I described in the report as "a stray Colonel"—and the fact that General Wright chose to ignore the "Fire in the hole" warning. When I got a copy of the report from the National Archives, I chuckled when I saw that each place where I had written something Control had disapproved of, they had circled it.

At this point, a 101st trooper walked up to us carrying an RPG-7 that was bashed to hell. The nose cone had a huge dent in it and I could tell from the burnt rocket motor that it had been fired. It was a dud—a very rare occurrence. He stood there, holding it out like a peace offering.

"What the fuck are you doing?" I said.

"Well, I thought you guys would want this," he replied.

I took it from his hands—what else could I do? —told everyone to get behind something, and threw it in the same pit we had just used to blow the fuses, and while it was in the air, ran like hell to behind a pile of rubble left over from the partially destroyed TOC. The rocket warhead did not go off, so we set another shot, more sandbags, and blew that as well. I think that time General Wright got behind something.

After we were done, Paul and I waited for extraction. We were both in a daze, filthy dirty, and worn out by the bloodbath we had cleaned up, and the rest of the day's events. A flying crane—a big helicopter that looked like a large fishhook turned upside down—came in with a big sling beneath it. We were on the lower level of the LZ, so when the Crane landed, we really could not see what was happening.

I think it brought in ammo or new artillery pieces to replace those shredded by incoming 60-mm mortar rounds. What we could not see were GIs placing the NVA bodies in the sling. When the sling was full, the Flying Crane took off. As the helicopter lifted and made its turn, we watched it ascend, flying out over the jungle, probably about a half-mile from the perimeter.

We sat, dumbfounded, as the sling opened and dead NVA bodies tumbled into the dense forest below. It was raining dead. I have never forgotten this event. It seemed to be happening in slow motion, and though I guess it was necessary under the circumstances, it still left me shocked, in disbelief. It is my most vivid memory from Vietnam, and it haunts me now.

When I got the Daily Staff Journals of the 1st Brigade, 101st Airborne Division, about the battle at Fire Support Base Rifle, it did not mention how the bodies had actually been disposed of. What it did say, however, was this: "NVA bodies to be buried or disposed of after pictures are taken." That is right: "after pictures are taken." Somewhere, here in the States, some former officer has a picture of these bodies, and I would like to ask him why he would do something like that, why they were taken in the first place. It is another thing about Vietnam—like body counts—that never made sense to me.

It was a sick war, and the people who were in charge were twisted. Why would anyone want pictures of bodies fried to a crisp, or blown up, or shot to pieces? There were people like that over there, the ones who took ears or fingers from dead enemy, but no one in EOD was like that. By the time I left Vietnam, I had thousands of pictures and slides, but not a single one of a dead body, though I saw hundreds of them.

I did not write about "raining dead" in my incident report. It did not seem pertinent to the mission. I tried to blot it from memory as soon as I witnessed it. However, it has haunted me every day of my life since. I mean it.

There is not a day that I do not think about Fire Support Base Rifle and what I saw there—not just the NVA bodies dropped over the jungle, but the scene we witnessed and, as with the Qui Nhơn ammo dump attacks in 1969, the realization that the enemy came and went as they pleased, usually without detection.

The pain I feel is palpable, if fleeting. From the air as we flew in, we could see the burned-out hulk of the Tactical Operations Center still smoldering, the three ambushes by the NVA while we were on the ground, and the ride out with the body bags. I was helpless to do anything; we all were. That is why the War is still with me.

A few years ago, Paul reminded me of something that happened on our extraction chopper. It is funny how you remember some things and forget others. On the chopper were Paul, me, and two body bags with 101st soldiers from the ambush that had happened as we landed. We also had several ammo crates full of one-pound TNT blocks and a bunch of unfired RPGs. There was also one of the few unwounded survivors from the battle at Rifle—at least not physically wounded.

There was something in his eyes that told me something was not right with this man. He had a wild, glazed look with an emptiness that only men who have been in heavy combat can understand.

About halfway back to Camp Eagle, the 101st main base camp, the Rifle survivor suddenly stood up and totally freaked out. He was screaming, going nuts about being in the chopper with his dead comrades in body bags. One of the door gunners turned around and yelled, "Shut the fuck up and sit down."

We were a couple of hundred feet off the deck, the Song Nong River spooling out below, and this flipped out guy was screaming and jumping up and down. The door gunner was screaming and the chopper was rocking back and forth with the bloated weight of the bodies, plus the weight of all the ordnance we were taking back and all the jumping up and down. Paul gave me that "what the fuck now" look.

I leaped up, and grabbed the screaming infantryman by the throat, threw him to the floor of the chopper on top of the body bags, and sat on his chest. I told him I knew why he was freaking out, but he had to stop the screaming and jumping around or I would tape his hands, arms, and mouth. I sat on him all the way back to Eagle, talking not so much to him as to myself. He calmed down some. At Eagle, he was medevacked in an ambulance. I wonder how he is today—or how I ended up there, in the middle of all that violence, blood, and complete bedlam.

2

Everything Starts Someplace

This is as much about my life as it is about the War. It is also about events, some unbelievable, that I experienced during twenty-six months in Utah and Vietnam. You are probably thinking, "Utah?"

These events made me stronger, not weaker. I will always be a Vietnam veteran, and I will always have been in "The War." What I do not have to be is caught in the past while living in the present. That is something a Buddhist monk brought home to me when he met with us in Da Nang on my trip back to Vietnam in 2012.

We had gone to the Buddhist Chua Quan Am Pagoda. It means "Pagoda of the Goddess of mercy who hears and responds." It is one of the holiest places in Vietnam. Our interpreter had arranged for my group to meet with the Most Reverend Zen Master, Thich Hue Vinh, and his chief disciple. This guy is godlike to the Vietnamese.

They both talked to us and told us many things that gave us pause to ponder the truths they had put forth. The monk went around the room and each of us got to ask him a question. When he got to me—and I had been thinking long and hard about what to ask him—I said, "I am sure this is presumptuous, but I think that if I do not ask this now, I will never have another opportunity … Why are we here?"

He looked at me intently for a moment, then started laughing and slapping his knees. He turned to his disciple and, still laughing and, according to our interpreter, said something like, "I can't answer this; this is part of your final exam and you must try to answer him." The younger man looked at me carefully and said, "You are not asking the correct question. You should be asking, 'Now that I am here, what is my purpose.'" It was right out of *The Hitchhiker's Guide to the Galaxy*. It was immediately obvious that he was correct.

The title of this book refers to something I said to Paul Duffey as we flew into Rifle, as I mentioned in the previous chapter. However, it also describes the entirety of the War and the eighteen months I spent there. My purpose, once I got there, was to do everything I could to keep my fellow soldiers safe and, particularly that purpose was twofold in relation to the men I served with in EOD.

The title also mirrors seven months in the Utah desert at Dugway Proving Grounds, where I saw the same planning for the destruction of human life that I experienced in Vietnam. In fact, we used some of the weapons developed at Dugway in Vietnam, which was somewhat disconcerting. The title also describes much of my personal history after I came back.

I have been addicted to alcohol, drugs, gambling, work, and, most significantly, to the War. I do not mean that "The War" caused my addictions. I made choices, as we all do, and they were frequently and monumentally the wrong choices. Nevertheless, the War and Dugway played a role; I am now trying to understand what that role was, and what it is going to be in the future. I am hopeful, after my return to Vietnam in early 2012, that the War will eventually be less and less a part of my life.

Nothing is a coincidence; everything happens for a reason. This thought has been significant since I got out of the Army in June 1971. Before that, and after returning from Vietnam fifteen months earlier, I could not allow myself to think about the more fucked up aspects of my time in Vietnam. It would have interfered with my ability to perform my duties in a stateside Explosive Ordnance Disposal unit. Moreover, I still had not made up my mind about re-enlisting again.

Dave Silva, my therapist in an addictions program, and I, eventually had the "why aren't I dead—why did others die and I didn't" conversation. He looked at me for a minute and said, "Others died so you could live," another version of "everything happens for a reason."

Every combat situation is like a mathematical equation, and each usually requires a certain percentage of casualties. Sometimes, to even the odds, there are no casualties. Other times, they are catastrophic—some live, some die. I was in the percentage that lived. I believe that I lived so that I could continue a life in public service—teacher; public defender; capital defense investigator;

and volunteer service officer, assisting my fellow veterans with claims for disability compensation from the Department of Veterans Affairs.

Hell is a relative term. If you talk to any combat veteran, they could tell you stories of devastation and destruction. Each of us has our own private hell and has to find our own salvation.

One of my friends was in military intelligence, in the Phoenix Program, which involved the assassination of Vietnamese civilians thought to be Viet Cong officials. It turned out that many of those killed were innocent of any such connection, or were killed because of a grudge between the informant and the alleged "bad actor."

Anne was an Army nurse who spent a year up to her elbows in blood at an evacuation hospital. She probably saw even more bodies than I did—and I saw a lot. Jerry was the officer in charge of a graves registration unit—more dead bodies.

Bob fell off a cliff and now cannot stand to cross bridges or look over the side of the road into deep desert canyons. When I drove him to a VA appointment in Portland, he scrunched down in the seat so he would not see this deep canyon we had to cross.

I was blown up, almost blown up more times, and saw too many bodies blown to pieces. Like I said, each of us has our own version of what Hell looks like.

Veterans wonder what it all meant, many for their entire lives after coming back. I want to figure this out, now, so I can move on. Until now, I have not been able, probably been unwilling, to figure that out on my own, and have often been unable to listen to, or seek the advice of, others who might have been able to help. Despite hospitalization in 1987 for drug addiction and PTSD, despite the individual and group therapy, I had not found any better understanding of myself or much solace.

I had all but given up until I decided to go into an addictions program in 2007 after I had gone through withdrawal from prescription morphine. During one of our classes on anger, the counselor said, "Religion is for those who are trying not to go to Hell. Spirituality is for people who have been to Hell and don't want to go back." I thought he was talking directly to me.

When I started to write this, I was not sure why I was doing it. Now I think this is an attempt at salvation, redemption, or some kind of spirituality, to help me feel comfortable in my life—at least as comfortable as I am ever going to be.

Maybe this will help other veterans understand what happened to them, and that they are not alone. For some of us, aloneness has been a way of life. You think you have friends, but they really are not. You do things you think you enjoy and you go places because you think you want to, but you really do not. You just do them because it is expected, or because you do not know what else to do.

The War scarred me—it scarred many of us—just as it wounded an entire country. As much as the country has never come to grips with what happened between 1956 and 1975 in that god-forsaken war—and god-forsaken is the right term—neither have some of us who were there and experienced things that no human being should ever experience.

In my case, like many others, I volunteered for Vietnam and then extended my tour. I knew nothing about the personal consequences of going to war and had no idea of the damage the War would cause me. Despite professional success after the War, it has taken many years for me to understand just how damaged I really was. If I am professionally successful, how can I be screwed up? Despite decorations for heroism, meritorious achievement in combat, and wounds, I wondered what it meant. Even now, I am not sure.

This has nothing to do with America treating Vietnam veterans shabbily when they returned and for years afterward. It has nothing to do with anti-war protests. I do not give a shit about Jane Fonda. After forty-plus years, what is the fucking point?

It had to do with our perceptions of ourselves, from personal experiences of the War that we fought in and then stayed in long after we returned. Epictetus, the Greek philosopher, who lived about 1,900 years ago, said, "Man is not disturbed by events, but by the view he takes of them." I learned that from one of my addiction program counselors; it is true.

Now that most of the country supports our troops who served in Iraq, and those still serving in Afghanistan and other war zones, Vietnam veterans are being accorded some thanks and respect. The hypocrisy is not lost on us. The question is whether we are finally getting our due because we deserve it or because the country feels guilty. For some of us, I think it makes no difference; for me, it does.

I do not mean that in the context of whether the war in Vietnam was right or wrong; that is something about which I do not give a fuck. I mean it in the sense that, for a long time, I found little joy in life since returning, despite events that should have been joyful. I would exclude my wife, Mona, and my son, Jonas, but that is about it. There have been times, however, despite their loving concern for my mental health, that I have not allowed myself to feel good even about their love. I thought I did not deserve it, and sometimes I still feel that way.

I retired as a capital defense investigator in early 2003. In the last case I worked on, the defendant was charged with capital murder, robbery, burglary, and unauthorized use of a motor vehicle. The case went to the jury early on Christmas Eve, 2002. They returned "Not Guilty" verdicts on all counts just before midnight. As far as I know, it was the first time that a defendant in a capital case in Oregon had been acquitted of all charges and walked out of the courtroom a free man. It was a stunning victory, and I felt even better when the prosecutors stormed out of the courtroom.

It was a great rush; I had a glowing sense of satisfaction after the verdicts. I knew the reason we got the result was my investigation. These feelings lasted about five minutes. After that, I did not care about the monumental accomplishment that should have brought me a lasting sense of pride. Now, when I think about it, my thought usually ends, "So what? No one gives a fuck."

Three weeks later, I turned down the investigation of one of the most gruesome murder cases in Oregon history—the killing of two small girls— and retired. Between the War and my job, I had seen enough blood and death, mangled bodies, and violence beyond description or imagination. If I had continued that work, I would have eventually lost my mind.

When I enlisted in the Army, I was bored with life in suburbia. I enlisted on a whim when a friend and I got drunk, woke up hung over the next day in our parked car, drove to Alexandria, Virginia, and enlisted.

We first went to the Marines, but they were closed. We walked to the building next door and joined the Army. We went without thought and paid no attention to the load of bullshit the recruiter sold us. This came back to haunt me later, when I got to my first duty assignment after Basic Training.

I drove to my parents' country club, where they were playing golf, and found them in the clubhouse with friends. I told them I had enlisted and that I was leaving, literally, on the "Midnight Train to Georgia."

My mom freaked out, because the war in Vietnam was starting to crank up in the summer of 1966. This was news to me. I had not heard about the Battle of the Ia Drang Valley, a place I would visit several times during my tour, even though it had occurred eight months before and been covered by the *Washington Post*, which we received daily. I was an uninformed dumbass.

My dad drove me to the bus station that night. I met my friend and we took the bus to the induction center in Richmond. We raised our right hands and swore to "defend the Constitution, against enemies foreign and domestic." Before we left for Basic Training, they discharged him for a medical condition. I was on my own, on the way to Ft. Gordon, Georgia. Since we had enlisted on the "buddy program," they told me I could get out of my enlistment. I did not.

I was not much aware of the war in Vietnam when I enlisted and could not have found it on the globe. In Basic Training, I learned that many of my instructors and drill sergeants had combat infantryman badges and combat patches on their right shoulders. After I learned what they stood for, that told me there was a war going on in some country I knew nothing about.

I do not remember hearing one word about Vietnam in high school, even though by the time I graduated in June 1965, American soldiers were starting to die in droves. By the time I enlisted on July 28, 1966, the toll was up to 5,732 and, somehow, I was completely in the dark.

I had no idea who the Viet Cong were, or that there was a South Vietnam and a North Vietnam. The North Vietnamese Army was a well-trained, heavily armed military force led by a general who knew what he was doing. I did not know that he had run the French out of Indo-China and had kicked the shit out of the Japanese during World War II. I would eventually find this out from firsthand experience in the Central Highlands and the Delta and Northern "I" Corps, places I would come to know in a bloody and savage way.

Few people knew in 1966 that American soldiers had been fighting and dying in Southeast Asia since just after World War II. In fact, the first American to die in Vietnam was OSS Major A. Peter Dewey, who was killed by the Viet Minh near Hanoi on September 26, 1945. Two CIA contract pilots were killed trying to resupply the French at Điện Biên Phủ in 1954. After that is when we took over from the French, who were soundly defeated and run of Vietnam out on a rail.

If you look at the Coffelt Database, the "official" list of all those killed in Vietnam, the first American soldier died in 1956, as I noted in the introduction. He was actually shot and killed by another Air Force member in a Saigon bar. Despite that ten-year "official" history, by the time I graduated from high school, I knew nothing about Vietnam.

Where did we get the idea that we would succeed where the French and every other invading force—including the Mongols, Chinese, and Japanese— had failed, particularly fighting the way we did? I used to wonder, "How the fuck can you sneak up on someone with a helicopter or a tank?" That is not something most of us ever thought about and, apparently, neither did five Presidents, Congress, and all of the generals and Ivy League analysts who planned and led this fiasco and lied about it.

They lied about the numbers, strength, and fortitude of the Viet Cong, the support of many of the Vietnamese people for them, and the military shrewdness and operational capabilities of the North Vietnamese Army. Although they say we never lost a major battle in Vietnam—which I assume is true—what did that matter in the end? It was like a very sick version of the expression, "We won the battle, but lost the war." We took ground and immediately gave it back. All you have to do is look at battles like the Ia Drang Valley, the Đắk Tô hill battles, and Hamburger Hill to know the truth of this.

When I volunteered for Vietnam, I was not thinking about these things. My need to get the hell out of where I was seemed more important than the Viet Cong and the North Vietnamese Army and all their mines, booby traps, and attacks on U.S. bases. Today, I wonder, "What the hell was I thinking?"

By any measurement, I should be dead and then some. I was blown up—literally—then almost blown up, and was in many situations where my survival was in doubt over the next few seconds. If I tried to write about every "unusual incident" I was involved in, this book would go on forever.

I was on the bomb squad—Explosive Ordnance Disposal. As we used to say, "E-O-Fucking-D!" Events supposedly "out of the ordinary" were "unusual incidents." Somehow, the regular, everyday dud or booby trap was usual, and the duds and booby traps where the enemy was trying to shoot us at the same time—well, these were unusual.

We did it day after day, and each time, that feeling of immediate pending doom was gone by the time we flew out or got back in our jeep and headed down some unsecured road for our base camp. It was kind of like the sixth minute after the not guilty verdicts in the murder case.

Do not get me wrong—I am glad I went and would probably do it again if I were twenty, even knowing what I now know. How weird is that? I guess that is why I went to Afghanistan in 2009 and spent six months there as an adviser to the Afghan Border Police on counter-narcotics operations along the Iranian border. I would have stayed longer, but my wife said I had to come home after the bad guys tried to bomb my driver and me twice.

I was in Vietnam from September 4, 1968, until March 24, 1970. Before that, from January to July 1968, I was at Dugway Proving Grounds in the Utah desert. I have been back for forty-seven years, but Dugway and the War have always been with me.

I do not mean they were there part of the time, that sometimes I went days or weeks without thinking about those experiences. When I say, "The War is always with me," I mean always. Dugway is another whole bag of shit; I volunteered for Vietnam to get out of Dugway. That should tell you something about how bad that place was.

There have been, of course, constant interruptions—mainly, my life—in these thoughts of war. Yet in between the interruptions, even if only a few seconds, I am back in those twenty-six months in Utah and Vietnam—the horrific things that happened to me, that I saw, or that happened to the men I served with.

I injured my left knee in an explosion and my right knee in an enemy attack; when they hurt, the war is there. If I see Iraq or Afghanistan on TV, I see Vietnam, even after spending six months in Afghanistan. There are more similarities between Vietnam and Afghanistan and Iraq than differences.

Vietnam veterans are keenly aware that when you cannot tell the enemy from innocent civilians, you are fucked from Jump Street. This seems to be lost on current war planners, just as it was during Vietnam. Even if the Taliban are using civilian shields in their homes when they attack, NATO forces must not call an airstrike and kill civilians. You just cannot do that. It does not matter what the reason, the logic, or the tactical advantage is.

When we kill civilians, we create people— their families—who want to kill us. This is exactly what happened in Vietnam, and during my recent trip back, our former enemies whom we met with made this clear to us. It was their driving force to fight us to the last man or woman.

When the sound in my ears from explosion-caused perforated eardrums is like a high-pitched radio wave—they call it tinnitus—I am thinking about Vietnam. When I take my diabetes medication—a disease caused by exposure to Agent Orange—I am thinking about the jungles we destroyed with that deadly chemical and the millions of gallons of other herbicides we sprayed and dropped.

Then, there are my brothers and sisters who have died horrible deaths since returning home, from diseases caused by these deadly chemicals. Also, there are the tens of thousands of Vietnamese who have died from these diseases and a fourth-generation of their children born with horrible deformities. The War has always been there for me and for many of my brothers and sisters who served there.

Why did I start writing this? Maybe it was withdrawal from prescription morphine. Maybe it was because of the stories I heard at the outreach center where I volunteered for five years. Maybe it was watching my friends, now sixty or older, who are also still trying to figure out how to get beyond all the bullshit.

From 2005–2010, I worked with a non-profit group originally made up of Vietnam combat veterans. Our primary task was to assist homeless veterans, and those at risk of becoming homeless, disabled, poor, or a combination of all of those. Many had substance abuse, alcohol, and mental health problems.

Maybe that has something to do with why I am writing this—hearing the stories of other people, day after day, tale after twisted, brutal tale. I am trying to tell their stories, as well, in the hope that America will understand, finally, how that war destroyed lives and continues to, to this day. I guess it destroyed my life a little, as well, or I would not be writing this; okay, maybe it was a lot.

From February to March 2007, I completed a program at a VA Medical Center in Washington, where I tried to come to grips with years of prescription-drug addiction, fueled by post-traumatic stress disorder. I am trying to have a good third marriage, mend my relationship with my son, and, to a large extent, save my life.

Long ago, those who served in Vietnam realized that if we do not take care of ourselves, no one else is going to help us. This is exactly how it was in Vietnam.

The men in your unit, at the platoon, squad, or team level were your family. You ate, slept, humped the boonies, and fought the enemy together. You saw your friends die or wounded in ways too horrible to describe. When all of these things were happening, you learned to ignore it. However, you did not learn to forget it.

I know some Vietnam veterans that came back, and they seem to be doing okay. In fact, if you look at the statistics, that is true for most of us. On paper, our resumes are impressive. I am a decorated combat veteran, law school professor, public defender, recipient of humanitarian awards, and I think I have the respect of my peers. However, some of us have never been the same since coming home. I have been one of those people and I am trying hard, now, not to be.

When I got back, where I grew up no longer felt like home. Since 1971, I have lived in thirty-seven different places. Today, I am working on that being a positive and life-affirming experience. I have not quite figured out how to do that, but I am working on it.

According to history, Union General William Tecumseh Sherman, speaking at the Ohio State Fair in 1880, told the graduating class of a group of cadets that, "War is Hell." He knew what he was talking about, too. During his famous march to the sea, he burned the city of Atlanta to the ground along with most of the rest of the Confederacy.

In many ways, it seems to me, that is what we tried to do in Vietnam— burn it to the ground, and, in so doing, we did that to ourselves as well. It seems like this is what we did in Iraq and are now doing in Afghanistan, which I know something about, having spent six months near the Iranian border in Northwest Afghanistan. Many of us were willing participants in this destruction of Vietnam, myself included. I tried to leave a softer boot print when I was in Afghanistan.

During my time in Vietnam, I personally detonated several tons of plastic explosives and TNT, destroying booby traps, dud ordnance, and ordnance that needed blowing up for strategic reasons. In addition, I helped blow 200 feet or so off the top of a mountain, destroying an enemy cave complex. Later, I probably helped change the environment forever in a large area of the South China Sea off the coast near Vũng Rô Bay when we dumped thousands of tons of bad ammunition there.

We did a good job, too—trying to burn Vietnam down—in between the massive "Arc Light" strikes by B-52s, napalm, and Agent Orange. Then there was the deliberate burning of villages believed to be havens for the enemy, and the use of every other destructive device we could shoot from guns, grenade launchers, artillery pieces, and rocket launchers, or drop from planes and helicopters. Individually, each of us was a weapon of mass destruction, given the opportunity. We had a lot of those.

During those twenty-six months with EOD teams in Utah and Vietnam, I participated in more than 700 "incidents," disarming and destroying chemical and biological weapons, booby traps, grenades, mines, dud artillery projectiles, rockets, and plane-dropped bombs from 250- to-2,000-pounders. I also dealt with anything else that could explode, or burn, or kill, or maim people in the most horrible ways imaginable, which they often did.

This will sound weird, but it was the greatest job I have ever had, and we were then, and are now, still considered one of the elite in all the military. Today, they use robots and all kinds of high-tech gear in places like Iraq, Afghanistan, the Balkans, and the Horn of Africa. They have jammers to block the electronic signal for remote detonators, and vehicles that can withstand huge blasts from mines and roadside bombs.

Back in the day, as I previously noted, we had an unarmored jeep or 0.75- ton truck, our hands, a bag full of plastic explosives, tools to fabricate shape charges, time fuse, fuse lighters, detonating cord, blasting caps, and our brains. You were right there, every time, over the device. It was always up close and personal.

It was an exhilarating, adventurous job. Our casualty rates were among the highest of any military occupational specialty and, despite the new technologies, it has remained that way during recent wars.

We lost forty-two men in Vietnam. So far, we have lost approximately 150 EOD men and women in the wars in Iraq and Afghanistan, and in the Horn of Africa; fifteen in 2010, and at least nineteen in 2011–12. The year 2006 was the worst year for EOD since the last year of World War II. I cry when I read these stories because EOD, like the Rangers, Special Forces, or the SEALs, is one of those jobs you are always connected to, long after your service is over.

EOD teams in Vietnam were no bullshit, no-nonsense outfits. Everyone's life depended on everyone else doing his job correctly. Every time we went out, there was absolutely no margin for error. On many occasions, we went into hot landing zones with the infantry, often after flying in by helicopter during a combat assault. There we were, trying to do our job, while the War raged all around us, and we had to ignore it.

I had forgotten about some of the things that happened to me in Vietnam. It was not until I started reviewing historical documents and talking to my former teammates that I recalled some of the worst events I saw or was involved in. I still had no memory of some of them, even after I read the report and saw my name in it. In one case, even my teammate did not remember what had happened, and he had written the report.

I am not trying to glorify what we did; I am just telling it like it was. I am not trying to justify the war because I did not care at the time whether it was right or wrong. Even today, I do not know if it was as wrong as the war in Iraq—at least in the way our soldiers were allowed to fight it—but I am glad I was in Vietnam and I am proud to have served with the men on my teams, and to have fought alongside men from the units we supported.

3

Arriving in Vietnam

When I left Utah for home to go on leave before Vietnam, I drove with a combat engineer, Chuck, who had a Comet Cyclone with a big-block Ford 428 engine, metallic gray with a black roof and a big cowl induction hood. It was faster than any car I had ever driven in.

Chuck was also on orders for Vietnam, and our families were in Virginia. I remember flying across the flatness of Kansas and Nebraska, late at night, where there were no real speed limits on the turnpikes. If I remember correctly, you could drive as fast "as conditions allowed," which we did.

When we crossed the Rockies at about 10,000 feet in early August 1968, it was snowing in a very strange way, if snow in August were not strange enough. It was about 75 degrees on the ground, and we could see the snow coming down but, about 100 feet above us, it melted into the bright summer day.

Chuck dropped me at my folks' place, and I never saw him again. If I could remember his last name, I would check to see if he made it back. I did not know Chuck at Dugway, but that does not matter. Vietnam veterans are tight. When we meet, even for a moment, most of us welcome each other home. It did not happen when we came back, and we try to make up for that on our own.

Sometimes, Vietnam seemed like that trip from Utah to Virginia with Chuck, especially the strange way it snowed when we crossed the Rockies. Vietnam went by in a blur, fast and furious. In between, there was a lot of weirdness, without the snow but with drenching, bone-numbing monsoons, things that made no sense, and, of course, the War. There was always the War. There is nothing weirder than war, not even snow in August.

My parents did not know I was coming home because I had not told them I was going to Vietnam. I felt that it would be best to tell them and my siblings in person. I did not tell them I had volunteered because I knew they would be upset as it was, especially my mom. She was equally upset when I volunteered to extend my tour for six months.

In Vietnam, I wrote her almost every week, and she saved all those letters, giving them to me just before she died, unexpectedly, in 1991. I lost the letters, probably threw them away during one of my fits—as when I threw out my medals. I wish I had those letters now, to help remember things long forgotten. I eventually replaced my medals, and I am proud to have them.

I spent three weeks at home on leave, yet have no memory of it. My folks had a family portrait done; I wore my khaki uniform with my EOD badge and the red Ordnance Corps ascot. I think they had this picture taken in case I did not make it back. It is on the wall in my bedroom, next to one of me receiving medals after the Qui Nhơn ammo dump attacks during the Post-Tet Offensive of 1969.

After leave, I left for Ohio, where my Utah teammate, Tom Allen, lived near Akron. I know I spent time with Tom at his home because I remember meeting his parents and his girlfriend, whom he married after the Army. I have no memory of anything we actually did, except a fair amount of drinking.

Tom and I took the train from Cleveland to San Francisco with five days left on our leave. The train had an observation car with large glass windows, allowing me to see the country in a way I had never seen it, to marvel at its beauty and vastness, wondering if I would ever see it again in that way.

There is something about watching the world go by from above it. It was the only time then, or "in country," that I contemplated my own possible death—even when I should have been killed, but somehow managed to live.

When we got to San Francisco, my elementary school friend, Bob Roberts, who had just returned from Vietnam, picked Tom and I up at the train station and took us back to his parents' house. As I remember, his dad was a Navy captain; I think he was a doctor, maybe with the U.S. Public Health Service. It is another memory that is very hazy. I do know that he wore a Navy-looking uniform.

Bob and I were best friends in elementary school, and then his dad was transferred to the West Coast. I spent many nights at his place when we were kids. They were Lutheran, and I remember going to church with them, thinking that it made more sense than Judaism. I do not feel that way today because I now believe that no religion makes any sense.

Maybe because Tom and I did not want to know, we did not talk to Bob about the War. We did not ask him what it was like, whether he had been in combat, and what had he seen. I do not remember if he seemed odd or different after coming back, but I had not seen him since the sixth grade, so I had no way of actually knowing if the War had changed him. He never brought it up either; that said something I was not aware of then, but fully understand now.

Before Vietnam, I knew quite a few Vietnam veterans from my various duty stations from Basic Training through my time at Dugway. I do not remember any of them telling "war stories," or discussing things they had seen or done. One of the NCOs at Dugway, Art Brosius, had just returned. Art did not talk about his experiences, and I did not ask questions, even when I got orders.

I did know, by then, that it was bad. It was in your face every night on TV. I had read about the Tet Offensive of 1968, and it had been on TV 24/7; I knew Americans were dying every day. Khe Sanh was ending about the time I volunteered for Vietnam. That is how crazy it was at Dugway. Even after the 1968 Tet and Khe Sanh, I still volunteered.

By the time I got orders for Vietnam, 32,549 soldiers were dead; I had followed the siege at Khe Sanh on television virtually nonstop. None of that translated into, "That might happen to me," when I saw bodies in flag-draped coffins, or wounded loaded onto med-evac choppers.

I never thought this applied to me. I was EOD and we were invincible. In the back of your mind, you knew that even a tiny mistake could kill or maim you. You also believed that this would not happen to you. If you thought that way, you could not do the job. You had finished the school when many others had not; that meant something in itself. Wearing that silver badge with the bomb and the lightning bolts was impressive, even to yourself.

Tom and I spent a couple of days with Bob, then signed in at the Oakland Army Base. It was a madhouse. The other men going to Vietnam were mostly in the combat arms—infantry, artillery, armor, and combat engineers.

Most had not had lengthy training or an assignment to hone their skills before deployment to the war. They had gone through Basic Training (lasting eight weeks) and Advanced Individual Training, which might have been another eight to sixteen weeks.

Some seemed freaked out and that, I guess, is not too surprising. EOD School had lasted almost six months, and I had spent another seven months in a stateside unit before Vietnam. I could have used more training and experience, but it was better than the nothing most combat arms soldiers had received.

Tom and I flew out of Oakland to Hawaii in the early morning hours of September 3, 1968. We deplaned for two or three hours. I will explain why I volunteered for Vietnam in the next chapter. You might not think it was a good reason, but it was better than staying where I was.

Tom and I walked around the airport, smoked cigarettes, and ate burgers, as if we were going on vacation. Those were the days; you could smoke everywhere and put your butts out on the floor. I think they still allowed smoking on airplanes, but I do not think we could smoke on the charter plane we took to Vietnam.

That brings up an interesting possibility. I flew to Vietnam on "Flying Tiger" Airline. We flew from Oakland to Hawaii to Okinawa to Vietnam. At the same time, the woman who is now my wife, Mona, was a flight attendant for "Flying Tiger" on that route. What are the odds she was on my plane? Maybe that is something my math genius son can figure out someday. Like I said, in the beginning, I do not believe in coincidences and, somehow, there was a connection between Mona and me, even then.

When we left the States, we wore starched, stateside fatigues and black boots with a mirror shine. When I left Vietnam, my jungle boots had no color left in them, and the leather parts were tan, not black. My jungle fatigues smelled funny and were faded almost to colorless in spots.

In Vietnam, I never had boot polish. When I had to attend an awards ceremony to receive medals, I knocked on hooches in other units to locate some. They had inspections. We never did.

Tom and I did not talk about it—the War—not even then. "Gee, I wonder what it will be like." Walking around the airport, we chatted about everything except the War—how we were glad to be out of Utah; family; baseball; girlfriends; and everything but Vietnam.

We had heard a lot about the Viet Cong and IEDs in EOD School. Of course, back then, before "Army Speak" got in the way, we called them mines, booby traps, or anti-personnel devices. For some reason, it did not register, at least not for me. It was just one of many courses, and I did not see it as having a deeper meaning than, say, "Applied Physics Principles." Maybe we were in denial; maybe we had to be.

More likely, we were not thinking about going to war. I was not thinking about it when I volunteered. I just had to get out of Utah, and as the saying goes, "Any place is better that here." Even after Vietnam, I still think I was right.

In the Utah desert, Vietnam was the last thing on my mind. I was trying not to die from lethal chemical and biological weapons.

We thought we would be safer in Vietnam than in Utah. We convinced ourselves that we could hear the enemy in Vietnam, unlike the chemical and biological weapons leaking all over Dugway. The Qui Nhơn ammunition supply point disproved that theory.

Approaching Biên Hòa Air Base, soldiers stared out the windows, Tom and I included. We talked about how it looked and acted as if we were landing at LAX. Landing, it looked peaceful. I did not know there were combat aircraft— jets, helicopters, and cargo planes—everywhere. Everyone was thinking about landing planes taking fire or soldiers disembarking in the middle of an attack.

Walking down the ramp felt like walking into a blast furnace. It was like nothing we had ever experienced, even in the blazing, skin-blistering heat of the Utah desert. The air was thick and hot. It was like inhaling molten syrup; it burned my throat as I tried to swallow. It was hard to adjust my vision, as the heat seemed to sear my eyes. Even my eyebrows were sweating, and the humidity meant it was like taking a bath without the tub.

By the time I left Vietnam, I was immune to the weather, the heat, the humidity, the everlasting monsoons, the cold—yes, it was cold during the monsoons—the bugs, the snakes, the leeches, and the bats. I had also gotten used to the enemy because they were everywhere, just like the bugs, snakes, leeches, and bats. Yet I never got used to the spiders, which always seemed to be huge and hiding under my rack, or climbing out of one of my boots, or dropping on me from a tree in the bush.

It is hard to describe what I felt when the plane touched down, and I knew, absolutely, that I was in Vietnam, in a combat zone, and that people would eventually be shooting at me. I might have been deluded about some things, but I knew that my job was not going to keep me behind a desk.

I do not know why I was not scared then; maybe I was just an idiot. It was exhilarating. The War was right there, right in my face, as we walked off the plane and onto the tarmac. As I felt when I arrived in Afghanistan in 2009, I think I knew I was in my milieu. Many of the soldiers were craning their necks skyward, expecting a rocket or a mortar round to drop right on top of them.

These exploding death machines did regularly drop out of the sky. Some have the impression, even some Vietnam veterans, that the big rear bases like Tân Sơn Nhất, Long Bình, Cam Ranh Bay, Biên Hòa, and Da Nang saw little enemy activity, and everyone sat around in air conditioning and drank beer all the time. Well, they did have a lot of air conditioning and almost everyone did drink beer. However, places like Biên Hòa and Tân Sơn Nhất were not immune to the war, even with their air conditioning.

Tân Sơn Nhất, for example, was regularly attacked and was hit thirty-five times between April 13, 1966 and January 28, 1973. During those attacks, 533 rounds of artillery, rocket, and mortar fire landed on the base. Forty-five men died; 376 were wounded. Maybe it was not Khe Sanh or the Ia Drang Valley, but it was not a resort.

During the Tet attack on Tân Sơn Nhất, January 31–February 1, 1968, defenders killed 962 Viet Cong soldiers, both inside and outside the perimeter. Air Force men with no infantry training fought side by side with the grunts, killed the enemy, and died just as dead as anybody else.

NVA regulars made a concerted effort to take the Biên Hòa Air Base. The base would have been overrun if a handful of Air Force security cops had not held a key bunker for several hours, until Army infantry arrived.

Biên Hòa and Tân Sơn Nhất were part of a huge military complex that included the air bases and Long Bình, which was the main Army base for Vietnam. Here is where my memory gets a little confused. I know Tom and I reported to the 90th Replacement Battalion at Long Bình because that is what my orders say. I only actually remember that we went to some replacement unit at some base.

Looking around the air base, I saw soldiers in dirty jungle fatigues, full rucksacks, armed to the teeth, LAW rockets slung across the top of grunts' rucksacks, and grenades hanging from their web gear. Crossed bandoliers of M-16 ammo slanted across their chests. They carried their rifles by the handle on the breech. Near the end of my tour, I also carried a LAW when I went to the bush.

Some carried M-79 grenade launchers and M-60 machine guns. Belts of ammo crisscrossed the machine gunners' chests or wrapped around their waists. Their fellow soldiers carried extra belts of ammo. Helicopters to take them to the field were firing up, rotors cranking with that "whop whop" sound, choking smoke from the turbine engines belching out the back. A phalanx of Cobra gunships sat to their left, bristling with rocket pods, forward-mounted mini-guns, and 40-mm grenade launchers. It smelled and looked like war.

I had never seen a Cobra gunship before; they were a sight to see: skinny, rakish, and sinister. The gunner sat in the forward seat with the pilot crammed in behind him. One of those choppers had a nose painted to look like a shark with a big red mouth and long, sharp, dangerous-looking white teeth.

This was one badass helicopter, and they saved our butts more than once. It was easy to understand, looking at the Cobras, that Vietnam was a dangerous place, that it took weapons like this to level the playing field. Except, that almost never happened—the level playing field—especially crashing around in the jungle with hundreds of men and armored personnel carriers. I always felt safer with only seven or eight recon soldiers.

The Special Ops people—Green Berets, SEALs, Marine Force Recon, and the Long-Range Recon Platoons (LRRPs)—had the right idea, and brought the war to the enemy in a way the rest of the military seemed unable to do. I always wondered how you could sneak up on someone in twenty helicopters.

Bombing the crap out of some place a few hours before a combat assault was like sending the enemy an invitation that they were always glad to RSVP by mining the LZ, which we then had to clear so people could land. It was all like some kind of weird ballet.

There were times when Vietnam seemed like any regular place with no war. You could drive down a paved road with broken, yellow-passing and solid, no-passing lines, stoplights at major intersections, through picturesque villages with no sign or sound of the enemy or the War. People walked to the grocery store, couples held hands, and children laughed, playing in the dirt like children everywhere. There were baseball and soccer games; it was like Main Street anywhere. Nevertheless, the enemy was always in the back of your mind. You had your finger on the trigger, the safety was off, and you were always alert.

Tom and I walked along with the other soldiers—after that truck ride, I cannot remember how many of us there were—until we reached a set of barracks. A crew from the 90th Replacement Battalion lined us up in formation. After the lengthy flight from Oakland, and virtually no sleep, none of us was in a mood to move quickly.

We got in a relatively straight line and the man in charge read names from his well-worn clipboard. He called out Tom's name before he got to me, and had him get out of line and stand by a jeep. I was not paying much attention since I had not slept in thirty-six hours, could barely keep my eyes open, and did not notice that the jeep had red fenders.

Eventually, the soldier with the clipboard said, "Steinberg." I said, "Here," as in the third grade. He looked dead at me. I thought I was in trouble for not saying something military, like, "Yes, Sergeant!" with a loud and definitive emphasis on the "Yes." I had stopped all that "Yes, Sergeant" crap when I graduated from EOD School, another benefit of my military occupational specialty.

"Get out of line and go over there by the jeep," he said. "You and the other EOD guy are being picked up by your Control Team." I had come to Vietnam from a research and development operation at Dugway Proving Grounds. As far as I know, we did not have a Control Team, and they never mentioned it at school, so I had no fucking idea what he meant. I moved over to the jeep, wondering who these people were that were going to "control" me.

Waiting for the Control Team driver, Tom and I made small talk. We did not talk about the flight over, or that we were standing in the middle of a war zone without any weapons, no body armor, and no steel pot. I remember standing there thinking, "I have got to get a gun, immediately."

At that point, I was thinking about a flak jacket, but I never wore one—or a steel helmet—during the entire eighteen months I was in Vietnam. Call me stupid, but I always figured that when I was face-to-face with a booby trap or a 2,000-pound bomb, the weight on my mind was enough. I only wore a steel pot once—when I got some medals. The general who pinned the medals on me disapproved of boonie hats—go figure.

Tom and I stood there, smelling the air, mixed fuel odors, the intense heat, body odor, and the almost drinkable humidity that made your nostrils sweat when you inhaled it. Even the humidity smelled funny.

The weather and the heat were omnipresent and were just as much a part of the War as the enemy was. It was like living in a dream, taken from the relative calm of the Utah desert and thrust face first, upside down, into a surreal and dangerous environment. It was a lot like Dugway, in that way.

A small group of Vietnamese men and women walked by us new soldiers, men in pajamas, and conical hats, women in flowing *áo dài* or black silk pants and white blouses. They were small by Western standards. It was hard to imagine these small people carrying rockets, launchers, satchel charges, heavy machine guns, and tons of ammo by themselves. However, they did and often under the most unbelievable circumstances, like dragging artillery pieces up mountains at Điện Biên Phủ, then again, fourteen years later at Khe Sanh, and two years later, at Fire Support Base Ripcord.

With only a few hours in country, I wondered if they were friends, enemies, or both. Again, I wished for a weapon. Due to the inability to tell who the enemy was, who the innocent civilians were, some soldiers called all of them "gooks," "dinks," "zips," "zipperheads," "slopes," or worse. I heard Montagnard, Rhade, and Bru tribes-people called "nigger," or all of those things, interlaced with obscenities.

To many soldiers, all Vietnamese were the enemy because of the ever-looming question of, "Do they have groceries in that bag, or a grenade?" "Is our house girl a house girl by day, VC by night?" Sometimes it was both. Driving in Vietnam, even on the main drags, when small children approached with a Coke in one hand, you always wondered if there was a grenade in the other.

When you dehumanize the native population, it is easier to kill them, even the innocents, without remorse. If you call them gook or dink—or like today in Afghanistan—"raghead" or "camel jockey"—it is easier to kill them without regard to whether they are the enemy or just someone in the wrong place at the wrong time. To the best of my recollection, I never referred to the Vietnamese by these racist terms. It was just a foreign concept to me, and it was not how my parents raised me.

An SP4 (a specialist fourth class like a corporal, but allegedly, a technician) came out of the building where the jeep with red fenders was parked. He asked to see our orders. He did not wear an EOD badge, so I figured he was the clerk at the Control Team. He told us to climb into the jeep and stow our duffle bags. Some EOD vehicles did not have red fenders for safety reasons; the enemy knew who we were, and the rumor was that there was a bounty on us.

None of the combat teams I was with had red fenders on their jeeps, or blue lights. The enemy knew what that meant, and we often drove down very dangerous roads—paved and unpaved—by ourselves, in enemy-held territory. We wanted to look like every other goober driving a jeep. We did have a siren, painted olive drab, but I never used it.

We drove about a mile on the base, and came to another building, parked, and the clerk told us to grab our duffle bags. It was the clothing store, where we traded our heavy stateside fatigues and jet-black boots for lightweight jungle fatigues and green canvas and black leather jungle boots. These were the best boots I ever owned. I wish I could find a pair now and not a cheap imitation, but the real deal. I have seen ads claiming they are real, but I do not believe it, not after almost fifty years.

The clothing people issued us heavy green socks, green boxer shorts, green t-shirts, a green baseball cap, and a green belt. I wanted a floppy boonie hat, but they would not give me one. They issued cloth tags that read, "U.S. Army," for our jungle jackets. Nametags were stitched on the spot by a Vietnamese man at a sewing machine.

They told us that our black camouflage EOD badges would come from the Post Exchange when we got to one at a big rear base area. I soon learned that in any good-sized village near U.S. bases, you could buy anything you wanted sewn, embroidered, or stitched. For the moment, I pinned on my metal badge. It was still in my pocket when I climbed on the bird home, and I still have it today.

Soon after I got to my unit, I bought some Tiger fatigues, the ones worn by Green Berets, the Long-Range Recon guys, and Korean soldiers. I got them at the same little sewing shop where I got my black EOD insignia.

It seemed obvious that if you are going to blend into the jungle, you need to look like a tree, like the brush you were walking through. The lighter-green jungle fatigues provided as much camouflage as, well, they just did not. The fatigues were a light, watery green; most of the bush I went through was a darker, more vibrant green, and there were blacks and browns. The issue fatigues stuck out like a fading leaf in fall against the color of a dark green fir in mid-winter.

I am sure whoever designed them would have disagreed, but they were not there and probably never had been. It was like most planning for the War—done by people who had no personal experience and yet thought they could understand everything with statistical analysis.

There was one thing they did not have at the store—a gun. "Shit," I thought to myself. "What's a guy gotta do to get something to protect himself?" This was a constant thought until I got to my unit.

I have no idea why the military did not issue weapons as soon as we arrived in country. We trained on the M-16 and other weapons, including machine guns and grenade launchers. Did they think we would point them at each other if we needed to use them? Well, they did put the warning "front toward enemy" on claymores. I can only imagine why that happened.

When I flew by helicopter up the coast for 400 miles with a bunch of other soldiers, most of whom were also unarmed, what were we supposed to do if shot down or had mechanical problems and crashed in enemy territory? Use harsh language? I know that the Chinook only has a flight range of about 260 miles, so we must have landed somewhere to refuel, but I have no memory of that.

After we got our duffle bags stowed in the jeep, the control clerk told us where we were going. I was bound for the EOD Section of the 184th Ordnance Battalion, in a place called Qui Nhơn, the provincial capital of Bình Định Province. It was in the II Corps Tactical Zone, in the Central Highlands. The city of Qui Nhơn was on the coast of the South China Sea.

Tom was going to the EOD Section of the 191st Ordnance Battalion in Cam Ranh Bay, also on the coast of the South China Sea. As we left the clothing supply point, the control clerk asked us if we were hungry. We were, so he took us to the Enlisted Men's Club at Biên Hòa Air Force Base, where we were somewhat taken aback.

The EM Club was in a modern building with air conditioners in most windows. The Air Force really knew how to be at war. They had better quarters, better food, less war around their bases, and they just had better everything.

Some of the places I went, like LZ English or the Phu Bai Combat Base, got hit more times in six months than Tân Sơn Nhất was in seven years, nor did we have air conditioning in our clubs. The officers might have, but not the enlisted men, or the NCOs. In early 1970, we managed to get a couple of air conditioners for our bar in Phu Bai, but it took a lot of wheeling and dealing, and cost me a Russian sniper rifle from an NVA weapons cache that Denny Vesper and I had been called in on when I was with the 25th EOD in An Khê.

Inside the club, we—us FNGs (fucking new guys)—stood there, almost in shock. It was like being in the States. There was a restaurant called a canteen, pool tables, pinball games, slot machines, a music room with a complete spectrum of instruments, a record library and recording equipment, so you could make your own tapes and take them back to your hooch.

After I got to Qui Nhơn and, eventually, to an on-site team, I really learned how much better the Air Force had it than the Army and the Marines. I found the same kind of digs at Phù Cát Air Base, between Qui Nhơn and LZ English on Highway 1. We would always stop there on our way to the on-site team at LZ English.

We were in the middle of a combat zone, with no weapons, eating greasy cheeseburgers and fries, and washing them down with Coke with shaved ice in the cup. The burgers were full of that old-fashioned grease—not this new high-tech shit, but the kind that made your arteries harden while you sat there—and the fries were boiled in oil that drives your cholesterol up a hundred points just being near it. Maybe it was even delightful lard. The only thing missing was a young woman on roller skates in a short skirt taking orders. That was the last time I would see these things in Vietnam for quite some time.

If we were not at some big rear area base like Tân Sơn Nhất or the Qui Nhơn Support Command Base, we had zip. We had a little EM Club at the 184th's compound in the Phu Thanh Valley, a few clicks (kilometers) down the road from Qui Nhơn, where we were the guests of the 8th Transportation Group. It was a place to get a cold beer and listen to music but it definitely was not air-conditioned. I do not even remember any fans.

What I do remember is that it was always hotter than hell in there. Sometimes, the beer was not cold, but we were glad to have it, even if it was Pabst Blue Ribbon. I do not even really like beer, but it was better than no liquor, of any type, and if we drank a few, things seemed a little better, for a while at least. There were no burgers, no shaved ice for our soft drinks, no tape libraries, and no French fries. It was in a large Quonset hut, painted olive drab and surrounded by sandbags.

Even so, in from the bush, I spent a lot of time there playing music and drinking beer with soldiers from the 8th Transportation Group. My good friend, Roger McCormack, was usually with me if he was not at one of the on-site teams' locations.

Then, as if struck by lightning, I snapped back into reality. Would a rocket come through the roof? I had read enough to know that the enemy attacked the big bases. We all remembered the Tet Offensive of 1968, when VC guerillas briefly got over the fence of the American Embassy, and virtually every base in Vietnam was under attack, simultaneously. Then, there was the savage battle for Hue City. I was having a hard time swallowing by this point. I would learn five months later that the Tet Offensive of 1969 was as bad.

After that air-conditioned club, the heat was like walking into a steel foundry. It was sticky and thick, like maple syrup, but not edible. Sweat soaked my t-shirt and new jungle jacket and just rolled out of my pores—forget deodorant.

A hundred or more EOD missions later, sweat would be the least of my worries. Like the monsoons, we learned to ignore it because it had nothing to do with survival.

The heat, humidity, and torrential rains defined the War as much as the invisible enemy and their incessant attacks. The heat and damp stench that came with it, like the enemy, was everywhere and always there.

So, I was standing in the street outside the club and had all these thoughts racing through my young, impressionable mind—I was twenty—and I still did not have a clue about what it was really going to be like once I joined my unit. The Control Team clerk told Tom and I that we would fly out of Tân Sơn Nhất in about twenty minutes. Tom was flying to Cam Ranh Bay on a C-130, and I was going to Qui Nhơn on a CH-47 Chinook helicopter.

I had never been on a big helicopter, and Tom had never been on a C-130, a big, four-engine prop job that was the workhorse of the Vietnam War. All services used them for transporting troops, equipment, and ammunition, and to drop supplies by parachute to remote bases like Khe Sanh, or the Special Forces camps along the borders with Cambodia and Laos.

The C-130 was also used as a very large gunship, with a 105-mm cannon sticking out of the side, 20-mm Vulcan Gatling guns, and 7.62-mm miniguns mounted in the windows. This version was called the AC-130—the "Specter Gunship." I learned the true meaning of firepower when I saw one of these beasts do its thing. They used it in Iraq and are still using it in Afghanistan. U.S. forces used one in the Horn of Africa a few years ago, when Ethiopian troops routed Muslim terrorists from Mogadishu, Somalia.

I was starting to feel naked without the weapon I had fantasized about for the past two hours. "Jesus Christ!" I thought, "Now I'm going to fly 400 miles up the coast in a helicopter. Rocket-propelled grenades can bring these babies down."

The CH-47 is still hard at work in Afghanistan and the Horn of Africa. Then, and now, it was, and is, used to transport up to thirty-four soldiers, artillery pieces, and ammunition—anything that can be loaded inside or in a sling underneath the chopper, such as C-rations, warm soda and beer, lumber for bunkers, pallets of sandbags to reinforce the bunkers that the lumber would build, everything to survive at remote firebases, and landing zones.

Even though the beer and soda were hot, we were glad to see them. When they flew in with hot food in mermite containers, we were glad to see that as well, even if the ice cream was on top of the hot food. The Marines used a smaller, lighter version of the Chinook—the CH-46—called the Sea Knight. They got me and my teammates out of more than one bad situation.

Driving to the airfield, I turned to Tom and said, "Well, maybe we'll run into each other later." I really did not believe it. I had that feeling this would be the last time we would see each other, maybe ever.

Tom looked at me and started to say something, then just stuck out his hand and we shook, realizing that there really were not words to describe what we were feeling. I did see Tom again, during a very FUBAR (fucked up beyond all recognition) situation in the Qui Nhơn Ammo Dump, during the

Post-Tet Offensive of 1969. He came in for a few days with other members of his team to help us clean the place up after the VC blew it up three times in a thirty-day period.

That was the last time I saw him. I called him some years ago, but he seemed distant and I could feel that he really was not interested in rekindling our friendship. The War is one thing; the rest of your life is something else.

We pulled into a parking area near a terminal and saw Tom's C-130 warming up. Troops getting on were loaded with combat gear, their fatigues long past broken in. Tom grabbed his gear and climbed out of the jeep. A young soldier wearing a 1st Cavalry Division patch stopped by. He carried a full rucksack and an M-79 grenade launcher and looked very tired.

Our red-fendered jeep was marked "533 Ord. Det. (EOD Control)." The 1st Cav trooper walking by looked at it, turned, looked at me, and said, "Man, EOD. You guys are fuckin' crazy." Then he was gone, disappearing into the cavernous maw of the C-130. I wondered what he meant.

Soldiers had a relative view of who was crazy. The Cav soldier, and most others, thought we were crazy for doing what we did. We thought they were crazy for doing what they did. Everyone thought the gunship pilots and door-gunners were crazy. Then there were the med-evac choppers—they were unarmed.

The one thing I think that all of us eventually agreed on was that the War was crazy. It made no sense from the time we got there, and we absolutely knew it was crazy by the time we left. Of course, we were all a little crazy by that time, some more than others, and it no longer mattered how crazy the War was, or even what crazy meant. We were just glad to make it out of there alive.

Tom tapped me on the shoulder, nodded, and walked off to catch his bird. We did not wait for the plane to take off; the driver from the 533rd said, "Man, we gotta haul ass, or you're gonna miss your chopper." I remarked about what the Cav solider said, and the driver looked at me. "You'll find out what that means. You are going to a team that supports combat units. You will be in the bush a lot."

"You know, I'm just the clerk, but I think he's right. You guys are fucking crazy and the extra fifty-five bucks a month isn't enough. Next time you see me, I will ask if you remember this conversation. I'll be interested to hear your response." The next time I saw the control clerk, during the memorial service for the commanding officer of the EOD Team in Saigon, it did not come up. He knew not to ask about shit that no longer mattered.

We drove down another road to a helipad, where Chinooks, Hueys, and Cobra gunships were warming up. My first close-up look at a Cobra was mesmerizing; it was nothing but death and destruction, mounted on a narrow helicopter platform that looked barely wide enough to hold its two-man crew, sitting one behind the other. Even though I had seen one when we first got off the plane, this time I was only ten feet away.

The two pilots walking toward it looked like they might have been twenty years old, maybe younger. Some 222 helicopter pilots who died in Vietnam were nineteen and twenty years old. The two pilots saw the EOD jeep with its standout red fenders and waved. One of them yelled, "EOD!"

I learned over time that we were respected everywhere, admired by many, and, like the Cav soldier and the clerk, all thought we were crazy. That is quite a compliment, coming from men who flew into Hell at a high rate of speed, dodging heavy machine gun fire and rocket propelled grenades on a daily basis.

Some 11,827 helicopters saw action in Vietnam, Cambodia, and Laos. Of that number, 5,086 went down. Some 43 percent of all the helicopters that flew in the Vietnam War were lost. Between Vietnam, Laos and Cambodia, 2,202 pilots and 2,704 non-pilot crewmembers died—so, who was crazy?

One could ask, why volunteer to disarm booby traps, or blow up dud 1,000-pound bombs, when you could do something much less dangerous? I have the same thoughts about the maniacs who flew Chinooks, Sea Knights, Pedros, Cobras, the Hueys, the little Light Observation Helicopters, the OV-1 Mohawks and OV-10 Broncos, the Caribous, and the med-evac choppers in and out of hot landing zones, bullets penetrating their thin skins, sometimes hundreds of rounds, before they could get airborne.

The med-evac helicopters, because of some dumbass rule, were unarmed, despite the fact that the enemy ignored the red crosses on them and regularly shot them down, even when loaded with casualties, dead and alive. I was on Hueys many times, in and out of those same LZs, bullets flying everywhere and door-gunners returning fire until their barrels turned red-hot.

The jeep stopped in front of a Chinook, and the 533rd clerk got out and took a copy of my orders to the pilot. This was when I learned just how special EOD was to the military. Even though I did not have my official EOD identification card yet, the orders were enough. We had Priority 1 flight orders. Flying on an EOD mission, I went to the head of the line for a seat on any aircraft.

Once, a colonel and his aide voluntarily gave up their seats for my teammate and me. The pilot had climbed into the back of the chopper—another

Chinook—and said he needed two people to give up their seats for two EOD people. We were hitching a ride to a remote firebase in the A Shau Valley.

Several grunts started to get up, but the two officers rose and waved them all back to their seats. The colonel looked at me as he walked by and said, "Wherever you're going, and whatever it is you're going for, be safe. It's a hell of a job you guys do."

It had been a long road to Vietnam.

4

In the Army and Ending Up in EOD

The mission of explosive ordnance disposal is to identify, render safe, and dispose of explosive ordnance of all types, all sizes, and from all nations, including nuclear weapons once you attain the right rank and have enough time in the field. I went to nukes when I got back from Vietnam. As you might imagine, that is many bombs, rockets, grenades, mines, fuses, missiles, artillery rounds, and incendiary devices. IEDs and booby traps were only a small part of the instruction.

You had to learn them all to graduate from the school. I do not remember how many other soldiers—all branches, enlisted, and officers—started in my class, but less than half graduated. An Air Force officer who had graduated from some Ivy League college flunked out. It was very tough academically and, when I graduated, I felt I had really accomplished something, maybe for the first time in my life other than being a super-star in Basic Training. I will tell you more about that later.

What I learned in basic EOD School, and when I returned for nuclear weapons after Vietnam, has served me throughout life. It still makes me proud, and I remember my accomplishments when I take out my original EOD badge—a wreath wrapped around a shield with a bomb in the center and lightning bolts dissecting it on the diagonal— when I am sitting, alone, in my office, late at night.

I think about all the soldiers who wore that badge and did not make it back, as well as those who were severely injured. I think of the EOD men and women we have lost in Iraq, Afghanistan and the Horn of Africa. I have the badge tattooed on my upper left arm, along with "Vietnam" across the top and "1968–1970" across the bottom. The wreath is green, the shield is blue, the bomb is red, and the crossed lightning bolts are yellow. I wear it proudly.

I arrived at Ft. Gordon, Georgia, for Basic Training on July 29, 1966. I went to a company of all National Guardsmen or Enlisted Reservists from Wisconsin; I cannot remember which they were. What I do remember is that they had all joined their respective units because they thought it would keep them out of Vietnam. I was the only enlistee in the company.

The Guardsmen knew they were going to Advanced Infantry Training after Basic and definitely did not want to be there, because they also knew they were all going to Vietnam. Many of them were professionals—managers, plumbers, electricians, and a couple of lawyers (who did not want to be JAG officers)—and union officers. They had joined to avoid the draft and, presumably, Vietnam. They were a group of very pissed off men.

When we had our first formation—"A" Company, 3rd Battalion, 1st Training Brigade (how do we remember these things?)—SFC Gonzales lined us all up, yelling and screaming what "low-life, fucking scum" we were. This was before he made me the acting jack. I was in the front row, and he knew I was the only RA, so he stopped right in front of me. Then he said, "OK, Mr. Regular Army. You're my fucking Acting Jack." I wore a blue armband with sergeant stripes, and I was "in charge" when the DI was not around.

I thought I was cooler than shit. I was "best" at guard duty inspection and did not have to pull guard duty marching around a pile of tires in the motor pool. After the first week, they sent me to driving school to learn to drive the big trucks that took the troops to the ranges and the obstacle courses, and I never pulled KP.

The night the company went to the obstacle course, it was raining hard and the course was a sea of mud. While everyone else got dirty and soaking wet, I went back to the company area with the truck to pick up hot chow and take it back to the course.

I do not think the fix was in just because I was the only Regular Army trainee, because I really tried to excel and earn recognition for the first time in my life. However, who knows? Graduating from Basic, I was the honor graduate, maybe because the rest of my company did not care.

My dad came to see me graduate from Basic Training. I think he had to be at Ft. Gordon or some other Georgia base because he had businesses on the bases. Nonetheless, he came, and I seem to remember they let him take me to dinner the previous night. Once, again, I think being RA really paid off.

I ate it up; I enjoyed excelling, beating the crap out of other trainees in physical tests. As I said, many of them were professionals or college graduates who joined the Guard or the Reserves to stay out of Vietnam. Well, they were not George Bush or Dan Quayle, and Vietnam is where they ended up.

I was the fastest through the low-crawl, quickly slithering on my belly through sand and under barbed wire. On the overhead ladder, I flew down the bars, barely touching them as I went from rung to rung. At guard mount, I knew all my general orders, my weapon was clean and polished, my boots were spit-shined to a glassy finish, my uniform heavily starched and correctly creased. None of this means squat; in Vietnam, it meant less than that.

I had enlisted to be a Nike Hercules missile crewmember and believed I would be learning skills that would be useful after my discharge—what a joke that turned out to be. As I have said, however, at least three times, now, everything happens for a reason. If the recruiter had not totally fucked me over, trying, no doubt, to fill his quota, I would not have ended up in EOD. It seems that simple to me. So, in some perverse way that makes sense to me. I am glad I got fucked by the recruiter.

After graduating from Basic, I went to a missile site in the Everglades, many miles from any inhabited community, except one small place right out of *Deliverance*. They stationed me with inbred, racist, anti-Semitic pinheads from Arkansas, Louisiana, and Alabama, and the Battery Commander— CPT Patenaude—and First Sergeant Ford let all this go on with no concern, whatsoever. One scumbag from Arkansas—if you are reading this, you know who you are—was a loan shark. The command also knew this was going on. The CO was a weak-kneed douche, and the First Sergeant was a piece of shit. Those are their real names. I considered killing a guy from Alabama on guard duty, when I had a loaded M-14. He was talking about how, "You Jews killed Christ," and threatened me with a .45.

I had to get out of there, so just before my first year was up, I made a trip to the career counselor at Homestead Air Force Base, some distance from the missile battery site. He explained that I could re-enlist as long as it was for at least the same amount of time as my original enlistment—four years—which meant that I would be in for five years. It was a small price to pay. I could not get out of there fast enough.

The career counselor had my personnel records and examined my Armed Forces Qualification Test scores and said something like, "PFC Steinberg, your scores are very high. You could do pretty much anything you want to." I had no idea what I wanted; I just had to get the hell out of that intellectually devoid environment.

I asked the career counselor what some possibilities were, and he said, "Well there is one Military Occupational Specialty that they are really looking for good people for, and I'm sure you'd qualify for it. In addition, they give you a $1,000 bonus if you re-enlist for this MOS."

Well, that piqued my interest, so I said, "And just exactly what would this be? And I mean 'exactly,' since I don't want to get fucked again."

"Well," he said, "It's for Explosive Ordnance Disposal." I had no idea what he meant. He explained to me what EOD was (the bomb squad), how long the school was, and where it was located—Indianhead, Maryland, about 50 miles from my parents' home. Sitting there, I tried to comprehend "being on the bomb squad." It seemed inherently more dangerous than pushing missiles out of a silo.

Then I thought, "Hmm, the bomb squad. That sounds very cool." That was all the thought I put into it. There was not much difference between that decision and the decision to enlist.

Yet there was the $1,000 bonus, the extra $55 each month for hazardous duty pay, and the prestige of wearing that very cool badge the counselor showed me in his big book of Army jobs. "Where the hell do I sign?" I said. After I passed the physical and the psych exam, off I went to the school's first stage. If I remember correctly, they also sent me to see the dentist to make sure I did not have a mouthful of metal. Apparently, there were some bomb fuses that had anti-magnetic features—too many fillings, or braces, could potentially set them off.

I arrived at Ft. McClellan, Alabama, in late July 1967 for chemical and biological weapons systems. They gassed us with CS—tear gas—and showed us films of things like Army soldiers freaking out on the chemical agent, BZ—the codeword for government LSD, or something close to it. The idea was to gas the enemy and disorient them so they could not fight.

BZ was manufactured by Hoffman-La Roche and had actually been rejected by them because of extreme side effects. It was twenty times more powerful than LSD in its hallucinogenic effects, and the Army tested it on some 2,800 soldiers. The hallucinations and maniacal behavior it caused lasted six weeks in some of the test subjects. The family of one of the men who was given BZ, or LSD, without his knowledge, killed himself when he jumped off a thirteen-story building. The family filed a lawsuit seeking the exact details of their father's death, but I think it was dismissed because of a very fucked up rule called The Feres Doctrine, a Supreme Court case that held that you cannot sue the military for anything that happens to you while you are serving.

In the movie we saw, soldiers were walking around grabbing at things in the air that were not there, and one guy was up in a tree batting at God knows what. I think it was part of the CIA's "MK Ultra" (mind control) program, which ultimately caused people to lose their minds.

There was a movie of nerve gas killing test animals, something that would haunt me six months later, except it would not be test animals that died. We learned about the different chemical and biological agents, how they killed, how delivery systems worked, and how to decontaminate areas where they had been dispersed; it was a good thing I paid attention.

A couple of my classmates had mustard agent put on their forearms so the rest of us could see what it looked like on skin. My friend, Doug Rhodes, still has the little scar it made. They did this by lining us up and then swabbing a wet substance on our arms. They swabbed most of us with water, but a few got the mustard. No one knew which, so we closed our eyes and waited, expecting to see our arms blister like frying bacon. I got the water.

We learned how to protect ourselves when working with deadly agents that could kill you in the blink of an eye. We learned how to get in and out of butyl rubber suits, booties, gloves, and the hoods we pulled over our gas masks. We had to seal them as tight as possible with duct tape (what else?) covering every place that could leak—where your pants went over your booties, where your sleeves pulled down over the gloves, and where your mask hood draped over your shoulders. They said, correctly, that failure to properly suit up for a chemical or biological mission could be fatal.

We also learned how to use Scott Air Packs, a self-contained breathing apparatus with a chemical cartridge to filter your air. You had to change them every twenty to thirty minutes. They are still in use today, but are much more high-tech and the air supply lasts longer. Learning how to use this kind of gear taught us that this job was very dangerous. Upon that realization, in fact, two members of my class dropped out.

Knowledge of protection was an essential part of the EOD program and key to survival. This is not to say that those who died or were injured did not pay attention. Sometimes, your number is just up. No matter how careful, no matter how alert, shit just happens. It happened to me, and I was careful.

I met Tom Allen at Ft. McClellan. He had worked for a tire company in Ohio, and the Draft Board was after him, so he enlisted. We became fast friends.

From Ft. McClellan, we went to the main EOD School at the Naval Ordnance Station, Indianhead, Maryland, about 30 miles west of Washington, DC. For reasons unknown to me, it was known as, "Stumpneck." That was followed by a short time at Eglin Air Force Base, Florida, where we learned about ordnance dropped and fired from fixed and rotary-wing aircraft—bombs, rockets, grenades, anti-personnel bomblets, and their delivery systems.

At Eglin, we learned how to dig a mineshaft in sand in order to recover a 500-lb high-explosive bomb, though the one we dug out was not live. They called it, "Rigging and Digging." If you have not dug in sand, lining the walls with wooden beams and planks as you went down 20 feet, you really do not know what digging is.

In Indianhead, we started with applied physics principles, where we learned the basic chemistry of high explosives and incendiaries and why things explode or burn when exposed to oxygen. I learned about lead styphnate, lead azide, and mercury fulminate, explosives that make nitroglycerin look like water.

These explosives were used in detonators and blasting caps. Lead azide, usually stored underwater in rubber containers, will detonate from a 6-inch drop or exposure to static electricity. Its detonation velocity is about 17,500 feet-per-second. Mercury fulminate is extremely sensitive to heat, shock, friction, spark, and flame.

The best part was explosives, during which we learned how to use plastic explosives, TNT, and shaped charges to disarm or destroy booby traps, mines, and other forms of unexploded ordnance. Detonating (det.) cord was my favorite—it looked like a plastic clothesline, except that it was filled with the explosive PETN. We used it primarily to tie multiple charges together for destroying large piles of ordnance. It detonated at a rate of 27,200 feet-per-second—5 miles in the blink of an eye.

Of the shaped charges we trained on, absolutely the coolest were linear shape charges. They came in different sizes, widths, and lengths, were made of metal and were in a "V-shape" if you looked at a cross-section. They had vertical sides from the bottom leg of each side of the "V." With these, you could do amazing things such as cutting through something in the manner of an acetylene torch, but with explosives instead of gas. Back in the day, we had to fill the linear shape charges with C-4; today, they come pre-packed with the explosives between two thin walls.

We learned how to use special EOD tools, like a .50 caliber de-armer, which shot various sized and shaped steel slugs though fusing devices, hopefully at a speed faster than the fuse could detonate. Now, robots fire the de-armer; when we used them, we were right there on top of the item, setting it up.

When I came back to school for nuclear weapons after I returned from Vietnam, I learned that EOD tools for nuclear weapons were made of Molybdenum, because it did not spark, and could not conduct electricity. It was another one of those little points in time when you wondered exactly what you were doing there.

In the improvised explosive device course—I think they called it "mines and booby traps" back then—we learned how to disarm and destroy Viet Cong booby traps and mines made from command detonated artillery rounds and aerial bombs. The same types of weapons killed soldiers in Iraq, and are still killing them in Afghanistan. The fusing of devices used now is more sophisticated, but the principles are the same.

I learned about fuses, artillery projectiles, land mines, anti-personnel mines, grenades, rockets, and missiles. If it exploded or burned—like white phosphorous or thermite—we learned how to safely handle it, or disarm it, and destroy it, with as little collateral property damage as possible. This included ordnance from most other countries, including Russia, China, the rest of the Communist bloc, Britain, Italy, and France.

I found out, later, that disarming things was not always possible in the middle of a village in the Central Highlands or the Northern Coast near the City of Hue, even when the "rendering safe procedure" was "blow in place" under all circumstances.

Sometimes, when you did blow things in place, you accidentally destroyed private property. Sometimes, the collateral damage—when you had to disarm something, despite the "rules"—had human consequences, as well, not just for innocent civilians, but, far too often, to the EOD men working to save lives. That is what eventually happened to me.

We were existential doctors trying to make the world a little safer, so real doctors had less work. I think that was why grunts respected us and took pains to protect us—since every time we disarmed or destroyed a dud, a mine, or a booby trap, it was one less thing to worry about killing or maiming them.

The Naval Ordnance Station was old at the time I was there, though the main school building was newer. The barracks were bunk beds and lockers, and a community bathroom and shower, with a bar in the basement. The Navy has been there since 1890, then as the Naval Proving Grounds. Today, the Naval Surface Warfare Center develops explosives, propellants, and pyrotechnics there.

As it was a Navy facility, even though all services went there for training, you had to "talk Navy." When an officer entered the room, you announced, "Attention on deck!" The first time this happened, all the Army people sat around looking dumb. Doors were hatches and floors were decks. The latrine was a head. The rank structure was different, so a 2nd lieutenant was an ensign and a colonel was a captain. An Army captain was a Navy lieutenant.

It was confusing, but we learned it, in addition to our studies. That, after my less than stellar high school career, was a new experience for me. The way I learned to learn in EOD School helped me through college and law school, places I never thought I would be that resulted in accomplishments I never thought I would achieve. I owe all of that to EOD.

The drive and discipline I learned in EOD school has marked my life and professional careers—lawyer, teacher, investigator. In many other—maybe most other—aspects of my life, those qualities were often wanting.

I am trying to take that discipline and the skills I brought back from the War, and use them to be a better person. As I write this, the story is changing shape and form, and I better understand what happened to me over the past forty-nine years and, particularly, during my recent return to Vietnam.

As the military and the War changed my life in both good and bad ways, the bad seemed to outweigh the good, so much so that the good part was subsumed much of the time. Like the "Rigging and Digging" class, I am trying to shaft down to the bomb that has been my life, and render it safe.

Just outside the main gate of the Naval Ordnance Station was the town of Indianhead. Then, it was only a few blocks long, a few blocks wide. It seemed like there were more bars than any other type of business, and they catered to the EOD crowd. Some Navy instructors owned parts of a couple of them.

In the EOD bars, I really started drinking. I learned to drink scotch and soda, rum and Coke, Tequila, and, my favorite, Jack Daniels, straight up, no ice, water back. I do not think anyone ever asked for identification, even though the drinking age in Maryland was twenty-one.

On my teams in Vietnam, drinking was a part of our day. I was not drunk every night in the rear, but some were, and I was lit up more times than I care to remember. In Phu Bai, I started drinking whiskey, which eventually became a big problem after I got back.

EOD was a hard-drinking lot. EOD teams in Vietnam had the best bars, places where others wanted to come and drink, not because they wanted to get shitfaced—though that was a big part of it—but because we ran a good setup.

We did not allow fights—although once in Phu Bai, a Marine made the mistake of starting one with our big, weight-lifting, college tackle, Wisconsin farm boy clerk—and we made sure everyone went back to their hooch feeling as good as they could about being in a stinking, rotten place.

When we were not in class or studying, which was not very often, we hung out in the bar in the basement of the barracks, or one of the little bars outside the EOD School, usually drinking until we were stupid. This is where my first addiction began.

After jumping through all the right hoops, they pinned on my basic EOD badge on January 7, 1968. The next day, Tom Allen and I got orders for an EOD team at Dugway Proving Grounds, Utah. Neither of us had ever heard of it, and we both ended up wishing we never had.

5

Dugway Proving Grounds

Dugway was, and still is, the place where the United States developed, tested, and stored major chemical and biological weapons systems. Most testing was in the open air, and Lord knows how many tons of lethal shit has been pumped into the atmosphere in and around the Proving Grounds.

Just what is it they are trying to prove? Today, they still test these types of weapons there, but claim that none of it is open air and that everything is contained within vacuum containment chambers.

They had weapons and delivery systems there that had been around since World War I, maybe even earlier. There were mustard rounds of several varieties left over from World War I, and, as I would learn, many leaked. You may have heard of Dugway.

Dugway, originally built in 1942–43, was located way out in the Great Salt Lake Desert. On one side was the famed Bonneville Salt Flats. I had always hoped that I would get to see a land speed record set while I was there, but it did not happen. I did manage to crash a motorcycle on the salt, and, after skidding on my side for about 100 feet, melted most of the skin on my left arm. That was my last motorcycle.

Dugway is about 80 miles west-southwest from Salt Lake City, surrounded by three mountain ranges, and covers 798,855 acres (1,248 square miles, which is bigger than some countries and 34 square miles larger than Rhode Island). It is a desolate and depressing place, especially if you are twenty and like girls.

One of my jobs, along with the rest of my team, was to monitor and destroy weapons systems when they malfunctioned, typically during development.

Sometimes, they invented weapons with new types of fusing systems, which often failed the first time they were tested. Our job was to figure out what to do next.

Do you think that while they designed the latest biological or chemical killing machine, they thought about how to disarm it if it messed up? Well, of course not. That was why we were there, drawing that big $55-per-month hazardous duty pay. There were bio weapons systems that included anthrax as well as other lethal biological agents.

There was a rumor that they had developed biological agents and did not know what the hell they were, let alone how to kill them if they got loose. There were things that they tested inside vacuum chambers so that there was no chance anything would be dispersed into the air—at least in theory.

In Stephen King's bestseller, *The Stand*, most of the world's population dies when a bio-agent escapes from a secret military base. In the movie, it was in California. Like these rumored agents at Dugway, there was no known cure. I am sure King was thinking of Dugway because of something that happened there in March 1968. It is why I volunteered for Vietnam.

In the chemical area, there were weapons systems containing two types of nerve gas—VX and GB. There was mustard gas; AC, or hydrogen cyanide, which was called Zyklon-B by the Nazis and used in the concentration camps to kill millions; DM, or Adamsite, which causes you to vomit—the U.S. government used it against veterans in the "Bonus March" in 1932, reportedly causing the death and serious injury of several children who had accompanied their parents; CS tear gas; and my favorite, CK—cyanogen chloride—a highly toxic blood agent, which causes you to asphyxiate. They referred to this mode of death as "dry land drowning."

Apparently, in terms of our development and storage of AC, we did, in fact, learn something useful from the Nazis other than how to make better missiles and nuclear weapons. I wonder if the U.S. government ever told anyone— particularly Holocaust survivors—they were storing this stuff at Dugway.

In 1968, we stored a lot of nerve agents at Dugway. Much of it was antiquated, contained in rusting and leaking artillery projectiles and rockets. GB (or Sarin) was the non-persistent agent. It killed you and then dissipated in about fifteen minutes. VX was the persistent agent. It killed you and then hung around and continued to kill long after it was dispersed. As little as 200 micrograms can kill you.

I never thought about it then, and I am trying hard not to think about it now. This is sometimes impossible since I live in Oregon and am downwind of the Umatilla Army Depot where they recently destroyed nerve agents in large, purportedly safe, incinerators. Given what happened at Dugway, I am not happy about this, nor do I have any faith that it was ultimately safe.

Dugway was sort of like being in Neverland because I had not contemplated—never, never—that I would see the things I saw there. Several weapons systems I worked on defy conceptualization because they are so horrific. Why the hell would anyone—no matter how much they were paid—want to sit around and invent shit like this? What kind of soul does that person have? Any?

One such weapon was a large landmine containing 15.3 pounds of plasticized white phosphorus. It was about 1 foot, maybe a little bigger, across and about 5 inches high—the XM-54. It was painted light blue or green, which I thought a little strange, as though it had an interior decorator pick this color, while everything around it, including us, was olive drab or sand-colored.

The XM-54 could be command detonated or set off with a trip wire. In August, 1968, while I was home on leave from Dugway, they shipped about 200 of these beasts to Vietnam. "XM" means "experimental."

White phosphorus burns as soon as it is exposed to air and will just burn a hole right through you. This mine was a gigantic Bouncing Betty. When detonated, it was launched into the air by a propellant charge, raining a hailstorm of white fire on everyone within range. White phosphorus burns at about 5,000 degrees, and the grenade version will burn for sixty seconds once it bursts and exposes the filler to air. At Dugway, we destroyed a couple of them that were duds.

When I left Dugway, one of the things I thought was, "Well, I'll never see those fucking white fucking phosphorus fucking mines again!" I was wrong. My first team in Qui Nhơn provided EOD support to the 184th Ordnance Battalion. They had a big ammo dump.

As I will eventually explain in detail, they had the worst security problem keeping the enemy out of the dump. It was an impossible task, no matter how much security they had. You will see.

One day, I was in the office at the unit, and we get a call from our Control Team. I answered the phone, and whoever was on the other end said they needed to talk to me. Some of the white phosphorus mines had been planted around the dump as an experiment. Someone—maybe the enemy, maybe not—hit a trip wire and the damn thing had not gone off. It was presumed to be armed.

I guess they had not tested it enough at Dugway by killing dogs (mostly beagles), rabbits, and other animals. They wanted to see how it killed people, so they sent a few over to Vietnam. I was jinxed when it came to this stuff.

Control somehow knew I had worked on this device. The functioning—how it went boom—was still highly classified. We were to check it out, see if we could figure out why it did not go off, and blow it.

It never dawned on me to ask how they knew I had seen this thing before. Allegedly, the U.S. government keeps track of former EOD technicians because of what we know. If you can take them apart, you can build them. I wonder if they really keep tabs on those of us, like me, who were trained on nuclear weapons.

I got another team member, though I cannot remember who; we jumped in the jeep and headed for the dump. It might have been First Sergeant Lee Miller because my memory is that whoever I was with outranked me. We arrived at the dump and a team of security guards and an ordnance officer led us across the dump in jeeps, which I thought was a really bad idea, and out through the back gate; we then headed up toward the low hills that faced the east side of the perimeter.

The officer raised his hand. We pulled up and got out of the jeeps. He pointed to a wooden stake sticking out of the red dirt, with a yellow plastic ribbon at the top. "That's where it is," he said.

"Where are the other ones?"

He looked at me. "Well, they're out there, but we didn't mark them. I have a diagram of their locations."

I looked at this guy, incredulously, wondering how he had made captain. "Who planted these things?"

"Engineers," he said, shifting the blame.

"Is there some reason why you guys didn't mark them all before you called us?"

"We're ordnance, and we couldn't get the engineers back in here. That's why we called you." That was fair enough.

I took the Captain's diagram and looked it over, sharing it with my teammate; we talked out a route to the stake, hoping that the diagram was accurate. We grabbed our guns and a demolition bag, and headed off into the minefield, looking for the trip wires of the other mines we believed were in our path. I guess we were right because we did not blow ourselves up.

We got to the stake and saw immediately that the tripwire to the mine was broken. There were booted footsteps all around it. I turned over one of my jungle boots and looked at the tread, comparing it to the tracks in the damp earth. They were a perfect match.

This did not prove it was not the enemy, but it was more likely either an American or Korean patrol. That was who conducted night operations and ambushes around the dump. Obviously, they were not told about the mines, or forgot they were there, or they would have stayed out of the area— lucky them.

In the end, we noted that the wire had been broken, and the mine failed to detonate. This was a problem we also had at Dugway. I believe there was not enough sensitivity in the tripwire method to detonate the thing unless you tripped it dead on, with a lot of foot drag. A glancing or angled drag of the foot did not apply enough pull to function the detonator to the propellant charge. That was what I thought.

We set a charge of C-4 with non-electric caps and a fuse lighter about 6 inches from the mine on two sides. We did not want to take a chance on setting the thing off with ground tremors by being too close. You always had to consider that when a trip-wire device had not functioned, that the firing pin was lodged in the detonator. It could set the mine off if the firing pin was dislodged.

In fact, we had approached it the last 10 feet on our knees. The charge set off the propellant; the mine jumped 6 feet into the air and detonated, throwing molten white phosphorus a long way in every direction. We were behind our jeep about 100 yards away, and I heard the ordnance officer mutter under his breath, "Holy fucking shit!"

"Yeah," I thought. "Holy fucking shit." It was not that I had an opposition to killing the enemy, but I remember thinking, "This is no way for a soldier to die." I read that they never deployed this mine, and I am glad for that.

One of our major jobs at Dugway—fondly called "Bugway"—was to assist the monitoring of VX and GB weapons systems, looking for leaks. The major weapon that was stored at Dugway was the M55 rocket. It measured 78 inches in length and was 4.44 inches in diameter. The rockets were filled with about 10 pounds of either VX or GB. The bursters contained about 3 pounds of the explosive Composition "B" or tetrytol. Composition "B" is a mixture of the explosives RDX and TNT.

Over the course of a week, my team identified many leakers and then transported them to our demolition area. When the demo pit was full, we covered the bad rounds with old tires, soaked them in jet fuel, and set charges containing a lot of C-4 plastic explosives and white phosphorus grenades tied together with detonating cord. We added a series of electric blasting caps and moved to a rear area.

Then we detonated the pit, igniting the tires and jet fuel, causing the rockets to split open and set off their bursters—theoretically. The ensuing inferno was theoretically supposed to destroy the nerve agent theoretically.

The pit would typically burn for several days and take several more to cool down, after which we blew the rockets that had failed to detonate. The explosion and fire burst the rockets open, then detonated their bursters while the fire destroyed the nerve agent. Sometimes, the bursters did not detonate; they would split and the fire melted the explosives inside, causing a slag that would cover the ground and harden as it cooled.

After one such burn, Tom Allen and I checked the pit for unexploded and melted rocket bursters. One thing we learned was that the explosives in the bursters became very unstable if they melted and then re-solidified. I mean, very unstable. The explosives, in their solid form are virtually impossible to detonate without setting them off with a blasting cap, or some other explosive.

However, once they melted and hardened, just about anything could set them off, including stepping on it, which is what Tom did. He was not being unsafe; there was just so much of this explosive crystallized slag in the pit after a blow that you could not possibly see it all as you looked for bursters and unfired rocket motors. It was amazing we did not have more accidents like this.

While I was at the vehicle cutting charges, Tom was in the pit looking for duds when a burster exploded and a large piece of shrapnel penetrated Tom's butyl rubber pants. He was in the hospital for several days.

As I said, Dugway played a role in my volunteering for Vietnam. Here is why—on March 13, 1968, Dugway Proving Grounds had the worst nerve gas disaster in the history of the world, at least that we have been told about. Based upon all of the other lies and deceitful, illegal actions of our government over the years, why should we believe that Dugway was the worst?

An F-4 Phantom jet was carrying ordnance that was a delivery system for approximately 320 gallons (2,740 pounds) of the nerve agent, VX. Why they had to use that much—enough to kill millions—on a simple test is beyond me. Some portion of that amount ended up outside the test area in a valley between the Skull and Camelback Mountains. Here is what the Army has to say about VX:

VX is a nerve agent so powerful that a single drop on the skin can result in death within about 15 minutes. It works by disrupting the nervous system and causing breathing to stop. VX has a thick, oil-like consistency that allows it to be sprayed on plants prior to enemy troops marching through an area. It remains toxic for at least several days.

If it only "remains toxic for several days," then why did the Army buy the land from the rancher and permanently fence it off?

During a test that took the plane over civilian land in Skull Valley, Utah, the weapons system malfunctioned and dispersed the VX over an area of thousands of acres. The U.S. government denied this occurred and covered it up for many years. An official report in 1970, now public, however, had this to say:

> The Stone investigation shows that on March 13, 1968—the day before the sheep died—Dugway employees conducted three activities with nerve agents. One was a test of a single artillery shell filled with a chemical agent, and another was the disposal of about 160 gallons of nerve agent in an open burn pit. [This was a burn conducted by my EOD Team].
>
> The sheep deaths usually are linked to the third activity—a test in which a low-flying jet fighter sprayed nerve agent in a barren target area about 27 miles west of Skull Valley. Later reports indicated one of the tanks malfunctioned and some of the nerve agent continued to be sprayed as the jet finished its run and began climbing high into the sky.
>
> Dugway's meteorological reports indicated the wind was blowing out of the northwest at the time of the test, but later shifted to the west as a small storm front passed. These west winds could have carried nerve agent directly over the sheep herds.

My team was first on the ground after the accident. My memory is that we went in by truck, but we might have flown in by chopper. My memory is a little hazy on this. It was March 14. There were some scientists with us from a government agency and a university. I have no idea why they were there.

There were also a bunch of people from the Department of Defense. My fantasy is that they wanted to see how well the nerve agent had killed everything. When we went into the site, we were dressed in butyl rubber suits and breathing through gas masks, with Scott Air Packs in reserve.

Every living thing in the contaminated area was either dead or in the process of dying a horrible death. Some 6,400 sheep were dead or dying; some of those still alive were euthanized by veterinarians. Every orifice exuded bodily fluids—feces, urine, mucous, saliva, and blood. Every bird, lizard, snake, bug, and cockroach was dead. The sheepherder's horses and sheep dogs were dead.

The only reason there were no civilian casualties was that the sheepherders were not there. March 13, 1968 was a Thursday, and we heard that they were from Albania, or somewhere in Eastern Europe, where Thursdays were their official day off. I have no idea if that is why they were not there that day, but it was clearly a stroke of luck for them.

Their horses and herd dogs, however, were not so lucky; they were just as dead as the sheep. One of my teammates, who was there, reminded me several years ago that the herders were also involved in killing the hundreds of sheep still in the process of dying. They did this by cutting their throats.

In some ways, it was similar to things I would see many times in Vietnam at locations where the bodies of dead Americans and enemy soldiers lay everywhere.

I am not trying to demean the bodies of dead soldiers, and I am certainly not trying to compare them in any sense with the dead sheep at Dugway. Death is a very powerful visual, especially when it is more than 6,000 of anything.

When you see a lot of one thing—men, sheep, whatever—dead, in one place, at one time, it is sickening and horrible, something that stays with you forever. I have as strong a memory of the dead animals at Dugway as I do about the dead American, Viet Cong, and NVA bodies I stripped of ordnance at places like the Qui Nhon Airfield and Fire Support Base Rifle. Dead is dead, no matter what, no matter where. Whether the dead are killed by nerve gas, or incoming rockets and mortars, or bullets, in the end it is all the same.

Over the next week, the team supervised the cleanup and assisted an engineer group that gathered up all of the corpses with bulldozers. There were sheep, herd dogs, horses, and everything else that was alive before the VX hit them. They dug a giant pit with the bulldozers in the center of the land and shoved them in it. When that was done, the entire landscape was scraped into the pit.

As with the destruction of nerve agents at Dugway Proving Grounds, we piled on tires, jet fuel, and tons of charges, setting off the explosives and burning everything in the pit. The hole was then filled in. The land was marked as government property and posted with "keep out" signs. I am guessing it is still that way today.

The Army paid off the owner and denied that anything had happened involving nerve gas. Those of us who cleaned up the Dugway incident were debriefed and told that we could not disclose what we had seen, or what the cause was. We were told that we could not talk about what had happened, or what we did. Virtually everything the Army and Department of Defense has ever said about what happened at Dugway is just a complete lie.

I also heard that for several months after the accident, the Department of Defense tried to blame the F-4 pilot for what had happened—pilot error or some such bullshit. They did not want to admit that, like many experiments conducted at Dugway, the weapons system had simply malfunctioned.

There were apologists for the Army who claimed that physical and atmospheric conditions make the deaths of the sheep by VX impossible. One weasel claimed that the sheep were actually killed by a deadly pesticide that was, he claimed, coincidentally sprayed several miles away. I know what happened because I was there, and douchebags like this guy were not. I wonder how much the government paid him to spread this bullshit disinformation.

By the way, I was recently told that the owners of the land were related to Senator Orin Hatch and were powerful people in Utah. I do not know if that is true, but nothing about that event would surprise me, given the government's refusal for years to admit that anything happened.

Dugway sticks out in my mind, right up there with my worst experiences in Vietnam. Back in the day, I had as many nightmares about Dugway as I did about Vietnam. I actually did not realize how it had affected me; it was one of the causes of my Post-traumatic stress disorder. It was not until 2002 that I first wrote about Dugway's impact and how it led me to volunteer for Vietnam.

The day we finished cleaning up the Dugway disaster, several of us went to the enlisted men's club and got staggering drunk. That night, Bruce Stearns, a teammate, took me onto the roof of our barracks, and I got stoned on marijuana for the first time. I later heard that he was medevacked from Vietnam because of drugs. The rumor was that he was caught with his head in a plastic bag huffing glue. Maybe Dugway put him that far over the edge.

None of us were quite the same after the Dugway event. Today, Dugway's motto—you could not make this up if you tried—is, "caring for the environment is also our business." When I was there, the sign said, "Warning. Dangerous instrumentalities of war are being tested on this post. Do not handle any unidentified objects." I think it would be more fitting, today, if it were the motto of a unit I saw in Vietnam: "Killing is our business, and business is good."

The day after I got really loaded, I volunteered for Vietnam. I think Tom Allen did, too, but I am not positive. At least in Vietnam, I naively thought, we could see and hear the enemy. I sometimes tell people when I talk about Dugway that, "The thing about nerve agents is that you hear nothing, you see nothing, you smell nothing. You're just fucking dead." I think now, that the VC and the NVA were not so different. They were also silent killers.

You know how you hear that cockroaches can survive a nuclear blast? Well, guess what? They cannot survive nerve gas because they have a central nervous system. Everything that walked, crawled, flew, or slithered over the land that was contaminated died that day. Vietnam just seemed a whole lot safer. I think that was one of those occasions, like when I enlisted, when I did not think things through very well.

One last thing—as if stories about Dugway have not been and are still not weird enough, there is now a group of people who think Dugway is "the new Area 51," complete with "alien" activity and UFOs. One guy claims that when he traveled through Skull Valley, he "lost time" and apparently was involved in some secret government time experiment, or something; I go for the "or something" option.

6

Qui Nhơn

The flight along the coast of South Vietnam from the Saigon area to the inland port of Qui Nhơn—a distance of about 400 miles—was uneventful in the sense that nothing happened during that long ride. It was bumpy, and I learned that flying in a Chinook, strapped into a web jump seat, was an uncomfortable sensation, at least over that distance.

I learned to like it, however, for short, fast flights when I went into an LZ in the bush. The bird never actually set down; you ran and jumped from the rear ramp, which might be just barely touching the ground. Maybe the door gunners, firing from side windows, were tearing it up. Yet, on that first trip, there was none of that—just a lot of time to think, still wishing that I had a weapon.

What was my tour going to be like? Would it be dangerous? Would I see a lot of action? Would I have to shoot people and would I be shot at? I was not scared or obsessing. They were the questions any one of us must have asked when we first arrived in country.

No doubt some of the guys—maybe a lot of them—were shitting in their pants thinking about these things, scared about the possibility of death. Some of us would be killed, but I always knew it would be someone else. Even when I was blown up and did not die, I was not very surprised and, at the time, never had those thoughts about why and how I had survived.

That was not true in the years after I got out and had more time to think. It is not that you did not have time to think about these things when they happened, you just did not. You would have gone crazy if you had, and I guess some soldiers who contemplated these things when they happened, did lose their minds. As I described it in Chapter One, I witnessed such an event when we flew out of Rifle.

I gazed from my window in the Chinook as we flew up the coast. We were flying low enough to see farmers working in the fields and rice paddies. Kids were herding the family water buffalo; I wondered how many VC were watching us fly over, wishing for a clear shot. I had no idea what the other passengers were thinking since it was almost impossible to talk over the noise of a Chinook.

Even if it had been quieter, I am pretty sure that, like me, the others were lost in their own thoughts about being in Vietnam, flying over what everyone knew was enemy territory.

By their well-used gear, I could tell that some of my fellow travelers were infantrymen; I guessed returning from an operation, or on their way to a new unit. One battle-weary sergeant was wearing a patch with a single white wing with the "Airborne" tab. Like me, he focused on the ground passing below us and fingered the trigger on his M-16.

"Lucky bastard," I thought. "He's got a gun." I tapped him on the shoulder and asked what unit he was with, yelling above the noise the Chinook's beating blades made. He responded, also yelling, "The 173rd Airborne Brigade, 2nd Battalion, 503rd Parachute Infantry Regiment." Then I saw the black and green jump wings sewn above his left breast pocket, just below the Combat Infantryman's Badge.

He saw my EOD badge—I was still wearing the silver metal one—pointed at it, and yelled, "You're EOD. Where you going?"

"Qui Nhơn," I yelled back. "You?"

"LZ English—a shithole near a place called Bong Son." Of course, I had no idea where Bong Son was and had never heard of LZ English. "We have some EOD guys at the LZ," he commented loudly. "They've saved our asses a lot with booby traps and all the fucking mines. Maybe you'll get up there."

He was right and I, too, would learn what a shithole the place was, and just how dangerous the Bong Son Plains and surrounding environs could be. He was talking about EOD men who were about to become my teammates, and, I would discover, the booby traps and mines were the least of the problems in the Bong Son Plains and the An Loa Mountains. The young "Sky Trooper" looked away, refocusing his attention out the chopper window, never taking his finger off the trigger of his weapon. I wondered if he had the safety off.

When I think about Bong Son and all the other dangerous places I was in and out of, I am struck by the lack of understanding we had for the places where we would end up. Really, there was no way you could have prepared for this in your previous training, other than knowing that anything could happen. They did not teach us about things like living in the mud, being wet half the year from monsoon rains or how steaming hot it really was.

You went to Vietnam, and you thought you knew something about the place before you got there, even though your common sense, if you had listened to it, would have told you that you did not know jack shit. There are some things, no matter how much training or education you have, that you simply cannot prepare for—kind of like life. You think you know what it is, and then one day, you open your eyes and understand you really do not.

My path these past forty-plus years has been like that. Do not get me wrong, because it is not as if all of a sudden, I think I understand my life any more than I understand the War. Yet I am working on it, and instead of focusing on how all the bad things about the War affected me, I am trying to rely upon the positive things I learned—particularly, saving myself—to get me safely and peacefully through the next twenty or thirty years, or however much time I have left.

Some other passengers on the Chinook, like me, wore what appeared to be new fatigues. Many of them looked scared shitless, eyes shifting about, not talking with their fellow passengers. Their duffle bags were at their feet, although one soldier held his in his lap, squeezing it like he was afraid to let go.

This is how I was about the War forty-seven years later, holding on for dear life, afraid to let go, as though something terrible would happen, if I did. We could have been shot down on that ride to Qui Nhơn, but were not. Now I see that life is pretty much the same. I could be shot down every day, but I am not. I have obsessed about that a lot. I never thought about it in Vietnam, and I am trying not to now.

For myself, while I worried about the possibility of being shot down, or just being shot at, I was glad I was there. I did not know it then, never thought about it at the time, but I know now that I was made for it—made for the War.

It seemed like, for the first time in my life, I was doing something important, and I still believe that. I am not saying it was the War that was important because that is just not true. It was not then, and it is not now. Being there was what was important, and I am not sure, today, if I actually understand why. Maybe it was being with the men I served with.

I am not saying that the important thing I thought I was doing was fighting Communism, or aiding our so-called "allies" in the fight to stop the dominoes from collapsing all over Southeast Asia. I could not have cared less about any of that and still do not today. What I mean is that it was important to me, personally. Being there was important to me, personally.

I say that twice because it was the first time in my life I felt that I was a part of something larger than myself. Again, I am not talking about the War, but about the four teams I was with, the men who were on them, the job we were trained to do, and the desire to do it well.

While I was in Vietnam, I did not think that much about my family, or the friends I did not have back home, who, if they had existed, would have been worried about me putting myself in harm's way. Somehow, it was important that I be right there, right then, just at that exact moment, totally focusing on my teammates and the people who counted on us to do our job.

Later, this feeling would be replaced by the belief that other people's lives depended on what I did, and I grew to understand that they often relied on my understanding of a particular situation to make the correct decision. I took a certain pride in that. I have had the same thing happen to me, repeatedly, in my professional life, and yet have been unable to feel that same pride for more than a fleeting moment. I am trying to change that.

In 2007, during a reunion of EOD men who had served in Vietnam, one of my buddies from the War and I were talking about the time he came to Qui Nhơn to help us cleanup the ammo dump that the VC blew up three times during the Post-Tet Offensive. We had not known each other before then; he had been sent up from the team in Long Bình, just outside Saigon, to help us.

He said to me, "I remember when I met you when I got to your unit. I looked at you and thought, 'This guy is a soldier.'" By then, I had the "thousand-meter stare," and maybe that was part of what he saw. It is one of the greatest compliments anyone has ever given me and I know now, looking back, that he was right. I was a soldier. I think that is what I had a sense of when I was on that first chopper ride. It has taken me more than forty years to feel pride in what he told me in 1969, but I do, and it is a new experience.

Despite everything going on back in the States, I never questioned whether the War was right or wrong. Frankly, I did not give a fuck and I do not think it ever entered my mind until about six months after my discharge in 1971. I am not quite sure why that is since I have always been what most people would consider a liberal, and my family has always been in the "left-leaning" wing of the Democratic Party.

Even now, and despite everything I know about what we did wrong in Vietnam, I am glad I was there and, given the opportunity, would do it all over again. When we went into Afghanistan in 2001 to kill the Taliban and al-Qaeda, I actually sent the Army an email to see if I could get back in, maybe to teach at the EOD School at Eglin Air Force Base in Florida. They never wrote me back.

The Army was family, more so than my real family had ever felt up to that point in my life. I have to admit, however, that was mostly of my own doing since I was pretty fucked up as a kid.

Even in Basic Training, there was a shared sense of belonging to something that was important, that had purpose. That was how I saw it, even though most of the reservists in my company probably would not have agreed.

In this country, there have been times when it was not an advantage to be a Vietnam veteran. In many facets of life, it was a negative factor, largely because the media often portrayed us as drug-crazed killers. Unfortunately, we are seeing some of that occur, today, regarding our men and women who have served in Iraq and Afghanistan.

When a Vietnam veteran went nuts and killed someone, it was somehow important that he was a Vietnam veteran, and that it had something to do with the murder. When a pharmacist went crazy and killed someone, the story made little, if any, mention of the fact that he was a pharmacist, and certainly never connected the fact that he was a pharmacist to the fact that he was a murderer.

Much of this country's "love" for its veterans has been tempered for many years by its failing memory of abject rejection of Vietnam veterans. As long as people feel safe, they do not care about the plight of the veterans who never made it back on track after serving their country, particularly those who were in combat.

It is a sad state of affairs that we are finally receiving our due as a result of the Global War on Terror, and our young men and women back from Iraq and Afghanistan. I think this has had a lot to do with why so many of us, in the past, have not been willing to share our experiences, or publicly show that we were proud to have served our country.

When I did talk about my service and some of the things I had seen, most people did not want to hear it, and seemed embarrassed that I would even bring it up. There can be no wonder, then, about why so many of us have had mixed feelings about our service during a war everyone has seemed hell-bent on forgetting ever happened.

After a bunch of hours in the air, the Chinook finally touched down at the airfield in Qui Nhơn. I climbed off the chopper and was, again, struck by the heat and thickness of the humidity. I wondered if I would ever get used to it. The heat was almost intolerable; it was like living in a blast furnace.

Every place you drove, the dust—red and rusty looking—got into, and all over everything. It was in your eyes, hair, clothes; your weapon and your boots were totally encrusted in the stuff. When you drove down a road in the unrelenting heat, you saw heat waves rising from the pavement. The sun was so bright, it seemed like you would go blind without sunglasses and a floppy boonie hat, and even they offered only so much protection.

Qui Nhơn was the capital of Bình Định Province. In many ways, when you drove through it, it was like any big, dirty, smelly city in the United States. Traffic jams, too many people, air pollution, slums, trash everywhere. There was also the problem of drive-by shootings, or the occasional flung grenade, which is not very different from some major U.S. cities, today.

When I worked as an investigator, I was sitting in an alley in LA, waiting for a witness to return home. In the early evening hours, when gunfire erupted several blocks away, I was startled, but then shrugged it off—been there, done that, and my .45 was on the seat next to me. It reminded me of all those times a teammate and I raced through the streets of Qui Nhơn or Phu Bai in the middle of the night, ignoring the sounds of gunfire from across the city.

Qui Nhơn was a violent, crime-ridden cesspool, and not just because of the War. That was there before the War ever started. There were "slicky boys," who rode their fume-spewing mopeds alongside your jeep and ripped your watch right off your arm, or grabbed your camera out of the vehicle. There were pickpockets, prostitutes, and drug dealers on every street.

But mostly, it was a place infested with Viet Cong and North Vietnamese soldiers, and had been the site of the first major tragedy of the War. On February 10, 1965, just before the Marines came ashore at Da Nang, Viet Cong sappers blew up an enlisted men's billet in a downtown Qui Nhơn hotel.

Apparently, our war planners did not think such things would happen, so they did not have properly defended billets for their troops. Sappers got into the hotel, set their charges, and blew the place to hell. Twenty-three Army soldiers, mostly from the 140th Transportation Detachment, died in the blast

The CIA had warned the military in April 1965 that the Viet Cong were sending 5,000 soldiers into Bình Định Province, where Qui Nhơn was located. This warning was ignored.

I learned early that when the monsoons came, the mud was thick and could suck your boots off, especially when we were on-site at places like LZ English in the Central Highlands, or along the coast of the South China Sea at Phú Hiệp. When we went to the bush in the monsoon season, it was wet hell. We were soaking wet all the time; our socks were permanently attached to our feet. Our jungle boots had a canvas mesh up the side, so the water leaked in, but did not leak out very well.

No matter what you did, and no matter how many lectures you heard, you just could not keep your feet dry and eventually, like me, you developed a lifelong affliction called jungle rot. Sometimes, you would be going down a trail and the rain would be coming down so hard that you could barely see your hand in front of your face. At night—well, it was just plain fucking cold when it was raining in the Central Highlands or up north near the DMZ, especially if you were 3,000 feet up the side of a mountain.

Qui Nhơn was located in a triangle bordered from the southwest to the northeast, then to the northwest, by Route 441. On the west, mostly running from the southeast to the northwest was Highway 1, the main drag that ran all the way from the Delta to the DMZ. The city itself jutted out onto a peninsula that was surrounded by the South China Sea. The airfield where I landed, located dead-bang in the middle of the city and the south end of the airfield, where our unit was located, was just off Route 441.

I cannot remember who met me at the helipad and drove me to the unit. The 184th's buildings (called "hooches") were next to a 3-foot thick, 10-foot high wall, heavily sandbagged and topped with razor wire, just inside the airfield perimeter. The city was just on the other side of the wall and, as I contemplated that fact, I wondered just how safe it was there. I would learn, soon enough, not very.

Within five minutes of joining the Qui Nhơn team, I finally got that weapon I had been obsessing about. It was an M-16, a weapon I had not been trained on before coming to Vietnam. I had it down pat within about two minutes. I loved that gun, but eventually came into possession of a CAR-15, the carbine version of the M-16 and now known as the M-4, although not with all of the high-tech gear they come with, today. It had a collapsing stock and a short flash suppressor. I carried it until I left in March 1970.

Anyway, I immediately felt safer, although, as I eventually learned, this was a joke, because no matter how many guns you had, the pall of death was always there. They could protect you only so much.

During the last few weeks of my second tour, I carried my CAR-15, two bandoliers of magazines, a 40-mm grenade launcher, and a .45. If I went to the bush, I packed a couple of grenades and strapped a LAW rocket to my rucksack. I figured that if something was going to happen, I was not going down without a fight. Even with all that firepower, I did not feel safer.

Those of us who actually fought the War never really understood the futility of it. We did what we could to protect our comrades, and ourselves, and to come back in one piece. What we never understood was that the War could not be won, at least not the way our politicians allowed it to be fought.

The war in Vietnam had no front, it had no rear, and I guess you could say it had no sides. It was everywhere. Today, they call it "asymmetric warfare." No matter where you were—the bush, the villages, the streets of the cities, or the rice paddies—there it was. Even when nothing was happening, something was amiss, but you could not see it.

The enemy was there and not there, all at the same time. In the bush a firefight was almost a relief, because at least you knew, generally, where they were. That does not mean you could actually see them. It was often the case that you could not, so you hosed down the jungle with automatic weapons.

We never quite understood that when you cannot tell the enemy from innocent civilians, well, you are just plain fucked. Whether you fight from tree to tree in the jungles of Vietnam, or house to house in the desert cities of Iraq and Afghanistan, it is all the same war—same AK-47s, same RPGs, same IEDs, same fanatical enemy, and same pissed off families of every person we "accidentally" kill and then refer to as "collateral damage."

In Vietnam, every time innocent civilians died, their families became the enemy or, at best, they stopped cooperating with us and with their own soldiers. When we went into a village and the locals cooperated with us, the VC often killed them after we left. Clearly, that brought the locals closer to our cause—as if.

However, the biggest mistake we made in Vietnam was that when the enemy perceives itself as a force for national liberation—and the population perceives us as occupiers—no matter how evil the enemy actually is, they simply cannot be defeated, and will fight to the last man or woman.

All you have to do to know the truth of this is look at our own revolution and the fact that untrained shopkeepers and farmers defeated the most powerful military force in the world. The guerrilla tactics we used against the British Empire were the same as those of the VC.

During the Vietnam War, it is estimated that we killed more than 1,000,000 North Vietnamese and Viet Cong soldiers. This means that for every twenty-nine Americans killed, we killed almost 500 of the enemy. If you add in the approximately 200,000 South Vietnamese soldiers killed, the ratio is still one of us to four of them.

Of course, the infamous "body counts" that were supposed to show the American people how well the War was going were a perfectly useless statistic since, in the end, they meant absolutely nothing. Many body counts were flat-out lies.

It is hard to remember all the men on the Qui Nhơn team, but Roger McCormack and Doug Rhodes became my best friends there. Roger eventually married a woman from England and moved there after the War. I learned that he was back in the States in 2007, and we are in contact, again, almost weekly. Doug and I also talk and Skype regularly. We serve together on the board of directors of the National EOD Association.

Just before I went to Afghanistan in 2009, I drove across the country to Indiana, picked up Roger, and we spent the next three weeks together, including his returning to Oregon with me after stops at the National EOD Association convention and to see my son in Minnesota. Roger is the same crazy, irreverent motherfucker he was in Vietnam.

Our first sergeant was Lee Miller, who had been in EOD a long time. I saw him after I came back, and he was drinking himself to death. He died in 1987 at the age of fifty-three. There was Jerry Culp, Jim Young, Pat Gehringer, Ken Eskew, and later, Bill Petersen, Tom Nutter, and Larry Brooks. Larry died last year. Pat and I recently made contact after almost forty years. He retired a Command sergeant major and was still in EOD as a civilian at Redstone Arsenal. He helped me out with identifying a very sophisticated IED detonator I found in Afghanistan. I recently learned that Bill Petersen passed away shortly after I talked with him in 2007 about an event that was being planned in St. Louis for Vietnam EOD men. Tom Nutter, who retired as a chief warrant officer 4, passed away in 2016.

The CO in Qui Nhơn was Captain Russell Hunt. Captain Dennis Lorance replaced him near the end of 1968, or in early 1969. I tracked Dennis down in Texas and we had a great phone conversation. He reminded me that one of the things that impressed him was that I had returned to the field within days after being wounded twice. It was pretty cool hearing that from him.

Dennis was replaced by Roberto Stillwell, another good man. I will explain why Dennis left the team later.

Sergeant First Class Arnie Neiderhofer is one of the best men I ever met. We got back in touch in either 2003, or 2004, when I saw a post from him on a web site called Fragweb. At the age of almost seventy, he was a private EOD contractor in Iraq. I thought about signing up with him, but my wife and kid said I was out of my mind. So, I did not, but I wanted to.

There was Mike Lizak, Roy Judkins, Frank Matsuda (our clerk), and Ron Carlton, who died from Agent Orange-related cancer. Judkins and Lizak have also passed away. Matsuda, our clerk, was replaced by a soldier named Forman, who turned out to be a junkie. We had to get rid of him. I think that is why so many important unit documents, like the report of the action in which I was wounded the second time, were not in our files. I love all of these guys.

During my second week in Qui Nhơn, the Viet Cong hit the airfield near where we lived. The attack started with a barrage of incoming mortars and rocket-propelled grenades that came over the wall behind our buildings, some of which landed fairly close to our bunker. I was just in country, and here was the War.

Nothing I had been told up to that point could have prepared me for the adrenalin rush when the alert siren went off and the incoming started to fall, and the fear. It was weird being scared and excited at the same time.

It felt like a red-hot poker had been rammed into my brain; I was in overdrive. Running from our quarters to the bunker, I jammed a clip into my M-16 and jacked a round into the chamber. For the first time, I wondered if I was going to have to shoot at someone. It would eventually happen.

After the incoming, Viet Cong sappers entered the airfield and began throwing satchel charges at buildings, fuel areas, and at fixed-wing planes and choppers on the runway. Mortars, RPG-2s, and RPG-7s—rocket propelled grenades—hit all over the airfield. From our position at the south end of the airfield, we watched stuff blow sky-high and burn for the rest of the night.

Early the following morning, at about 5 a.m., my team was called out to deal with dud satchel charges, Viet Cong stick grenades, several RPG-2s and RPG-7s still on enemy bodies, and a lot of ordnance that had been thrown around the airfield from exploding helicopter gunships. This included 40-mm grenades, 2.75-inch high-explosive and white phosphorous rockets, and a lot of 7.62-mm machine gun ammunition. Our job was to disarm the devices, if necessary, and destroy them.

One of our other tasks—one that I would perform, again and again, at locations all over Vietnam—was to clear the dead bodies of enemy soldiers. This involved checking the bodies for booby traps and unexploded ordnance. Miraculously, no Americans were killed during the Qui Nhơn Airfield attack.

They were my first dead bodies—other than relatives in a casket—including several that were blown to pieces, shot many times, missing limbs and heads. There was blood and gore everywhere. That night, I pretty much stopped sleeping, and that has not changed in the years since, at least, not without medication.

The dead bodies on the airfield and the concomitant mayhem did not bother me. Somehow, even in the worst of situations, with shooting going on all around, I had a clinical approach to my job.

It was like Lamont Cranston had clouded my mind and allowed me to focus on the task at hand. More than once, this ability saved my life and those of others in close proximity. I think that mind-clouding thing followed me for many years after my discharge.

Later, when I investigated similar gruesome scenes after a murder, I was able to move through the crime scene with a certain detachment that allowed me to focus on the evidence. In Vietnam, this amounted to seeing damaged ordnance or a booby trap, and being able to consider all possible scenarios—a possible secondary device, or an alternate means of detonation not immediately visible. At murder scenes, I often saw evidence the police had missed.

Moving from area to area around the airport, we found that a number of satchel charges had failed to detonate, something that happened regularly. This was usually caused by bad Communist bloc blasting caps at the end of a pull-friction fusing device jammed into the explosive charge, usually TNT. A lot of this TNT turned out to be ours, taken from abandoned or stolen ordnance.

A lot of our ordnance, including large artillery projectiles and dud bombs that contained TNT or RDX, ended up in enemy hands. That was where they got much of the explosives they used to kill and maim us. They got it either because Vietnamese soldiers sold it to them, or because American and Vietnamese units abandoned LZs and firebases without destroying left-over ordnance that could not safely be removed.

On a little firebase called Davis, we found several bunkers full of ordnance abandoned the last time American or South Vietnamese units had used it for combat operations. After they left, the enemy would move in. They sawed these rounds open, steamed ("trepan" is the technical term) the TNT or RDX out, and then used our own explosives to kill us.

The design of the satchel charges was primitive, wrapped in a U.S. sandbag or similar material, but effective when the 1–2-pound charge did detonate. Typically, they were thrown into bunkers, or, as in this case, under aircraft; the blast effect was devastating, particularly on a human body confined within a typical perimeter bunker.

These bunkers were often reinforced with thick wooden beams, many layers of sandbags and, sometimes, a final layer of cement, making them all but impenetrable from the outside, but so well built as to contain an interior blast that would kill everyone and collapse the bunker.

We worked a long time to clean up after the attack on the airfield. Some items we blew where we found them, like dud 40mm high-explosive grenades. These were American ordnance, fired from an M-79 grenade launcher.

The grenade, itself, was the warhead of a 40-mm shotgun shell that separated from the casing when fired. They did not need to travel very far to arm—9 meters, if I remember correctly. We considered them armed if separated from the casing.

Those grenades killed and wounded many EOD men. At An Khê, near the beginning of my extended tour, Boyd Kidd and Jimmy Willis were wounded at our demo area when a 40-mm round they had placed in the pit went off for no apparent reason. It was a miracle they were not killed.

The day after the airfield attack, we received a call on a dud grenade on the perimeter of the airfield. I went with Captain Hunt. On the perimeter, an MP took us to a spot just inside the three rows of concertina and razor wire, and pointed to an M-33 grenade hanging on the outermost section of razor wire. Captain Hunt asked if I was ready to handle this thing. I said yes.

I picked my way through the first two sections of wire and stood up between the second section and the razor wire. Apparently, one of the perimeter defenders had thrown it during the attack the night before. The spoon had flown off; the grenade hit the wire and hung with the wire between the striker and the fuse detonator. What are the odds?

I looked at the grenade for a minute or two, then took out my blasting-cap crimpers and carefully slid the flat end between the striker and the detonator, then lifted the grenade off the wire, yelled "Fire in the hole", and heaved the grenade, crimpers and all, as far as I could. Everyone got down just before the grenade went off.

Shortly after, I was promoted to Specialist Five, and soon after that, our Control Team moved us to the Phu Tai Valley, where we lived in the compound with the 8th Transportation Group, at a place called Camp Vasquez. I think Control decided the airfield was too unprotected, and that we would be safer there.

Eighth Group gave us a patch of ground in the southeast corner of the compound; we had to build our own hooches and bunker.

7

Bong Son and LZ English

Several years ago, while doing internet research about EOD in Vietnam, I found a story from the 173rd Airborne Brigade's newspaper from the November 11, 1968 (Veterans Day) issue about Arnie Neiderhofer and me at our on-site team base at LZ English.

Stunned is probably not descriptive enough about the feelings I had when I read the story, almost forty years later, especially since I have absolutely no memory of the interview. Yet, there it was, in black and white, with my name in it, on the screen of my computer monitor: "EOD Means Daily Danger". This was true, even if it sounded a little hokey. Still, why was it there? Did the young soldier who wrote it save it all these years, then post it on the web? I am sure that I will never know the answer.

While the story talks about the fact that working with the 173rd was extremely hazardous—200 calls each month—it also points out how idiotic and surreal things sometimes got. That was two guys handling 200 calls a month, meaning an average of between six and seven each day, almost exclusively mines, booby traps, and duds as large as 2,000 bombs dropped by planes.

Then there were caches of enemy ordnance and weapons, usually found deep in caves that were typically booby-trapped. If you consider the fact that some calls took an entire day, or even two, then there were probably days when we had ten calls.

"EOD Means Daily Danger"
By Sp4 L. A. Gillis

QUI NHƠN (November 11, 1968)—A Paratrooper almost stumbles on a crudely made Viet Cong mine; a GI suspects that his vehicle has been booby-trapped.

For the men of the 184th Ordnance Battalion's Explosive Ordnance Disposal Detachment working for the 173d Airborne Brigade, such situations are typical in a routine day.

"EOD teams receive some of the most intensive training in the Army," said Sergeant First Class Arnold Neiderhofer of Texas City Texas. "In all of Vietnam there are only 150 qualified EOD men." Qualified EOD personnel learn to be experts. Each two-man team is charged with deactivating a myriad of explosive devices devised by the enemy.

Working with an Airborne unit which is constantly on the move keeps the explosives experts busy. On the average, they answer close to 200 emergency calls each month. "These emergency calls," explained SP5 Stuart A. Steinberg of Fairfax, Virginia, "become routine after a while. I'm not nervous when I handle explosives because I've had good training and enough experience to know what to look for."

The 21-year-old Steinberg tells the story of a Paratrooper who walked into the EOD tent with a live grenade in each hand. "Both pins were pulled and the guy who brought them in looked like his eyes were ready to pop out of his head he was so nervous. All I did was put a paper clip in the slot where the pins were supposed to be and that was the end of that emergency."

You could not make stuff like that up, even if you tried and, yet, there it was, right in an official military publication.

I have no idea after all these years why this guy had two grenades with the pins pulled. I suspect it was some kind of initiation for an FNG (fucking new guy) to see how he would respond to a bad situation. It was probably the LRRPs. We should have found the perpetrators and kicked their asses for pulling a stunt that could have had deadly consequences, especially for us.

The story then goes on to recount the types of incidents we ran into on a daily basis, sometimes multiple times in a single day.

On another [occasion], a 173d Long Range [Reconnaissance] Patrol spotted a Viet Cong squad sawing a 500-pound bomb in half. The paratroopers wiped out the squad and called in the EOD team to deactivate the bomb. "A 500-pound bomb," said Steinberg, "is packed with 175 pounds of explosive material. With that they can make hundreds of grenades or even blow up a bridge."

"The enemy will use anything he can lay his hands on, canteens, bamboo, C Ration cans, to make a mine or booby-trap," said SFC Neiderhofer, holding up a plastic canteen [that had been] stuffed with TNT which had ten steel spikes taped to it. "We found this on the perimeter of an evacuated enemy base camp. It is a very simple version of our claymore mine and packs just about as much wallop. Charlie can really put together some nasty mines with artillery rounds," said Neiderhofer, "and he is a master at concealing them."

"When it comes to camouflage," added Steinberg, "Charlie knows his business. He even uses green monofilament fishing line to trip some of his booby-traps. If he doesn't have that he'll use a piece of vine."

The night I found the article, one of those *Twilight Zone* things happened that totally freaked me out. Finding the story was weird enough, but what happened next just was just plain dumbfounding.

After reading the 173rd article, I did more online research about LZ English and the 173rd, looking for information about operations and events during the times I was there at the on-site team. I started thinking about Arnie Neiderhofer and the time we had spent together at English when my wife called to me from our bedroom.

Mona was going through boxes of photographs and memorabilia we each had accumulated over many years, before and after we met in 1993. I walked into the bedroom, and she said, "Look what I found in this box, with the pictures of Jonas [our son] when he was a kid." I had put some pictures inside a one-quart-sized baggie to protect them. I almost started hyperventilating.

In the baggie was a picture that I have no memory of putting there or even having. It was a black and white Instamatic photo of Arnie Neiderhofer and me sitting in front of the hooch at LZ English. It was the same hooch where we did the interview with the 173rd reporter. I was a kid with his first mustache.

I used to have many of these black and white Polaroids. I had hundreds of them. All the rest of them, every single one, have completely faded out over the years. This is the only one that survived.

The first time I drove into Bong Son, the location of LZ English, base camp for the 2nd Battalion, 503rd Parachute Infantry Regiment, 173rd Airborne

Brigade, I realized this was where the "Skytrooper" I met on my chopper ride to Qui Nhơn was stationed. Riding through the town to the turnoff for LZ English, I remembered his statement, just six weeks earlier, that maybe we would run into each other there. I did not see this guy, but I did run into someone I had gone to high school with, Jim Chaconis, who was with the Long-Range Reconnaissance Platoon (LRRPs, for short).

Jim eventually got a leg blown off, I think by a claymore intended for the battalion first sergeant. It had been planted under the first sergeant's hooch and set with a trip wire across the doorway. If I remember correctly, Jim had gone into the hooch to see the first sergeant and set off the mine.

Approaching the bridge over the Song Lai Giang River, coming into Bong Son, you were immediately struck by the firepower around two heavily fortified bunkers at each end of the bridge. When I say fortified, I mean to the point of being able to withstand multiple hits from rocket propelled grenades. At each end of the bunkers was a "Duster," a tracked vehicle with twin 40-mm cannons that fired at an ungodly rate.

Directly in front of each bunker was a 2.5-ton truck (a "Quad 50") with four .50-caliber machine guns mounted on a turret in the truck's bed—talk about death and destruction. When fired at close range, they could obliterate anything in their path. When the bridges or English got hit, a regular occurrence, and all these guns went off, along with the artillery, the noise was deafening and could almost suck the air from your lungs. I cannot remember if it was Americans or the South Vietnamese Army guarding the bridge; maybe it was both.

Here is how bad it was in and around Bong Son and LZ English, from September 7, 1968 until August 10, 1969, when I was transferred north to the 25th EOD. During the time I was with the Qui Nhơn team and "on-site" at LZ English on a regular basis, the 2nd of the 503rd had seventy-one men killed in action. Just down the road, at LZ Uplift, the 1st of the 503rd was located. We did ops with these troopers too, and for a time, we kept an on-site team there, as well. They lost sixty-three men. The 1st of the 50th Infantry, which also operated out of English and Uplift, lost twenty-six men and the 1st of the 69th Armor Regiment lost nine.

I have written about the rain in Vietnam and the fact that it was constant for months at a time. Well, there is rain and there are typhoons. I went to LZ English for the first time in October 1968 and soon learned what being wet really meant. On October 14, 1968, Typhoon Hester, by then a tropical storm, hit the Bong Son area, and it was like being in a Hell that had flooded in some grotesque joke on Satan by God.

It rained 3 feet in about a week. We could not get out of LZ English by vehicle because most of Highway 1 had flooded. Other than a couple of missions by chopper during the few lulls in the deluge, there was essentially no EOD support for the 173rd or the other units in our AO. Lee Miller and I were stuck in our hooch at the LZ, not the most waterproof building in town, and bored out of our minds. I remember reading the same two Zane Grey and Louis L'Amour books about five times each.

The year 1968 was one of the worst typhoon years ever. Normally, the season ran from June through December; in 1968, it essentially lasted the entire year. This may be one of the reasons I keep talking about how wet it was, even though, at the time, I do not remember hearing that we were experiencing a typhoon. All I knew was that it seemed to be raining all the time. If I had bought stock in the sock and foot powder industry, I would have been a millionaire.

The area around Bong Son Village, the plains surrounding it, and the An Loa Mountains to the west, were deadly and dangerous places, controlled by the Viet Cong and NVA at all times of the night and day. We were on alert most of the time, and got mortared and rocketed on regular a basis. Moreover, there were ground probes, incoming small arms and automatic weapons fire. We spent a lot of time in our bunker.

Any sense that we controlled even a small part of the countryside around English and Uplift was non-existent. We deluded ourselves in the bush, with dozens of heavily armed infantrymen and cobra gunships flying over our heads, into believing that, somehow, we had an advantage over the enemy. If we had thought otherwise, the reality of the situation would have driven us crazy.

Bong Son was a sleepy little town, if you let appearances fool you. On some days, if you were "downtown," it looked pleasant. It was hard to believe that the town was riddled with Viet Cong and their sympathizers. You saw a few lawn chairs, the hardware store, and dudes on the corner hanging out, smoking, and probably planning that night's attack on the LZ, kind of like the gangs in any modern urban area. The only thing missing was people barbecuing, with beers in their hands.

There was a great little restaurant in Bong Son that made the best baguettes I have ever had. The owner had been a baker for the French when they had a base there in the fifties. His baguettes had a toasty, crunchy crust, and were light and tender on the inside. When it was still warm with a little butter and a slice of cheese, it was heaven—well, as close as you were going to get to heaven in Vietnam.

Pulling through the gate into LZ English, the red dirt road went a short distance, maybe 100 yards, and then made a 90-degree right turn into the main body of the base. Our hooch and bunker were on the inside of that curve. On a slight hill above the back of our quarters was a Vietnamese Army artillery outfit with big 155-mm howitzers.

When they all went off at once, usually about 2 a.m., things fell off the walls. Our weapons and ammunition fell, and one time, a grenade rolled across the room when it bounced off a table. Eventually, I got used to this and was able to occasionally sleep through it. I would wake up in the morning and find C-ration cans and other objects that had been on tables the night before lying on the floor of the hooch. One night, my CAR-15 bounced off its pegs above my bed and hit me in the head.

On the outside of the road curve coming into English, no more than 50 yards from our bunker, was the water point—huge bladders of potable water—and water trucks that brought the water in from either Phù Cát Air Base, or Qui Nhơn. Our bunker was located to the left of our hooch, just outside the roadway. It was heavily reinforced with claymores to the front, facing the water point in case the VC tried to come through the wire to the south and east. This happened twice while I was there.

The VC regularly launched mortar and rockets attacks on the water point, and the helicopter airfield, which the chopper crews called the "Crap Table." I have no idea why, unless it was because the pilots who flew the 173rd choppers always rolled the dice when they flew out on a mission.

When the VC tried to hit the water point, sometimes the rounds were "long," and would pass over the water point and walk up the road to our hooch and bunker. If their target was the chopper pads, they landed just across from our hooch, maybe 200 yards out.

Each time there was incoming on the LZ, which was regularly, we got called out, usually about three in the morning, sometimes while the incoming rounds were still falling. Our guys immediately launched counter-mortar and rocket fire, but it was rare that they actually hit anything. Sometimes, as soon as the counter-fire ended, the VC or NVA were launching a new barrage from a different location.

I later learned that a lot of herbicides were used around English and Uplift, as well as in vast areas of the Bong Son Plains and the An Loa Mountains. By destroying vegetation, the military believed—I mean, really and actually believed—they could deny the Viet Cong the ability to sneak up on the LZ.

Above: Fire Support Base Rifle before the attack.

Below: Ed Vogels, 101st Airborne Division, carrying an M-60 machine gun at Rifle before the attack.

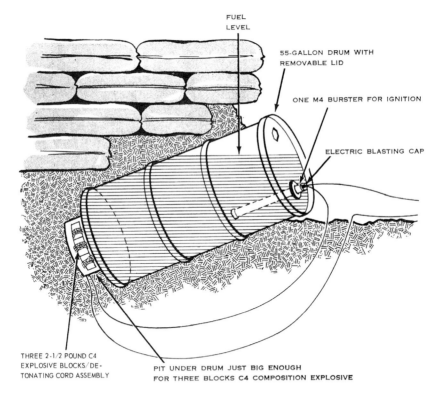

FUEL LEVEL

55-GALLON DRUM WITH REMOVABLE LID

ONE M4 BURSTER FOR IGNITION

ELECTRIC BLASTING CAP

THREE 2-1/2 POUND C4 EXPLOSIVE BLOCKS/DETONATING CORD ASSEMBLY

PIT UNDER DRUM JUST BIG ENOUGH FOR THREE BLOCKS C4 COMPOSITION EXPLOSIVE

Figure 22. Flame fougasse (55-gallon drum).

Above: Fougasse container like those used on the perimeter at Rifle.

Below: The author (on the left) and Paul Duffey after clearing Rifle of rocket-propelled grenades and satchel charges.

Right: The author waiting for extraction from Rifle.

STU STEINBERG –
2-11-1970
LZ RIFLE
THE "THOUSAND METER STARS"

Below: 184th Ordnance Battalion (EOD Section) office and quarters on the Qui Nhơn Airfield.

Above: 184th EOD Section's bunker at the Qui Nhơn Airfield.

Below: Camp Vasquez, Phu Tai Valley, where the 184th EOD Section moved after the attack on the Qui Nhơn Airfield.

Above: The author and Jerry Culp working on the 184th EOD Section's new building at Camp Vasquez.

Below: Roger McCormack (in front) and Mike Lizak in the 184th EOD Section's day room.

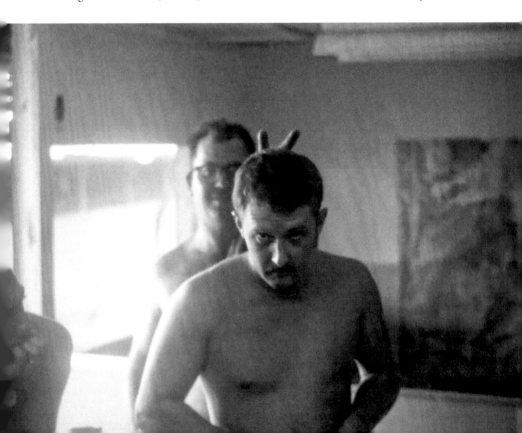

Masthead of the 173rd Airborne Brigade newspaper that published the article about the author and SFC Arnold Neiderhofer while on-site at LZ English.

Above: Aerial view of LZ English.

Left: The author and SFC Neiderhofer outside their quarters at LZ English.

Above: Ha Tay Special Forces Camp in the 506 Valley.

Below: View from the 184th EOD Section's location at Camp Vasquez of the Qui Nhơn ammo dump going up from 5 miles away.

Above left: View of mass detonations in the Qui Nhơn ammo dump as the author and other members of the 184th EOD Section arrived at the dump's main gate.

Above right: Qui Nhơn ammo dump of 105-mm high-explosive artillery rounds that mass-detonated.

Below: Bed of 0.75-ton truck the author was driving after 81-mm high-explosive mortar round detonated.

Above left: Doug Rhodes stands guard while 184th EOD Section members take turns in mountain pool.

Above right: Mountain pool we discovered while clearing area for demolition of damaged ordnance from Qui Nhơn ammo dump.

Below: Typical pile of damaged ordnance from Qui Nhơn ammo dump prepared for demolition.

Above: Shot of damaged ordnance detonates. The picture was taken from the EOD bunker about 1.5 miles away.

Below: 184th EOD Section members and unknown EOD man from another team preparing to escort a load of damaged ammunition to Tuy Hòa and then dumped in the South China Sea.

Above left: The author on an operation with the 173rd Airborne Brigade in the Central Highlands.

Above right: 25th EOD bunker at the An Khê Combat Base.

Below: Letter of commendation for IED removed from Tuy Hòa theater.

DEPARTMENT OF THE ARMY
533d Ordnance Detachment (EODC)
APO 96491

AVCA—OD   8 June 1969

SUBJECT: Letter of Commendation

Commanding Officer
184th Ordnance Battalion, EOD Section
APO San Francisco 96226

1. This letter of commendation is in recognition of the fine example of technical ability and hard work displayed by SSG Michael D. Lizak and SP5 Stuart A. Steinberg, of your organization, in preparing the Intelligence Report on the Viet Cong Variable Delay Device acquired by your unit on 14 April 1969.

2. It is abilities such as these that keep the field of Explosive Ordnance Disposal far above the rest of the technical fields of the Army in dedication and professionalism.

3. Copies of this report will be distributed to all US Army EOD units in Vietnam.

GERALD W PACK
Major, OrdC
Commanding

Above: Mang Yang Pass on Highway 19 between An Khê and Pleiku.

Below: Summit of Hamburger Hill. The picture was taken by Gary Raines 287th Ordnance Detachment (EOD).

Above: Joe Jimenez and the 287th EOD's bar in Phu Bai.

Below left: Home of the 287th EOD at the Phu Bai Combat Base.

Below right: Booby-trapped Bouncing Betty in village school's floor.

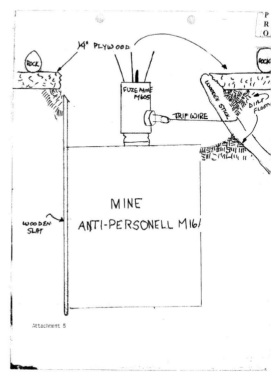

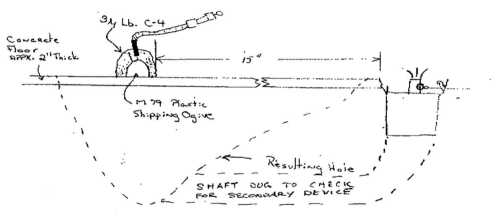

Above: How we fabricated a shaped charge to get under the booby-trapped Bouncing Betty to check for a secondary device.

Left: Author's citation for the Bronze Star for Heroism at Fire Support Base Davis for disarming a booby trap as the enemy was attempting to detonate it.

DEPARTMENT OF THE ARMY
HEADQUARTERS, UNITED STATES ARMY SUPPORT COMMAND, DA NANG
APO San Francisco 96349

GENERAL ORDERS   2 March 1971
NUMBER   132

1. TC 439. The following AWARD is announced.

STEINBERG, STUART A 224-62-2546 SPECIALIST FIVE USA 267th Ordnance
Detachment (EOD) APO 96308

Awarded: Bronze Star Medal with "V" Device (First Oak-Leaf Cluster)
Date of Action: 24 January 1970
Theater: Republic of Vietnam
Authority: By direction of the President under the provisions of
           Executive Order 11046, 24 August 1962, para 5 AR 672-5-1.
Reason: For heroism, not involving participation in aerial flight, in
         connection with military operations against a hostile force.
         Specialist Five Stuart A. Steinberg distinguished himself by
         exceptionally valorous actions on 24 January 1970, while
         serving as an Explosive Ordnance Disposal Specialist at Fire
         Support Davis, Republic of Vietnam. His mission was to
         render safe and dispose of all hazardous explosive ordnance
         found. While employing professional expertise and rapidly
         completing his precarious assignment, he noticed a North
         Vietnamese Army Regular pulling on a long piece of commo
         wire that was attached to a 155mm projectile. Completely
         aware of the NVA's attempt to initiate the improvised mine,
         Specialist Steinberg ran to the wire, grabbed it, and cut
         it with his wire cutters. Upon closer observation of the
         mine, it was shown to be capable of destroying the two
         helicopters nearby, bringing harm or death to personnel
         in the area, and resulting in a serious setback in the
         operation. This type of complete disregard for one's
         own personal safety for the benefit of the objective and
         the fellow members of his team, is truly in keeping with
         the highest traditions of the military service and reflect
         great credit upon himself, his unit and the United States
         Army.

FOR THE COMMANDER:

OFFICIAL:

J. N. TAKANE
MAJ, AGC
Adjutant General

C. E. CONRAD
COL, GS
Chief of Staff

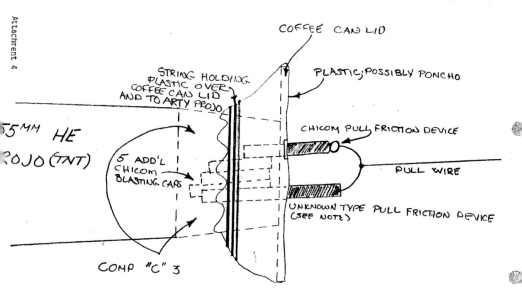

Above: Diagram of the fusing system of the booby-trapped artillery round at Fire Support Base Davis.

Below: How the booby trap at Fire Support Base Davis was located in the middle of the landing zone and where the enemy soldier who was attempting to detonate the device was located.

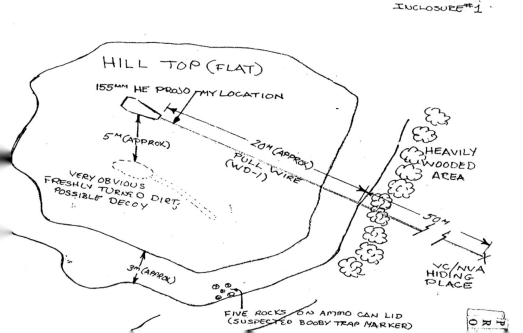

Above: The author and Tom Miller working on building the 287th EOD's new bar.

Left: The author at the 287th EOD's area on the Phu Bai Combat Base.

At Qui Nhơn, the Viet Cong blew up the ammo dump three times between February 23 and March 23, 1969. Each time, the 184th Ordnance Battalion added more guard towers, perimeter bunkers, and roving dog teams, had infantry patrols inside the dump, and ambushes set up outside the dump.

They even brought in Korean Marines, just about the baddest motherfuckers around, who never took prisoners, and they could not stop the VC. This area had also been heavily defoliated and, as with the areas around LZ English, a fat lot of good it did.

When they hit English or Uplift, our job was to look for duds and to check every set of mortar tail fins sticking up from the ground to make sure the round was not still attached, buried in the hard, red dirt. Then there were the dud rocket propelled grenades—the venerable RPG-2 and the RPG-7. These were some badass weapons that have been around since 1961 when the Russians started giving them to North Vietnam.

The RPG-7, which has a longer rocket motor and a more powerful explosive charge than its little brother, could knock the turret off a tank if it was hit right, and it often did. What it did to sandbagged-bunkers, even if reinforced, was criminal. These weapons were, and still are, major league weapons of mass destruction. I saw newer, more sophisticated versions when I was in Afghanistan; they are still as lethal.

Although more sophisticated, today, in Vietnam, the launchers were covered with wood sections so the gunner's hands did not get burned when he fired the weapon. The handle behind the trigger guard was also made out of wood. Despite the appearance of being made in some Vietnamese garage, this weapon was deadly in its simplicity.

RPGs were very dangerous when they became ineffectual, which was not that often. They had a base-detonating fuse with an anti-disturbance device. So, if it was a dud, and lying on the ground, sticking out of a sandbag on a perimeter bunker, or the side of a person's head, it could go off if you tried to move it or even touch it. In Phu Bai in late 1969, or early 1970, one of our NCOs set off an RPG-7 fuse in our workroom when he dropped it; this fuse had come from a round that had never been fired. He ended up with an ass full of shrapnel.

I am not kidding about the dud sticking out of someone's head. That actually happened in the 67th Evac Hospital in Qui Nhơn. While I was stationed in Qui Nhơn, Lee Miller, our first sergeant, and another member of the 184th, removed an RPG-2 from an Army of Vietnam soldier's head in the Evac Hospital's emergency room. It made it into *Stars and Stripes*.

Doug Rhodes and Roy Judkins helped take dud 40-mm HE rounds out of soldiers' heads twice within three days. Rod Wilkinson and I worked on a 40-mm high-explosive grenade that had become ineffectual after it went through a soldier's head. It was sticking out of the top of his head. I will talk more about that, later.

I saw an RPG-7 totally blow the crap out of a Sheridan Assault Vehicle while I was on temporary duty with a team in the Delta, heaving its 152-mm gun tube about 20 feet from the vehicle's burnt out shell. The Sheridan fired a 152-mm HEAT (high-explosive anti-tank) round with a load of RDX explosive behind a shaped cone. It had a long nose that contained a piezoelectric crystal, which, when crushed on impact, immediately—in a microsecond—sent an electric charge to the base-detonating fuse.

The Sheridan was a real war-machine, all cranked up, because it was also armed with a 7.62-mm machine gun and a .50-caliber heavy machine gun. When the Sheridan got hit by the RPG-7, the blast penetrated the armor like the proverbial hot knife through butter. Then all the ammunition inside exploded seconds later; you knew it was coming when the vehicle was hit and you also knew that the crew would not survive.

The 506 Valley was another bad place. It was named for Route 506, which ran right through the middle of it. It was located north and west of LZ Uplift and west of Highway 1, the major north–south road in Vietnam. The south end of the Valley and Route 506 came out on QL 1, about 5 miles south of LZ Uplift. The VC controlled this place, and it was a hotbed of enemy activity. The 173rd units in and out of there were in constant contact.

At a place called Ha Tay, there was a Special Forces camp with Montagnard troops (tribal people). LZ Pony was located in the same area. Ha Tay and LZ Pony were at the north end of the 506 Valley. Driving up Route 506 between the mountains on both sides of the Valley was not unlike driving through parts of the Shenandoah Valley in Virginia where I grew up, except for the enemy soldiers hiding along the way who were continuously trying to kill you.

The 506 Valley was one of those places you tried to stay away from, since going there meant something bad had happened. The Special Forces camp was frequently hit, and had been almost overrun on more than one occasion. It was located where Route 506 intersected with Highway 3A. We were in and out of there on several occasions, usually to take care of duds after an incoming attack.

I think that the Ha Tay camp eventually became part of LZ Pony, an artillery base that supported the 173rd Airborne Brigade and the 4th Infantry

Division. I am not totally sure about this, but, then again, my memory for some things is not that great.

During my first on-site tour at LZ English in October 1968, Lee Miller and I flew into Ha Tay after a call from the Special Forces commander. He said one of his patrols had run into an unmarked minefield, and a couple of their indigenous soldiers were killed. The patrol had stopped where they were. They were unsure of where the minefield began and ended, and mines could be all around them.

This was not an unusual situation; the French and the South Vietnamese Army had laid mines all over the country, never marked them, and never kept records of where they were. They still kill Vietnamese civilians today, as do the anti-personnel bomblets we dropped as interdiction weapons. The unmarked mine problem was something I ran into over and over again.

When we landed at the Special Forces Camp, their CO briefed us, and we headed out of the perimeter with a couple of Green Berets and about a dozen indigenous soldiers. We moved about 2 km east, into the hills, to the site where their other unit was trapped. We did not fly because chopper noise would give away our position; this was an area totally controlled by the enemy.

This was my first venture into the bush; this was really it. This was the War. I carried my M-16, a couple of bandoliers of ammo, and one of our canvass bags slung over my shoulder, full of C-4, blasting caps, fuse igniters, detonating cord, and time fuse, as well as probably a few shaped charge containers.

Lee Miller had the other bag. We were separated by about three of the indigenous troops since it was not a good idea that we stay together in a situation like this. Shit happens, and one of us needed to be around to complete the mission, if possible.

We crossed the open area outside the wire, no doubt defoliated with one of the herbicides we dropped all over Vietnam, particularly around Bong Son. The area around Ha Tay and LZ Pony had 47,290 gallons of the stuff dropped on it. Another 87,293 gallons was dropped around Bong Son; 69,703 gallons had been sprayed around LZ English. It is a wonder any of us are still alive, although many, many of us have either died from herbicide-related diseases or have one now, like me.

At the veterans' outreach center where I volunteered, I was a service officer for Vietnam Veterans of America. This means that I am accredited by the VA to handle veterans' claims for disability compensation and pension. I still do that work out of my home office and, right now, I have three clients with prostate cancer; one of them also has bone cancer. There is one with non-

Hodgkin lymphoma, one who had lung cancer, two with leukemia, and one who has had non-Hodgkin lymphoma twice, lung cancer once, and probably now has prostate cancer.

Now, I have clients with ischemic heart disease and Parkinson's disease, which were recently added to the list of illnesses presumed to have been caused by herbicide exposure in Vietnam. It also looks like the VA is about to add bladder cancer and thyroid problems to the list of diseases presumed to be caused by herbicide exposure. In 1978, I was one of the original plaintiffs in the Agent Orange litigation; I had bladder cancer in 1983.

There are at least five of my clients with Type II Diabetes; I also have this disease. I have about fifty clients who are Vietnam veterans; 26 percent of us have herbicide-related diseases. Vietnam is the war that just keeps on killing.

We cleared the open area outside the Special Forces camp and entered the dense bush leading to the foothills. Low, rugged mountains rose steeply as we worked our way along narrow trails. To avoid leaving footprints, we stayed off them and traversed in a zigzag fashion. We were about a click into the hills when the Green Beret leading the column stopped and signaled for the rest of us to do the same. Another Special Forces solider popped up from the bush to the left of the trail below us and motioned us to follow him.

Some 50 yards into the dense undergrowth and trees, we saw an open clearing, probably a makeshift firebase or landing zone sometime in the past, or maybe it was bombed years before and then covered by growth. We came to the edge of the clearing; the column split in two, one going left around the clearing, the other right. Miller and I went right toward a group of CIDG forces and the other Green Beret. We could see the two bodies of the dead CIDG soldiers about 150 feet into the clearing; their uniforms shredded by shrapnel.

Trying to locate who knows how many mines would be a foolish waste of time. Miller decided to clear a path to the bodies so the Green Berets could retrieve them. It was my first experience of "Leave no man behind."

The thing about clearing a minefield in Vietnam was that there was no easy or good way to do it. Mine clearing had not changed much since the Civil War, especially since we were not running around in the bush with a mine detector. We did it the old-fashioned way.

Miller and I dropped our explosives bags, pulled out our K-Bars (Army issue knives), got down on our knees, side-by-side, 4 or 5 feet apart. Using the knives, we probed the soft dirt of the clearing, slowly and deliberately, hoping not to hit a mine in the wrong way. We moved foot by foot toward the dead soldiers, me poking the ground from left to right, Miller from right to left, sort of meeting in the middle between us.

Halfway across the clearing, Miller stopped and said he had hit something. He told me to back up about twenty feet the way I had come and to lie down on the ground. Both EOD men often did not go "in" on the actual incident together. One man worked, the other watched, ready to offer suggestions. I watched my first sergeant dig carefully, clockwise, gently probing and lifting out dirt as the knife loosened it.

Miller put down his knife and looked back over his shoulder. He said something about the type of mine it was, though I do not remember if it was a conical mine, a Bouncing Betty, or something else. I do remember that it was French; this would not be the last time I was in an unmarked French minefield.

The French had many small outposts in the Central Highlands during their Vietnam days. Apparently, in their haste to leave after the fall of Điện Biên Phủ in 1954, they decided it was not important to record where all these mines were buried.

Whatever the device was, Miller disarmed it, and I rejoined him as we continued to clear a path to the dead soldiers. We reached their location and cleared a circular area around the bodies without locating another device. The SF soldiers and two of their men came in through the area we had cleared, picked up the dead bodies, and moved them back to the edge of the clearing for extraction by helicopter. They secured an LZ and, within minutes, two Hueys came in, picked us all up, and flew us and the bodies back to the camp.

This incident was uneventful in that we were not shot at and never saw the enemy, but it was my first experience with that "clench your asscheeks" feeling in enemy territory. I do not mean that we were afraid; we were hyper-alert, trying to pay attention to the entirety of our surroundings. They call it hypervigilance when you keep doing it long after you are out, and many of us do, even forty-eight years later.

On December 11, 1968, a chopper from the Casper Aviation Platoon went down while supporting the 173rd Airborne Brigade's 1st Battalion on an operation out of LZ Uplift. As the chopper flew over an LZ in the bush, it took several hits from RPGs, lost its tail rotor, and then was hit by anti-aircraft fire.

The chopper went nose-first into the trees, then crashed to the ground. The rescue operation of the pilots and crew, and two high-ranking 173rd officers, was the stuff that legends are made of. "Pedro" crews (HH-43 Huskie helicopters) out of Phù Cát Air Base performed heroically, taking constant enemy fire until all of the crew and passengers were recovered. It was one of the largest rescue operations mounted during the entire war.

When this happened, I was on a two-week on-site deployment at LZ English with SSG Mike Lizak. Mike was one of my instructors at EOD School. He has gone now. He died young, I think from complications of diabetes and losing most of a leg to a mine on an oil pipeline.

Answering the call on the afternoon of December 12, Mike and I were assigned to go to the 1st of the 503rd's Battalion Command Post at LZ Uplift. They had not told us the details of the mission as the VC or the NVA frequently monitored the Uplift and English phone calls.

Moments later, a helicopter landed on the road in front of our hooch, picked us up, and flew us down the road to Uplift. It seemed a little weird that they would send a chopper for us since Uplift was not that far away—maybe 5 miles—and we normally drove there when we had an incident from that small LZ. Once we arrived, we understood why the details were kept secret, and that time was of the essence.

One of EOD's jobs was to go to the sites of downed aircraft—both rotary and fixed-wing—to destroy what might be left of the aircraft, its radio gear, and guns and ammo that had not, or could not, be removed. Before that, we had to clear the area of booby traps, particularly around the aircraft. Sometimes, they called us in to do this when the aircraft was to be recovered because it had not been severely damaged. In this case, however, the Casper chopper was totally crunched, deemed not salvageable.

The VC and NVA knew that someone would come to survey a crash site, so they often hid little surprises for whoever that might be. The NVA and VC had a bounty on EOD men, since we often disrupted their well-designed plans to kill U.S. and allied soldiers. We frequently found secondary devices buried under, or attached with a hidden trip wire, to the device that had been discovered. A lot of non-EOD soldiers, who thought they could do the job we trained for six months to do, were killed by not finding the secondary device.

The way we destroyed things like the downed Casper helicopter was to use a combination of plastic explosives on the aircraft and thermite grenades on the radio and guns. Thermite, when it burns, will melt down just about anything, often in a matter of seconds.

A thermite reaction occurs when aluminum is oxidized by another metal, usually, iron oxide. As one source noted, thermite grenades are used as incendiary devices to quickly destroy items or equipment when there is imminent danger of them being captured by enemy forces."

The grenade is comprised of thermite and pyrotechnic materials required to get the thermite burning. In addition, because EOD teams' publications for rendering explosive ordnance safe were highly classified—the nuclear weapons publications required a Critical Nuclear Weapons Design Information (CNWDI) clearance—we had our safes wired with large, flat thermite packs for melting everything into a pile of molten slag.

We encountered no enemy on our mission. Considering what had happened the day before to Casper 721 and the other birds involved with the rescue of the 721 crew and its passengers, it was pretty amazing.

Every bird involved in the rescue was hit by enemy fire on multiple occasions. We flew in and landed near the wreck site. There were four or five infantrymen with us from the 1st of the 503rd, plus a gunship cruising overhead the entire time.

I took the point as we worked our way along a small trail to the crash site, looking for booby traps and mines, with Mike behind me. I did not see any, which does not mean they were not there. That was how Mike lost his leg on a fuel pipeline near Qui Nhơn in September 1969.

We got to the site, set our charges, and hauled ass. After we took off, the pilot circled the area until we were sure the shot went. The blast threw molten thermite high into the air; when the smoke cleared, there was nothing left of Casper 721, except a big crater burning with the thermite residuals.

I would like to say most of our unusual incidents were this uneventful, but that was not the case. In 1969, before and during my time in Phu Bai during my extended tour, the 287th team handled 2,155 incidents. Of that number, 186 were unusual.

The unusual ones did not include flying into some remote area of the A Shau Valley to blow up a dud 2,000-pound bomb after an airstrike. That was "usual." I am not making this up. It was not that they ever said the other 1,969 incidents were "usual," but what else could the implication be when they required us to describe some as "unusual?"

The unusual incidents did, however, include those where the possibility of death or serious injury was right in your face, from the time you hit the ground—and, sometimes in the air—until you flew back out. I am unclear, today, how any incident that took us into places like the A Shau Valley could ever be considered "usual." The unusual incidents also included those where someone was injured or killed.

Sometimes the incidents involved investigating explosive events that killed American soldiers by accident, negligence, or deliberate acts, such as "fraggings". On July 14, 1969, I was at LZ English with Arnie Neiderhofer when a soldier from the 173rd Airborne Brigade suffered hand injuries when the blasting cap from a claymore mine went off after he had removed it from the mine. This followed an incident on January 12, when another 173rd soldier blew himself up on the perimeter when a claymore had detonated as he rolled up the firing line without removing the blasting cap from the mine.

A claymore is triggered by an electric blasting cap connected to a length of wire leading back to the plastic blasting machine, called the "clacker", at the other end. When the handle on the clacker is depressed, it sends an electrical charge to the cap and detonates the mine. After the second event, we ran a series of tests on electric caps to determine if radio frequency energy or static electricity could detonate one.

We used a comb run through our hair to create static electricity; this failed to cause several different electric caps to detonate. We then dragged open leads to several caps along the ground; this also failed to cause a detonation. We then exposed open leads to the caps to radio frequency energy from three different size radios. The PRC 25, the standard field radio carried by soldiers in the bush, was located six inches from the cap leads, and we keyed the mike as if we were sending a call. Nothing happened.

We then repeated the experiment with the two larger radios, the VRC 46 and 106, this time from 25 feet from the open leads. Nothing happened. However, when we brought the unshunted leads into the radio van and keyed the VRC 106 with the leads four inches from the radio, the cap outside detonated.

In the end, we told the 173rd command that this was such a remote possibility, and given that there had not been a VFC 106 near the two detonations on the perimeter, that the two incidents were probably caused by carelessness. We then instructed the 173rd command to remind their soldiers of the proper way to de-arm a claymore.

In early February 1969, I was, again, at the 184th's on-site team location at LZ English with Mike Lizak. On the day I arrived at English, Mike and I were assigned to clear a large tunnel complex discovered by elements of the 173rd. The tunnel complex was located in one of the small foothills of the An Loa Mountains bordering the Bong Son Plains, one of the deadliest area of operations (AOs) in Vietnam.

We flew into the LZ near the top of the mountain and humped up the hill to the complex entrance. Tunnel rats had done the basic clearing of the tunnels. When we entered the tunnels, I was amazed at how high they were;

we hardly had to bend over to cross the tunnel system and locate the weapons, ammunition, and ordnance we eventually found. The thing was lit with small bulbs and run by a generator, which the tunnel rats had cranked up.

The arms cache was located really far in, on the second level below the entrance. There were RPG-2s and 7s, 122-mm rockets, 60-mm and 82-mm mortar rounds, Chicom stick grenades, homemade claymores and road mines, satchel charges, AK-47s, SKS carbines, RPD machine guns and ammo, and lots of TNT and C-3 plastic explosive.

As we examined the cache and the many boxes of ammunition, we saw two trip wires between boxes of RPG-7s at the bottom of a stack of boxes of Chinese 82-mm HE mortar rounds. The monofilament lines—almost transparent—came out from between two crates, crossed the dirt floor for about a foot, then disappeared under another crate on top of a fourth crate. We made sure there were no other trip wires, or other suspicious looking stuff, in, on, or around the cases of mortar rounds, then began to lift them off the pile, one box at a time, piling them up about 10 feet away in a side tunnel.

Now, we were down to the boxes of RPGs, two in each case, with the wires running between them. Eight RPG-7s, if they were to detonate all at once, would kill both of us, and, no doubt, set off most of the rest of the enemy ordnance in the tunnel.

We talked about the situation and figured that the trip wires were attached to the undersides of the two boxes, and then separately rigged to another trip wire that went into the ground attached to a device like a grenade, with the pin pulled, or maybe a pull-friction fuse on a claymore mine.

The claymore is a dangerous little item that caused mayhem and death when detonated facing the direction of enemy soldiers; both sides used them. Usually, the VC and NVA variety were handmade and conical in shape. Ours were rectangular curved plastic shells, about 10 inches long, 4 inches high, and 1 inch or so thick.

They were to be planted in the ground, facing the suspected route of the enemy, on two sets of small bipod legs. They were packed with C-4 plastic explosives and in front of the C-4 was a "wall" of steel balls. The VC claymores were typically filled with nails, bolts, nuts, and anything else they could cram in there.

As I noted above, the claymore is armed with an electric blasting cap, and set off with a hand-held blasting machine. When detonated, the steel balls blast outward on a 60-degree arc, and anything within 100 meters, or so, are shredded. They could do damage up to 250 m.

People within 50 m were dead and usually seriously torn up. Embossed on the front of the U.S. claymores was a warning I always got a kick out of: "Front Toward Enemy." At least that way, when the inevitable happened, they could say, "We warned you." Of course, I always wondered why the military had put those words on the claymore in the first place. I assumed that when they were first manufactured and sent to the field, some dumbass had pointed the device in the wrong direction.

Since we knew we were going to blow the crap out of everything in the tunnel, we decided there was no reason to disarm whatever was under the RPG crates. We moved all the other ordnance into two central locations inside the tunnels, while the infantry removed the weapons. One pile was in the side tunnel with all the mortar rounds, the other around the two boxes of RPGs. Before we did anything else, the 173rd Public Information Office had a photographer come into the tunnel and take pictures of everything.

We set the shot with about six 40-pound ammonium nitrate cratering charges, many cases of C-4, WP grenades, and a lot of detonating cord, all of which we had flown in from LZ English. Then we strung more cratering charges throughout the tunnel complex. We cut twenty minutes of time fuse and set it off. We left the tunnels, humped back to the LZ, and were extracted by choppers.

I will never forget what happened next. As we flew away from the mountain, the chopper did a slow turn so we could make sure that the shot went off. It did. It was another one of those "slo-mo mini-cam" moments. The explosion was deafening; the smoke plume was lost in the heavens, looking like a nuke had gone off. We could see that one side of the mountain had been blown away and, as we watched, and the smoke and dust cleared, we saw the entire top third of the mountain collapse inward.

It was like Mt. St. Helens, except the destruction was manmade. We actually changed the environment in this one shitty little corner of the world, and never looked back, or thought twice about it.

8

The Qui Nhơn Ammo Dump

This is, by far, the longest chapter of the book. The events described occupied four of the eighteen months I spent in Vietnam. This is about the Qui Nhơn Ammunition Base Depot, which the VC blew up, to one degree or another, on five occasions between February and September 1969.

Although I talk mostly about my team, I want to be clear that every man in the 184th Ordnance Battalion performed heroically and with great courage during these events. In the cleanup that followed, sixty-one EOD men from all over Vietnam came and helped in this dangerous, mind-numbing operation.

The commanding officer of the ordnance battalion, Lt. Col. Albert A. Busck—he retired a full colonel—recommended the entire battalion and my team for the Valorous Unit Award. It was approved by the next command and then, apparently, the paperwork disappeared for some time. I checked with the Army and learned that, in 1973, after Col Busck had asked what happened, it was disapproved by some pinhead who wrote that the actions during the three attacks on the dump did not involve actual enemy action. I wonder who this jerkoff thinks blew up the dump. I intend to do everything I can to see that this award is made.

During the week before the enemy's Post-Tet Offensive of 1969, I was in the mountains west of the Bong Son Plains on a combat operation with the 173rd Airborne Brigade. It was raining like hell; it was cold, and we were moving down a trail across a ridge. We were back in the column, as usual, when I heard the platoon leader send word from up the column that we were taking a break.

The platoon radio operator came up to me and said, "Specialist Steinberg, you're not going to believe this," and he extended the radiophone toward me. "What?"

"Man, we've got the rear on the hook, and they say your mother is going to call you at the MARS office when we get back to English." I did not believe him, figuring it was a practical joke by the rest of the team back in Qui Nhơn.

I grabbed the phone from the RTO and said to the person on the other end of the radio, someone back in the 173rd rear area, "Who the hell is this?" He said he was PFC something-or-another and that they had received a call from the Red Cross in Saigon about a family emergency; that my mother was going to call me on the MARS line.

I apologized and when we finished our job, I flew back to English to await the call. My first thought was that something had happened to my dad or one of my siblings. I was sitting in the MARS hooch when the phone rang and the soldier running the operation handed me the phone. "Mom? What the hell ..."

My mom then told me that my grandfather had passed away, and our Congressman had arranged for me to come back to the States on emergency leave for ten days. You do not get emergency leave for a grandparent. You get it for your spouse, child, parents, maybe a sibling, but not your grandparents. However, our Congressman was a very powerful politician, and he made this happen. My folks were bigwigs in local politics, so they knew him pretty well.

My mom then explained how the Congressman had arranged for her to come to the Pentagon where they made a phone connection through the MARS system (Military Affiliate Radio Service) and they called some place in Australia. Australia then called Vietnam, and whoever answered the phone called the 173rd HQ at LZ English, which patched the call through to the 173rd MARS office. They did this in cooperation with ham radio operators.

Mom asked if I knew where Phù Cát Air Base was. I said I did and asked her why. She told me that our neighbor and good friend back in Fairfax, Virginia, Col. Alex Smith, was the base commander or a wing commander—I do not remember which—and that all I had to do was get to Phù Cát. He had arranged for me to fly on a transport to Okinawa, where I would catch a military ride to Travis Air Force Base near Sacramento, and then a civilian bird home.

When we got back to LZ English, I hitched a ride with some 173rd medics to Phù Cát and flew to Okinawa on a C-141 Starlifter, loaded with wrecked jet aircraft, and a lot of shot up, crashed helicopters. I was the only passenger on this cavernous flying machine. I strapped into a red-web jump seat in the cargo bay. It was cold as hell.

I landed in Okinawa, on February 21, and called the Army EOD Team there. They came and picked me up as my ride to Travis was not until noon the following day. I was still in Tiger fatigues, floppy boonie hat, carrying a full rucksack, and had my CAR-15 and two bandoliers of ammo when I landed. I ditched my grenades at Phù Cát because they would not let me on the plane with them. The EOD guys took me to their quarters and I stowed my gear. Then they took me to the infamous Naha District where we got very drunk in some prostitute-packed, sleazy bar.

During my time in Vietnam, the members of my units, particularly the younger guys like me, would occasionally go down to the local den of iniquity for some 33 Beer, and either a blowjob or sex with one of the local prostitutes. Usually, I went with them. These sleaze palaces also had massage parlors, steam baths and a barber who would cut your hair, shave your face, and clean your ears and the hairs in your nose, all with a straight razor. Being a barber is a good cover for a spy because you hear a lot of gossip, but it would be counterproductive to cut my throat.

When we went to these places, the girls said things like, "Hey, GI, I love you too much. You number one. I give you good sucky fucky." I never took them up on the "sucky fucky" offer because of all the stories about VD so bad that, if you got it, the military sent you to some island somewhere, and that was where you stayed, never to be heard from again. Forever. They told your family you were missing in action. I may have also heard that it made your dick shrivel up.

So, when approached and asked if I wanted "sucky fucky," I always said "no" and then the girl would start screaming at me that I was, "Number 10,000," which meant that I was a complete asshole. I never got VD, so I think I did the right thing and did not care if I was Number 10,000. I did, however, know a lot of guys who did not follow "Steinberg's Rules of Engagement," and they did get the clap.

As we left the bar in Naha, a drunken driver jumped the curb and hit one of the EOD guys I was with. He flew through air and hit a phone pole about ten feet off the ground, then fell to the sidewalk. The driver was a drunk Marine, and my host was critically injured. I never learned his fate.

Very early the next morning, February 22, 1969, I was informed that the VC had launched their Post-Tet Offensive and all transports were being routed to Vietnam loaded with ammunition, new helicopters, gunships, and artillery pieces.

I could not go on to the States; I would have no way to get there for days. The shit would hit the fan in the Qui Nhơn area because it was a major U.S. base, and they had gotten pounded during the Tet of 1968. I also knew my team would soon be up to their eyeballs in difficult and demanding work.

I called my mom and told her my decision. She did not understand, but my dad, who had been an infantry company commander in World War II, did. I caught one of the very first planes leaving Okinawa. It was loaded with ammunition and headed for Qui Nhơn because of the 184th's ammo dump.

My team was responsible for any EOD matters in and around this dump, and they came up a lot. I landed in Qui Nhơn and caught a ride out to my unit in the Phu Thanh Valley. When I walked into the hooch late that night, everyone looked at me. The first sergeant, Lee Miller, said, "What the fuck are you doing back here?" Upon my response, my teammates made a universal decision that I was out of my mind.

Maybe I was. People ask, "Whatever possessed you to go back before you had to?" I have tried to explain about being a part of a close-knit group of men—all volunteers—to do a very meaningful, if hazardous, job.

If we disarmed a mine or a booby trap, we probably saved lives. If we blew a 1,000-pound dud bomb out in the bush, we stopped the enemy from turning it into dozens of smaller explosive devices to be used against allied soldiers and civilians, which they did every day, of every week, of every month, of every year we were there. If I had not come back from Okinawa, others would have to pick up my share of the load and take the chances I should have been taking. That knowledge, even if you never actually consciously thought about it, drew the team together, almost like a family. It never dawned on me not to go back. Besides, then I would have missed being inside an ammo dump three times while it blew up.

EOD teams slept in the same place—everyone, including the officer, the senior NCOs, and the enlisted men. We ate together and drank together. We did everything together, and we were equals in every sense. Our officers never treated us as if they were our betters.

In most other units, the officers were in the Bachelor Officers' Quarters, sometimes located some distance from their enlisted men, and the senior NCOs were in their separate quarters. We did everything as a closely-knit unit. Because we often were in perilous and enemy-infested situations with only one other man, we eventually became individually close to each member of the team. That was why I went back instead of taking that free vacation.

During the 1969 Tet Offensive, between February 14 and 22, 1969, there were no coordinated attacks. However, 273 Americans died during those nine days. The day after the 1969 Tet Offensive officially ended, and for the next month, things were totally out of control. According to *Time* magazine, more than 350 U.S. soldiers were killed each week from the beginning of the month.

On February 23, 1969, the Viet Cong launched major assaults by attacking 110 targets in South Vietnam. On February 23, March 10–11 and 23, 1969, the Viet Cong penetrated the perimeter at the Qui Nhơn ammo dump and blew the place all to hell. Maybe the Tet of 1968 was worse; it is the one everyone always talks about because of the attack on the U.S. Embassy in Saigon. Yet the Tet of 1969 was no cakewalk. No matter how much they increased perimeter security after each successive attack on the dump, the VC still got in.

The VC got into the dump again, on July 11, 1969, and evaded dog teams, the tower and bunker guards, and twenty—yes, twenty—Korean ambushes outside the perimeter. This occurred at 4.15 a.m., and our team was in the dump by 5.15 a.m. They also got around ground sensors placed around the dump, and at two other locations in the Qui Nhơn area. The sensors were useless in keeping the VC out of the dump, the tanks farms, and the signal stations on the top of Vung Chua Mountain.

The VC also got in and blew the place up one more time in September 1969, after I left for another team. In January 1971, they blew it up one final time. This time, one EOD man from the 184th—SSG Louis Payne—was killed, and eight were wounded, several seriously enough to be medevacked back to the States. Ultimately, like most of the rest of Vietnam, the military could not protect this place no matter what they did.

Back to the July 11 event. As we conducted the search for additional satchel charges, we discovered one on a pad of 105-mm high-explosive ammunition. We disarmed the device and put it in the jeep for later destruction. When we examined it, we saw that the blasting caps had detonated, but, for an unknown reason, failed to set off the plastic explosives they had placed inside two one-quart American-issue salad oil cans.

Walking around the outside of the pad, we and our infantry escorts from "D" Company, 58th Infantry, discovered bare footprints in the red soil. We followed them out to the perimeter and discovered that the VC sappers had avoided the dog teams, sensors, and all the guards by tunneling under the perimeter and coming up out of the ground between two guard towers, inside the dump.

They planned it just right so that their exit hole was in both towers' blind spots. Man, these guys were good, for people running around in shorts and sandals made from old tires. When our team got to the perimeter, we saw the entrance to the tunnel that went back under all the concertina and razor wire, avoiding small anti-personnel mines (called "Toe Poppers") and claymore mines.

On both sides of the tunnel opening, Viet Cong propaganda leaflets hung on the wire. Beneath each leaflet, was a large pile of, well, shit. Then we noticed that the enemy had wiped their asses on the leaflets before hanging them on the wire—kind of a very clear message of, "Hey, fuck you! We can do this any time we want." It was disconcerting, as you can probably imagine. In the report of this event that I recovered from the National Archives, I noted that the command of the ammo dump left out the part about the great steaming piles of enemy dung.

In addition to ground sensors, the VC evaded forty-three manned guard towers, up from the twenty-nine that existed when the dump went up on February 23. There were twenty "ambushes in the area around the [ammo] depot"; there were six dog patrols inside the dump; and three roving infantry patrols, also inside the perimeter. Not only that, but starting at five minutes after midnight, there was regular and fairly constant illumination fired over the dump by a nearby artillery unit. There were also roving "pad patrols" of ammo humpers going from pad to pad throughout the night. Despite all that, they still got in, blew the place up, once more, and disappeared into the night.

Here is the final rub. On July 4, 1969, seven days before the sappers got into the dump, Korean intelligence reported to the Qui Nhơn Support Command that thirty members of the Viet Cong 5th Company, 300th Sapper Battalion, had been seen on Vung Chua Mountain overlooking the city, the dump, just about everything, from that vantage point. I could not find a single mention in the reports from the National Archives that they ever sent in an infantry patrol, let alone bombed the area where the sappers were spotted.

As I note over and over, it was utter futility to try to stop the VC from blowing up the dump on multiple occasions. I think this observation in the report on the July 11, 1969, attack makes the situation crystal clear: "To gain access to the [Qui Nhơn Ammunition Base Depot] the enemy was required to pass three [Korean] ambushes. The [Korean] ambushes observed no movement nor heard any sound."

Back to February 23. My team was located about five miles from the dump in Phu Tai, a small village in the Phu Thanh Valley, where we lived with the

8th Transportation Group. I had just returned from Okinawa, and the team sat around drinking and bullshitting until the early morning hours.

That night, the Viet Cong blew up the Qui Nhơn Ammunition Base Depot. It was the beginning of the Post-Tet Offensive of 1969. Our ammo dump was not the only victim that night in the Qui Nhơn area. Simultaneously, the VC hit the Vietnamese Army Ammunition Supply Point in the Depot Defense Sector on the other side of Qui Nhơn.

Two South Vietnamese Army EOD men were killed in the Vietnamese dump. Multiple locations around Qui Nhơn received small arms, rocket, and mortar fire throughout the night and into the following day. On the dates of the three attacks on the Qui Nhơn ammo dump, across Vietnam, 209 soldiers were killed on February 23, 1969, 103 were killed on March 10–11, and another thirty-two on March 23. So, do not try to tell me the Tet of 1969 was not as bad as the better-known Tet of 1968.

The first major explosion at our dump, at 2.20 a.m., was like being in an earthquake, except that it was also raining hot steel all over the area around the ammo dump. Shrapnel and base plates from artillery rounds fell as far away as our compound, 5 miles from the ammo dump. Within minutes, the CO of the 184th Ordnance Battalion, Lt. Col Albert Busck, called out my unit. He was not only a great commander, but he loved his EOD team.

The entire unit in Qui Nhơn except the clerk responded in jeeps, with military police gun-vehicle escorts. I do not remember exactly who was there, other than First Sergeant Miller and CPT Lorance. We would have had four men at on-site teams, two at LZ English and two at Tuy Hòa. So, five of us went into the dump that night.

During the trip, we were pelted with falling debris. Parts of the dump continued to explode as ordnance flew from one pad to the next. Shrapnel and burning debris rained down on the roadway as we and our MP escorts flew down QL 1, weaving and swerving to avoid falling objects. It is amazing that none of us were hit during this insane ride, nor did we get a flat tire and flip over at 70 miles per hour

Before we entered the dump, several pads of ordnance had exploded; we could barely breathe the sulfur and nitrate-fumed air. It permeated everything, including our hair and clothes; you never quite got it washed out. As we entered the dump, pads of ordnance were exploding, and the Vietcong were still inside the wire setting satchel charges. Yet no one ever—I mean ever—saw them, not even a glimpse.

The first pads that went up at 2.35 a.m. were Nos 92, 95, and 103, all of which contained 105-mm high-explosive artillery rounds.

The VC picked pads they knew would cause havoc throughout the dump when they mass-detonated. These pads were exploding while we checked other pads and looked for satchel charges, rounds flying through the air over our heads with a "whooshing" sound as they flipped end over end. Patrols from "D" Company, 58th Infantry, searched high and low for the enemy, but they never caught them. This was a theme through all the occasions that the dump was blown up.

The shrapnel was thick; explosions on the three pads were continuous. The Ordnance Battalion brought in fire trucks to put out fires on pads burning from rounds blown out of the other three pads, but the flames and fires, by this time, were too intense, and the trucks could not get close enough to lay out their lines.

About 3 a.m., pads 93 and 96, and a small arms pad, began to burn from all the stuff blown out of pads 92, 95, and 103. Dozers tried to quell the new fires when pad 85 began to burn, and the fire became so intense that the rounds on No. 85 began to cook off, throwing even more ordnance into the air, coming down all around us, as well as falling into more pads.

It was impossible to extinguish the small arms pad fire, which was zinging M-16 and 7.62-mm machine gun ammo all over the place. It was raining bullets as if some huge swarm of psychotic bees were everywhere, except that they had trails of red phosphorous shooting out of their asses.

By 4 a.m., rounds and shrapnel were flying everywhere, and fires burned out of control. A patrol from the Provisional Guard Command came in and extracted the tower guards in the northeast corner of the depot. By 5 a.m., wounded were being brought into the small triage area set up outside the main gate, and "Dustoff" evac choppers came in to med-evac the first three. Fifteen minutes later, one of the battalion's warrant officers was medevacked for a heart attack.

It is amazing more of that did not happen, given the utter chaos going on. At 5.30 a.m., we were still checking pads for satchel charges; things were still exploding, and I cannot understand why none of us were wounded or killed that night. During the actual explosions on February 23, March 10–11, and March 23, we did not have a single EOD man wounded. That would change when we got to the cleanup.

At 8.30 a.m. on February 23, it seemed like no additional pads would detonate, despite the fact that fires were still burning out of control. We pulled back to the dump offices near the main gate and were just starting to take little rest, have a smoke, and slug down some coffee when it started all over again.

By 8.45 a.m., pads 91 and 99—more artillery projectiles—were on fire and at 9 a.m. they mass-detonated. All efforts to put out any of the fires ended; the shrapnel was virtually unending as more and more rounds began to explode. We made a decision to get out of there, except things did not go exactly as planned.

At 9.45 a.m., pad 65 burst into flames while First Sergeant Miller and I moved right in front of it. It had taken almost thirty minutes to move from one side of the dump to that location, dodging exploding ordnance and fires. One second, pad 65 was fine; the next it was a storm of mortar rounds. Then, between 9.45 and 10 a.m., pads 98 and 94, also artillery rounds, began burning from shrapnel falling on them like red hot rain; they started cooking off within thirty minutes.

The battalion commander ordered everyone out; we were all—EOD, ammo humpers, firefighters, grunts, and guards—more than happy to oblige. It was the right decision. We had been in the dump without a break for almost seven hours and were completely wiped out.

Six hours after we pulled out of the dump, at 3.30 p.m., pads 101, 102, and 97 went off almost simultaneously. The tower guard and a patrol from D/58 reported seeing "smoke in the hills" west of the dump and it may well be that those detonations were caused by incoming mortar or rocket fire. We never found out. There were so many holes in the ground, ankle deep shrapnel all over, that we never even considered looking for rocket or mortar frag.

The battalion requested, and got, a slug of gunships from Lane Army Airfield at Qui Nhơn, and within three minutes, they were blasting holy hell out of the mountains and, just for good measure, tore up the ground beyond the perimeter surrounding the dump with miniguns and 40-mm grenades.

According to the after-action report of the February 23 attack, "sixteen pads of [HE ammunition] and one small arms area w[ere] destroyed within sixteen hours." At 5 p.m., the 2nd Battalion, 26th Infantry Regiment, Republic of Korea (ROK) Capital Division, began an operation in the area west of the Qui Nhơn dump.

For three days, they looked for the enemy and found none. They did, however, find evidence that 10–12 VC "had recently been in this area for several days." That is several days that they managed to avoid the many infantry patrols and ambushes and eventually blow up the dump.

As my EOD team moved through the dump that night and early into the next day, ammunition was exploding everywhere, yet none of us were wounded or killed. I said that already, but it seems worth repeating because, though I am not religious, I recognize that it was a miracle that during the three times the dump went up, and the four months of cleanup, we did not lose an EOD man. That was not true for the Ordnance Battalion, however.

During the time we spent in the dump on February 23–24, "D" Company, 58th Infantry, on loan from the 4th Infantry Division (who eventually became part of the 75th Infantry Regiment (Rangers) in II Field Forces) provided us with security.

Ammo company members attempted to extinguish multiple fires on pads of ammunition that had not yet exploded. In some cases, they did this with hand-held pump fire extinguishers that had to be constantly filled with water. All of these guys (not just us) continuously exposed themselves to this particular kind of hell on earth for most of a day.

During those first sixteen hours, my team moved through the pads not exploding, as well as those on fire, looking for satchel charges still cooking. I cannot remember if we found any, but it really does not matter since it would not have added that much more danger inside an ammo dump that was blowing up.

The Qui Nhơn dump was one of the largest ammunition storage facilities in Vietnam. Every type of ordnance except bombs was there, to be used by combat units in the II Corps Tactical Zone, which comprised most of the Central Highlands. We had 103 pads of ordnance, including 105-mm, 155-mm, 175-mm, and 8-inch artillery projectiles, large shells loaded with high explosives, white phosphorous, and unconventional munitions that contained small anti-personnel bomblets or flechettes, small steel darts flung at high velocity when the casing broke apart after firing. There were also illumination, CS (tear gas), and smoke rounds that had the effect of setting other ammo on fire when they went off near high-explosive ordnance.

There were grenades you threw, and shoulder-launched and gunship-fired 40-mm high-explosive grenades. There were 2.75-inch-high-explosive and white phosphorous rockets; 60-mm, 81-mm, and 4.2-inch high-explosive, illumination, and white phosphorous mortar rounds. Then there were the millions of rounds of M-14, M-16, .30 cal. carbine, M-60 machine gun, and .45 cal. pistol ammunition. There was also claymore mines, anti-personnel mines, Bouncing Betties, high-explosive anti-tank mines, 3.5-inch rockets, 66-mm LAW anti-tank rockets, and 90-mm, 106-mm, and 152-mm high-explosive anti-tank (HEAT) rounds. All of this ordnance was contained in an area that covered many acres, and it was exploding all around me and my team members.

We started cleaning up the dump on February 25. It still burned in several places and rounds and small arms ammo were still cooking off. The worst were white phosphorous (WP) rounds, exploding as the phosphorous burned from exposure to air. This is why they paid us the big bucks—that extra $55 per month. In the areas deemed "safe," which really did not exist, we began to remove damaged WP rounds, two or three at a time, and take them to a small demolition area we had set up inside the dump, but away from the pads.

We would blow the rounds we collected, go back for more, and then repeat the process over and over and over. We did this in two-man teams, but left one man at the unit to answer incoming calls and inform callers that we would be somewhat tied up for the next few days. Every couple of days, you got to stay at the unit and mostly you slept and ignored the phone, letting the clerk handle the calls.

If we had an answering machine, the message would have been something like, "Hi, you've reached the 184th EOD. We are not here right now because we are out trying to get our asses blown up or set ourselves on fire so you can continue to get ammunition. Please leave your name, unit and the type of incident you have. If it's worse than an exploding ammo dump, we'll get back to you as soon as we can."

By the third or fourth day, our control team came in to assess the situation, and they started sending for men from other teams to assist us. The Control people were shocked at the level of destruction and surprised that none of us had been injured or killed.

Many areas still smoldered; rounds cooked off on a regular basis. No matter how prepared you thought you were, you were not. Each time something cooked off, you jumped out of your pants, and usually hit the ground. That was one reason why my startle response is so exaggerated. I jump at almost any unexpected noise, not just loud ones; sometimes, the phone sets me off.

From February 25 through the daylight hours of March 10, we worked hard clearing the devastation from the attack. We worked long, brutal, sweaty hours; the smell of cordite, tear gas and white phosphorous was constant. The ground still smoldered, littered with tens of thousands of rounds of damaged ordnance and small arms ammunition.

Sometimes, slight breezes carried the acrid stench of CS tear gas into our work areas, burning our eyes and skin. There was not a thing we could do about it. We were not going to don gas masks when the temperature was consistently at 100 degrees or higher.

In the middle of all of this, on February 27, the Viet Cong and NVA launched attacks on thirty U.S. installations throughout Vietnam and attacked nine cities and towns, including Qui Nhơn. As the team was still knee deep in the dump, Doug Rhodes and I became the EOD Team for all of Bình Định Province for three days.

In seventy-two hours, we handled more calls than I can remember, mostly blast sites, mortar tail fins sticking up from the dirt, and 107-mm and 122-mm rocket shrapnel and burned out motors. We got virtually no sleep during this time; on the fourth day, we went back to the dump.

By late afternoon of March 10, heading back to our hooches, we were about as worn out as anyone has ever been; I certainly was. We were slowed down, destroying a few rounds at a time inside the dump, and began to make plans to move large quantities of damaged ammunition to a larger demolition area down the road. None of us thought it could possibly get any worse than it had. We were wrong about that.

Returning to the unit that evening, we settled in to drink some cold beers—just like the evening of February 23—grill some steaks, and relax to the extent we could. The calm did not last very long, maybe five hours. The March 10–11 attack began at 10.50 p.m., when a satchel charge detonated on pad 89, which contained 105-mm artillery illumination rounds. It burned furiously.

By just after 11 p.m., infantry patrols scoured the dump looking for sappers, but, apparently, missed them, because, at 11.20 p.m., an explosion was reported on pad 28, full of 81-mm high-explosive mortar rounds. This became a problem for me two months later when I ran into one of these rounds we had missed during the initial cleanup.

Pad 28 burned violently and exploding mortar rounds threw molten fragments throughout the area. By 11.35 p.m., pad 90 (2.75-inch HE and WP rockets) went off, immediately causing explosions on pads 68, 83, and 84 as some rockets launched when their motors caught fire.

That was when we arrived at the dump—rockets flying through the air in all directions, and the "red glare" that Francis Scott Key described when Ft. McHenry went up, was live and in color and right in our faces. At 11.45 p.m., MSG Miller and I found a satchel charge cooking on pad 29, another pad of HE rounds. Lee ripped out the blasting cap and he tossed it over the pad's berm, recovering it the next day and destroying it.

As Miller and I moved to the next pad, another satchel charge exploded, and pad 28, not more than 100 yards away, blew in a mass-detonation, throwing 81-mm high-explosive mortar rounds and more 2.75-inch rockets throughout the entire depot. It was as if the sky had opened up and God was raining down exploding, fiery lightning bolts at us.

We were blown to the ground by the blast, and even though shrapnel fell all around us, we were not scratched—another miracle. At 11.46 p.m., the dump commander ordered everyone out, and I cannot say that we were unhappy with that decision. By 1.25 a.m. on the 11th, pad 90 was still exploding and the rockets were landing everywhere.

Rockets shot out of the dump, arcing into the air, then fell back to earth, landing outside the dump perimeter, or sailing into the foothills a few hundred yards away, starting fires in the dry foliage and jack pine. The rockets sometimes detonated when they hit the ground, as if launched from a helicopter gunship, as intended.

At approximately 3 a.m., when the rockets stopped flying every few minutes, we went back inside the dump to look for satchel charges. The flying rockets had not completely stopped, but it was deemed safe enough for us—not the rest of the dump solders who did not get that big fifty-five bucks—to return.

I do not know who actually made these decisions, but my guess is Captain Lorance and MSG Miller. I do not think the battalion commander would have ordered us back in when he was not sending his ammunition people. Yet, this is what they paid us for and what we were trained to do.

While I was in EOD School, none of my instructors ever said, "And, oh, by the way. You will be up to your asses in exploding ammunition inside an ammo dump." Even if they had, you could never be prepared for something like this. Yet when these kinds of situations arose, you never hesitated to do the job. I do not remember being scared, as that term is commonly understood, and I do not know if that is because I was an idiot or just did not let fear affect my ability to do my job.

From 2.21–2.58 a.m., the area outside the dump perimeter was pummeled by friendly artillery fire. They thought maybe this would finally kill the sappers, who were, no doubt, from the same VC unit that blew up the dump on February 23, and again on March 23. At 4 a.m., while shit was still going off all over the place, we moved back inside the dump and kept checking the remaining pads for satchel charges.

At 5.17 a.m., pad 68, another HE pad, began to burn, probably from the rockets still going off, and the dump was again cleared of all personnel at 5.30

a.m. As the infantry patrols pulled back from their positions inside the dump, and redeployed outside the perimeter, they began to receive small arms fire. They called in a fleet of helicopter gunships, which suddenly appeared and hosed down the area with mini-guns and rocket fire. That lasted for twenty minutes.

We were still outside the dump at 7.05 a.m. when pad 68—full of 8-inch HE artillery projectiles—exploded in a high order mass-detonation. The good news was that this explosion was so powerful, that it actually extinguished several fires in the depot area. The bad news was that it threw these 200-pound projectiles from one end of the dump to the other, and many of them landed outside the perimeter.

At about 7.30 a.m., we reentered the dump while pad 68 was still burning and high-explosive rounds were still detonating. Continuing to search for satchel charges and booby traps, we discovered that the sappers had gotten into the dump by cutting their way through three rows of concertina wire, put in place just one week earlier. They were able to do this while tower guards, roving infantry patrols, and dog teams covered the dump; no one saw a single sapper.

Today, December 4, 2007, I just got off the phone with retired Colonel Albert A. Busck, commanding officer of the 184th Ordnance Battalion when the dump went up, all three times. He remembered me as "the guy who got blown up," an event I will discuss shortly. He said, "When I saw your truck, I couldn't believe you survived." Then he reminded me of another one of those weird events I had forgotten. You ask yourself, "How could I not remember that?"

In the early morning hours of March 11, while we were clearing the dump after the second attack, then Lt. Col. Busck and his driver were on one of the dump roads in his jeep. Al led from the front, and was admired and respected for that.

Several hundred feet away, ammo people bulldozed burning pallets of 105mm high-explosive rounds away from the pad, hoping to avoid another large mass-detonation of an entire pad. Let me repeat that—they were moving burning stacks of 105-mm high-explosive rounds with a bulldozer.

These rounds were more than capable of destroying a bulldozer and, yet, these guys acted like it was just another day at the office, and people thought EOD guys were nuts. As they moved a pallet, several rounds detonated.

A large blade and the armor plating on his cab protected the driver. When the rounds went off, they threw a single HE round through the air about 200 feet, and it bounced off the hood of Lt. Col. Busck's jeep and landed, dead bang, in his lap. He started laughing, telling me this, and said, "My driver turned to me and said, 'Sir, do you know that you're on fire?'" We both laughed, and I said, "You know, Sir, we're both pretty lucky to be having this conversation."

"No kidding," he said. He told me that he still has scars on his legs from the burns.

In between the ammo dump attacks on March 10 and 23, ten VC sappers got into No. 2 Petroleum Oil and Lubricants Tank Farm on March 20 and blew the remaining four tanks still in use after a similar attack on January 3, 1969. EOD was called in to check for additional satchel charges, like we did not already have enough to do in the dump. I cannot remember who I was with on this incident.

Avoiding massive walls of flame and the oily smoke that only a petroleum fire can produce, we found no satchel charges. We did discover blood trails, leading us to believe that their own explosives had wounded some of the sappers.

On March 22, Korean infantry patrols and ambushes around the dump were withdrawn for a "higher level" security mission. The next night, the VC, once again, got into the dump and, once again, blew the hell out of it.

Even without the Korean infantry, security was so beefed up after the February 23 and March 10–11 events that this seemed impossible—how little we knew. Everything done to clean the dump after the first two attacks was undone by the third attack.

On this night, "D" Company, 58th Infantry, had seven patrols inside the dump and another platoon in ambush outside the dump, and the night before on a trail believed to be used by the sappers. A Korean recon team and Korean Special Forces also had two patrols and four ambushes in the area just southwest and west of the dump's perimeter.

At 8.30 p.m. on March 23, part of the D/58 ambush reported movement on the trail they were observing. At 9 p.m., they opened fire on four VC and killed two, while seriously wounding a third. The fourth VC solider escaped to a position in front of part of the ambush and joined six other VC. For reasons not explained, the ambush did not engage these seven enemies. This was the only time before, during, or after, the three attacks on the Qui Nhơn ammo dump that the enemy was seen.

By 9.30 p.m., the ambush leader reported that he could hear movement and voices, and that they were moving south, in the direction of the ammo depot. He also reported movement to his east and west. At 9.45 p.m., reinforcements from the Qui Nhơn Provisional Guard Command deployed to the northeast area of the depot. By 10 p.m., seven dog patrols were posted.

Somehow, all this security and the successful ambush failed to stop the sapper attack on the dump, and failed to detect any of the seven VC the D/58 ambush had reported on a trail leading to the perimeter.

At 11 p.m. on March 23, a guard tower reported an explosion in its area and pad 76 started burning. As ammo dump personnel fought the fire, pad 64, containing 155-mm HE artillery projectiles, mass-detonated, more than likely from a satchel charge, and started pad 76's fire anew. At that point, pad 76 detonated. The ammo dump was cleared of all personnel and, once again, we entered the fray.

As we arrived, the detonations from pads 64 and 76 blew up the Operations Office for the 820th Ordnance Company, and set the generator on fire, cutting off all lights in the dump. Dustoff med-evac choppers, trying to land to move the wounded, had to pull back because of the fire and exploding ammunition.

At 11.30 p.m., everyone (including us) evacuated, leaving only essential security personnel behind. At about 3.30 a.m., we re-entered the dump and began looking for satchel charges.

My teammate and I (I forget who it was) moved down the road toward a pad of burning 8-inch rounds about 200 yards away. Three ammo men entered the pad in an attempt to put out the fire and, as they did, it exploded; the blast blew us off our feet and shrapnel flew everywhere. If we had been moving any faster and been closer to that pad, I probably would not be writing this.

It was another of those events you cannot explain in terms of why are you still alive. The three ammo men who had entered the pad as it detonated were all killed. The only thing found the next day was part of a jawbone. I do not know if they ever identified which man it belonged to.

One of them was CPT William J. Ahlum; the other two were SP5 Michael L. Berry and SP4 Jerry Lee Peterson. According to the official report, "Three personnel who were last seen in the vicinity of this pad are missing and presumed dead." The next week, the *Army Times*, which reported those who had been KIA the previous week, listed the three men as, "Missing, Presumed Dead." You could not make this up if you tried. Where did they think they were? Des Moines?

After the 8-inch rounds went off, we left the dump to regain our senses and our hearing. This is probably how my tinnitus began.

At 4 a.m. on March 24, we reentered the dump while pad 76 was still exploding and many fires still burned. We thought pads 77 and 78 were also burning due to the huge flames in the area, and dense smoke that made it almost impossible to breathe.

It turned out that it was just smoke from the detonations on pads 64 and 76. Unlike Dugway, we did not have the luxury of Scott Air Packs. We went through most of the pads that were not on fire and removed pieces of hot fragmentation and rounds blown in from pads 64 and 76, so that fires would not begin.

Of the three attacks on the dump, the March 23 event—with the exception of the three men killed—was the "best of the worst" since only the two pads had gone up. Despite that, thirty-seven men were also wounded that night, accounting for 77 percent of the men wounded during the three attacks.

I do not know exactly what to say about the whole ammo dump thing that went on for months after the three sapper attacks. It was like something out of *The Twilight Zone*; nothing seemed able to stop the VC from getting into the dump and not one was killed, captured, or wounded. I would like to say it was the worst thing that happened to me—being inside an exploding ammo dump three times in a month—but it was not, not even close.

On May 13, 1969, I was almost killed, just when my team and EOD men from all over Vietnam were almost finished cleaning up the Qui Nhơn ammo dump. Roger McCormack and I were examining a pad of 8-inch high-explosive artillery rounds when we discovered an American 81-mm mortar round that had impacted with a stack of ordnance and lodged itself between two rounds.

This might sound like a weird occurrence, but it was not the strangest thing we saw after the three attacks.

The round was probably thrown into this pad when pad 28—containing this type of ordnance—went up during the March 10 attack. The mortar round was a high-explosive projectile armed with an M-524 fuse. The 8-inch artillery projectile is a very, very big bullet that weighs 200 pounds and is packed with explosives. The pad was full of pallets of these rounds. The fuse in the mortar round has what is called a "bore-riding pin," which is the only thing blocking the detonator from the spring-loaded nose plunger. It is removed before the round is dropped down the mortar tube.

It is possible that when these rounds are thrown by another explosion, like in the ammo dump, the bore-riding pin is ejected and the round is fully armed as if shot from a mortar tube. It could also have been that the round flew through the air and the bore-riding pin ejected when the round slammed into the artillery projectiles. In the end, it really did not matter.

This is the condition the round was in when Roger and I found it. In addition, the plunger was damaged from impact and jammed down into the fuse-body, possibly forcing the firing pin into the detonator. Obviously, we could not blow the round in place because of its location.

Roger and I tied a lengthy piece of commo wire around the tail fins, backed up the truck, got behind it, and jerked the round from between the 8-inch rounds. Even at that distance, we heard the round as it hit the concrete floor of the pad, and bounced several times before coming to a rest. I assumed the round was safe to move to our small demo area inside the dump for destruction. I was wrong about that.

It could be that this was my one and only mistake in Vietnam. I am not trying to imply that I was, otherwise, perfect, but I prided myself on assessing each particular unusual event and making the best decision on how to handle it. Looking back today, given the circumstances, I would do it the same way, even if I knew I was going to get fucked up.

My CO, CPT Dennis Lorance, came up with SSG Mike Lizak; I told him what had happened and what my plan was. CPT Lorance agreed that I would move the item to the demo area several hundred yards away and destroy it.

I backed our 0.75-ton truck into the pad, dropped the tailgate, then moved the large spare tire to a standing position against the canvas back of the driver's cab. I placed several sandbags on the floor of the truck and put the mortar round on top of them, covered the round with additional sandbags, and closed the tailgate.

I drove out of the pad and turned right, heading for the demo area. Some 50 feet later, I heard a large bang. What happened next occurred in the blink of an eye, though it seemed like slow motion.

The mortar round had exploded. It was so close that, as the blast perforated both of my eardrums, it sounded far away. I thought, "Boom?", turned to look, and saw a ball of fire coming right at me; the round had detonated directly over the gas tank. Both doors were blown off, and the windshield blown out in the initial detonation. I had to jump from the moving truck.

Engulfed in fire as I tried to jump through the driver's door opening, the blast hit me and blew me out of the truck. I hit the hard-packed road on my right knee, my head colliding soundly with the ground, and rolled down an embankment. Just before losing consciousness, I heard a lot of buzzing in my ears; it felt like the wind was rushing through my head.

Lying on the side of the hill, I regained consciousness and thought, "Oh, fuck, the truck will go into a pad and blow the thing up." I was worried that

I would cause more work for my teammates. I could barely see the road, but down-range I watched as the burning truck turned slowly to the left and went down over the same berm I was lying on.

This is how God—or whatever—looked out for EOD men. In Vietnam, at least in that dump, they had a large pond where fire trucks would recharge their tanks while fighting fires. It was right down the road from where I lay. The burning truck went over the berm and into the pond, putting out the fire. I thought, "Holy shit!"

Then Mike Lizak bent over me and yelled, "Are you alright? Can you hear me?" I could hear radio-crackle and someone was yelling about a dust-off. I tried to get up on my elbows, but I had no strength and fell back to the hard-packed ground. I thought I was dying. Then I lost consciousness, again.

I have no memory of the med-evac ride to the medical aid station down the road from the dump.

The only reason I am still alive is that the spare tire, which I had propped up against the canvas behind my seat, had absorbed most of the blast and shrapnel. I had second and third-degree burns, particularly on the backs of my ears and neck. I took some shrapnel in the back, my inner forearms, and my eardrums were perforated. Jumping from the truck, I tore up my right knee, a major-medical problem today. It took several weeks to recover from these injuries, mainly because of the perforated eardrums.

A few years ago, CPT Lorance reminded me that I actually returned to the field within three days, and worked until a week later when I was injured a second time during an incoming attack on the compound we lived in with 8th Transportation Group.

Our control unit screwed over CPT Lorance because of this incident. They felt we should have figured out some way to destroy the round without moving it off the pad of tens of tons of high-explosive artillery shells. After all, they taught us in school that we were never supposed to mess with this round when armed with the 524 fuse, and to always blow it in place, if the bore-riding was missing. Whoever invented that theory had never been to Vietnam inside an ammo dump where they found this piece of ordnance in this condition and in this kind of location.

They transferred CPT Lorance from Qui Nhơn to a desk job at Control in Long Bình for a while, and he eventually took over the 133rd in Chu Lai. I guess he had to do penance and a bunch of Hail Marys before he was deemed properly reformed and sworn to follow the company line.

That was no way to treat an officer who led by example. He allowed his experienced men to make decisions when the situation called for it. My guess is that the regular Army pinheads at U.S. Army Vietnam and 1st Logistical Command did not care for Dennis because he was an ex-enlisted man who had gotten a field commission.

This is an example of the way the military treats people who choose to think for themselves once they realize that what is written in official publications is not necessarily the best answer in all situations. These things have not changed.

It took four months to clean up the dump. Our primary task was to check the thousands of tons of ordnance damaged by explosions or subjected to intense heat by the many fires burning in the dump all three times it was hit. To destroy this mass of damaged ammunition, the engineers cleared a large area about a mile down Highway 1 from the dump.

In early March 1969, on the day we were set to begin destroying the damaged ordnance, we went to the area, a large plain of elephant grass at the base of a low mountain range about a kilometer off QL 1, the major north-south highway. To get to the demolition area, we turned west off QL I and took an old two-track road to the site. While several of my teammates and I waited for the engineers, we discovered one of the few things of beauty I saw during my time in the War.

We got out of the jeeps, carrying our weapons, and began to check the tree line at the border of the plain and the base of the mountains. One of us heard rushing water; we went deeper into the tree line to the base of one of the mountains. Moving around a wall of stone and dense vegetation, we saw where the sound came from. Out of a crevice about 50 feet up the mountain wall, a small but powerful waterfall crescendoed into a clear pool below.

We took one look, got out of our filthy, stinking fatigues, and took turns, two at a time, jumping into the pool and relaxing.

The other two team members kept watch because we were in an area heavily traveled by the Viet Cong. Too soon, we heard the engineer trucks carrying bulldozers and graders, and we had to return to the realities of the war.

For the demolition area, we cleared a space about the size of a football field and dug a huge pit in the middle. Over four months, we trucked huge amounts of bad ammo to this site and blew it up. From April 26–May 25, 1969, for instance, we destroyed 3,756 pieces of explosive ordnance that weighed 18.5 tons.

While we were cleaning up the dump, a total of sixty-one EOD men from the other thirteen teams and Control came for one or two weeks at a time to help. That was how big the job was. Among them was my friend, Tom Allen, from Dugway. Also among them were Jim Austin from the 59th in Quảng Trị, killed in 1971; Tim Roumph, also from the 59th, wounded in the dump by an exploding white phosphorous round; and Dave Tipton and John Claffy from the 3rd Ordnance Battalion, EOD Section, in Long Bình. Claffy was wounded when a damaged mortar fuse exploded; the same fuse in the round that almost killed me.

During the few days after the dump was first attacked on February 23, 1969, we destroyed 12,465 pieces of ordnance, weighing 34.27 tons. During the three explosions and subsequent cleanup, three men were killed and forty-eight were wounded.

Other than the ambush high up in the hills above the dump, not a single VC was confirmed to have been killed—or even seen—despite artillery barrages and gunship fire on all of the areas inside and outside the dump's perimeter. Every member of my team was decorated at least twice for heroism, meritorious achievement in combat operations, or for wounds received in action.

During the three attacks, twenty-three pads of high-explosive ammunition exploded, along with a couple of pads of small arms ammunition. Of the average total tons of ordnance in the dump during the three attacks—almost 19,000—more than 11,000 tons (22,000,000 pounds) were destroyed. In all, there were fourteen Bronze Stars awarded for heroism and four for meritorious achievement; there were twenty Army Commendation Medals given for heroism and seven for meritorious achievement.

Forty-eight men, including myself and fellow EOD-men John Claffy and Phil Kirwan, received the Purple Heart. I received the Army Commendation Medal for the dump explosion on March 10, another for the period February 23–March 23, which covered all three explosions and part of the cleanup.

Tim Roumph, who was wounded when a fuse in a piece of a WP round detonated, did not get his Purple Heart. In 2015, I took his case to the Army Board for the Correction of Military Records, and they denied him the award. They said that, after all, "it was an accident" and he was just "doing his job" as an EOD specialist. By that logic, no infantryman killed in a firefight should get the Purple Heart because he was just "doing his job."

By the end of the cleanup operation, we had destroyed 403.75 tons of ordnance—that is 807,500 pounds of dangerous stuff that had been exposed to explosions and fire. During the destruction operations, we handled every single one of these damaged rounds and sustained no injuries other than blisters and very sore muscles.

We had to deal with white phosphorus rounds still cooking off well into May, three months after the original attack on February 23. During the dump cleanup, we disposed of 70 tons of leaking and damaged white phosphorus rounds.

We transported every single one of these items in containers filled with water and destroyed them inside the dump, far away from pads with high-explosive ammunition. To get them into the large containers, we had to pick them up using heavy flame-resistant gloves. Many were smoking as we did this, so the threat of detonation was always there.

The sides, tops, and bottoms of the containers were covered with plastic explosives and detonated, completing destruction of all WP rounds without incident. In addition to the 404 tons of ammunition we destroyed by detonation, we trucked another 375 tons of 105-mm and 155-mm HE artillery rounds to an area near Tuy Hòa on the coast, then took them out to sea in Navy barges and dumped them overboard. I wonder, today, about the environmental damage this must be causing forty-seven years later.

During the cleanup after the three attacks, we hand-carried 2,011 90-mm, 106-mm, and 152-mm high-explosive anti-tank (HEAT) rounds from locations inside the dump to our demolition area in a safe part of the dump. We handled thousands of 66-mm LAW rockets, also a type of HEAT round.

We had to do it this way because many of the fuses were thought to have armed as the rounds were thrown around the dump, many of them exposed to fire. If the nose fuse was crushed, you had to assume the base-detonating fuse had armed and all of them were damaged. Virtually all had crushed nose fuses.

We were still regularly disposing of bad ammo as late as June 25, 1969. From incident logs, it appears that the last event we handled at the dump related to the attacks was on July 19, 1969, when a damaged fuse was found in the dirt of one of the pads. I guess we really did, as the 173rd reporter had noted in the November 1968 interview, "live a life of daily danger," although it sometimes went on for months without a break.

During my time in Vietnam, this reality never entered my conscious thoughts. I have no idea why.

9

More Time in Qui Nhơn

On May 19, 1969, six days after being wounded in the ammo dump, I was wounded a second time while still recovering from the mortar round event. I was at the unit Command Post in Phu Tai, and felt good enough that evening to head up to the enlisted men's club operated by the 8th Transportation Group, whose compound we lived in.

I grabbed my rifle and a couple of clips, and Roger McCormack and I walked up the slight rise to the club, about 200 yards from our quarters. Until then, the compound had not been hit since we moved there in early October 1968. The walk was a bit of a strain because my injured right knee was still sore and tender.

My punctured eardrums had not quite healed, and it felt like wind was rushing into my head; the tinnitus was bad, too. I call it "radio waves from outer space," but I cannot figure out what they are trying to tell me. Maybe if I put aluminum foil over my head it would stop. The tops and backs of my ears and the back of my neck were still crusted over and painful from second-degree burns. I smeared Vaseline on them, which caused a very creepy feeling when my sweat mingled with it.

Eighth Group was responsible for handling trucking from Qui Nhơn, up the coast along Highway 1 and then west on Highway 19, through An Khê and to Pleiku, and then on to Kontum and Duc Co. They also had routes further north on Highway 1 to places like LZ Uplift and LZ English.

The road to An Khê and Pleiku was particularly dangerous. Eighth Group had three battalions and, during the War, had lost 120 men. Larry Dahl, an

Eighth Group driver, won the Medal of Honor for smothering a grenade blast to protect his comrades.

The Group's units were constantly under enemy attack along their routes and the 8th had a large number of gun trucks mounted with M-60 and .50 caliber machine guns. They even had one truck in the 27th Transportation Battalion mounted with a mini-gun, salvaged from a helicopter gunship. With all this firepower at the Eighth Group compound, we felt pretty safe.

Roger and I entered the club, got a beer and went to the music room, where they had musical instruments—electric guitars, a bass guitar, an old, decrepit upright piano, and a set of really beat up drums. The drumsticks had been made in one of the villages and they were slightly bowed, but the people who played them did not care. They were just happy to jam and drink some beer.

I cannot remember how long we were there, but it was dark when we walked up there and it was dark when we hauled ass back to the CP when the shit hit the fan. Plus, it was raining like hell, and it was chilly.

Our Command Post was at the far south end of the compound, next to the perimeter. To the immediate west, right outside the perimeter, there was a huge rock escarpment that shot about 300 feet straight up to a small plain which ended at the low hills surrounding the valley that Highway 1 ran through south to the ammo dump and then to Tuy Hòa.

About 10 p.m., Roger and I were sitting in the club, playing guitar with a couple of soldiers from the 8th, working on our second beers, when we heard a loud explosion and the place went completely dark. Not just the club, but the entire compound was plunged into a wet blackness. The alert siren sounded; everyone jumped up and ran through the darkened club, out the doors, toward their various units.

Running from the club down the hill, limping and in pain, toward our bunker, I slipped a magazine into my rifle and was pulling the charging handle to the rear to get a round into the chamber. Incoming mortar rounds began hitting the far west side of the compound, and rocket propelled grenades were launched from the plain right at the edge of the stone escarpment above our hooch, CP, and bunker.

Unknown to me—or I had forgotten it was there—a large pile of PSP ("pierced steel planking" used, among other things, to make short runways on remote firebases) was stacked up in the path between the club and our bunker next to the CP. I think it was about 8 feet high. I was running, getting my rifle loaded, limping in pain, when I ran headfirst into the PSP, knocking myself cold. I regained consciousness as Roger and Doug Rhodes were dragging me through the wire to the next compound, where the 51st Medical Company had an aid station. I think maybe Bernie Duff, a medic I met online, may have worked on me as well, since he was with the 51st at that time.

There were ruptured ligaments and blood vessels in my left knee, which was hugely swollen and a large laceration to my left thumb that required eleven stitches to close. They used a huge needle to drain my knee.

When it is cold, the thumb still hurts. That is where scar tissue crosses the lower part where it attaches to my hand, and then runs all the way up the thumb and turns red. I cannot touch the heel of my left hand below the little finger with my thumb.

As I was taken to this small 51st Medical Battalion aid station in the middle of the night, no mention of these injuries found its way into my official medical records, which were in a drawer back at the unit Command Post. If it had not been for CPT Lorance's monthly report, which I retrieved from the National Archives, there would be no record of this event. His report clearly states that my injuries occurred "during a red alert."

I mention this because the paperwork for my second Purple Heart never got sent up the chain-of-command. Our clerk, who was a junkie, was not doing his job at this point, and CPT Lorance was being investigated for my injuries in the ammo dump. I tried to get the Army Board for the Correction of Military Records to correct my records, but they turned it down because there were no orders, and our clerk had never submitted the casualty report. They ignored CPT Lorance's report.

This was also my first experience with a Spooky gunship, a converted C-47 transport plane outfitted with mini-guns and a Vulcan, six-barreled 20-mm Gatling gun. These babies could crank it out and were the forerunners of the AC-130 "Specter," which also carried a 105-mm howitzer. On the way back to our CP from 51st Med, an Air Force "Spooky" came in and just blasted the shit out of the plain above the compound where the incoming rounds had come from.

On July 6, 1969, there was a fire on the pipeline south of Qui Nhơn that ran from Vũng Rô Bay to the city of Tuy Hòa. It was caused by Vietnamese civilians trying to pilfer fuel from the line; the ensuing inferno incinerated five of them. Maybe if we had provided the Vietnamese people with more support, like fuel, these kinds of events could have been avoided, or not.

I stood there, watching the flames as they licked their way upward toward the sky, while the homes of the people who lived there fell to the ground, leaving nothing but burning cinder, ash, and smoke. It was a sad, terrible situation that we were helpless to stop. You did your job and moved on to the next one, forgetting as best you could, to work without distraction—that was the job.

On July 8, 1969, at 4.40 p.m., Mike Lizak and I were called out on another pipeline explosion and fire near a village about 18 miles northwest of Qui Nhơn. The pipeline was 6 inches in diameter and 50.6 miles in length. We left the unit with an MP gun-jeep escort and headed north on Highway 1 then east on Highway 19, which ran east and then north, to An Khê, Pleiku, and Kontum. Someone wanted us to check the area around the pipeline—which, we were told, ran through the village—for booby traps and satchel charges.

This line carried fuel to aviation units at An Khê and Pleiku, following Highway 19, a very dangerous stretch of road. We turned off the highway and followed a dirt road about one-and-a-half miles to the good-sized village. The fire, as it turned out, was in the village. The pipeline was back down the road and had not exploded, nor was it on fire.

The fire had been caused by the mass-detonation of between 300–350 gallons of JP-4 (jet fuel) in 5-gallon gas cans that the villagers had tapped from the pipeline, a regular and dangerous occurrence. The village was virtually destroyed and, according to the report, the homes of 1,000 people were burned to the ground.

All the many ways there are to cause massive damage with brute force and overwhelming firepower, were equally devastating in creating havoc on the Vietnamese. Some were caused by us and our allies, others by the enemy, and still others by the Vietnamese people to themselves. The event in this village was one of those. I am pretty sure this was the same pipeline where Mike Lizak lost a leg to a mine in September 1969.

The Central Highlands, where the 184th operated, was a bad place. You did not hear as much about it in the news as you did about "I" Corps, home of the A Shau Valley and Hamburger Hill, or the Delta, with the Iron Triangle. Qui Nhơn was in Bình Định Province. It was a hotbed of enemy activity during the war; 2,349 soldiers died there.

Pleiku Province (now known as Gia Lai) was where the cities of Pleiku and An Khê were. Another 1,084 men died there. The Central Highlands was the scene of the Battle of the Ia Drang Valley, where 151 members of the 1st Cav died between November 11–13, 1965. The Battle of Đắk Tô (the "Hill Battles") in Kontum Province lasted from November 3–22, 1967. During this savage fight, 376 men died, mostly from the 173rd Airborne Brigade. There were 1,685 soldiers killed in Kontum Province.

Mike Lizak has passed away. Former SSG Roy E. Judkins, who was with Mike and I at the 184th, has also passed away. Roy Judkins is the only Army EOD man ever to get the Distinguished Service Cross. The only higher decoration is the Medal of Honor. He and Doug Rhodes removed a dud 40-mm HE round from a guy's head in a hospital emergency room in Qui Nhơn, carried it outside, and blew it. Two days later, Roy carried a wounded 173rd paratrooper out of a minefield, while Doug provided cover fire. Doug was awarded a Bronze Star with "V" Device for heroism. It took until 1996 for Doug and Roy to get their awards; it is sad that Roy passed away shortly afterward.

10

On-Site at Tuy Hòa

On April 14, 1969, Mike Lizak and I were at the 184th's on-site team near the City of Tuy Hòa at the Phú Hiệp Base Camp, taking a break from the ammo dump when we got a call about a suspicious device found under a seat in the Tuy Hòa civilian movie theater. Tuy Hòa was one of those very strange places that actually made the war bearable.

Even though the 173rd Airborne Brigade, MACV, and Special Forces all ran combat operations outside of the city, the war never came to Tuy Hòa. At least that was how I remember it. There was an air base there, as well, but I do not remember ever going there. Other than during the Tet Offensive of 1968, I guess it was like an unspoken rule between the two sides that the City of Tuy Hòa was off limits for matters resulting in death and destruction. One VC bomb-maker, however, apparently did not get the memo.

There was a very nice French restaurant in Tuy Hòa; we used to go there for lunch during lulls, usually with some advisers from the MACV (Military Advisory Command Vietnam) compound. It was a little strange being there; it was like you were actually somewhere else, like any city anywhere but there. There were linen table cloths, real silverware, and waiters who took your order.

The Vietnamese who ate there were not like other locals, assuming they were locals; they seemed more refined than the typical Vietnamese we ran into. They dressed well, their hair was meticulously cut, and they spoke either French or better than average English. I thought they were educated NVA or VC officers, since I never met a South Vietnamese soldier who looked or acted like these guys.

Vũng Rô Bay, the deep-water port at Tuy Hòa, was one of those places you dream about. There was a pristine white sand beach, the deep blue water of the South China Sea and a small compound off the beach where the transportation guys who ran the port, MPs and some Seabees lived. There was a long pier where big tankers came in and downloaded oil and fuel into a pipeline that went north to Qui Nhơn.

Mike and I arrived at the theater in downtown Tuy Hòa. Two MACV advisers and two Vietnamese Army MPs met us. One MACV adviser said that someone had found a lunch pail under their seat, with smoke coming out of it with a very acrid odor.

The Vietnamese carried thin metal lunch pails with two sections and a top. The lower section was for boiling water and the upper section, which had small holes in it, was for steaming their food. There was a little handle to carry it, like the handle on a bucket.

Mike and I entered the darkened theater, and one of the advisers took us to the seat. We asked him to leave. Mike looked under the seat with a flashlight. He kneeled on one knee and, after peering under the seat, turned to me and said, "Yep. It's a lunch pail; it is smoking and the smoke smells like acid burning something."

We agreed that this was probably an improvised explosive device and made a decision to remove it from under the seat and carry it outside. Normally, we would put C-4 near such a device to blow it. However, we decided that the people of Tuy Hòa would not be happy if we blew up their only theater.

Thinking that there might be an anti-disturbance device, we had to determine if the IED was safe to move. The handle, like any bucket handle, hung downward, touching the floor. Mike sent me to the jeep for a length of wire. I cut off about 50 feet and took it back inside. He put a loop around the pail and loosely tied a simple knot. We laid the wire out as far as we could and got behind a row of seats. Mike slowly pulled on the wire until he got tension, then, even more slowly, pulled the wire toward him, trying not to knock the can over.

He reeled in about 5 feet of wire. The device did not hit the floor or detonate, so we went back to the seat. It sat on the floor between the seat and the seat in front of it. We decided to pick it up and carry it outside.

I do not remember who picked it up and carried it outside, or where we placed it on the sidewalk. I asked the MACV advisers to have the MPs clear the area for several hundred yards since we had no idea what we were dealing with. Then I told them and the MPs to pull back with the crowd.

Mike asked me what I thought; I said we needed to remove the top remotely to see inside.

I went to the jeep and got two sandbags and about 100 feet of commo wire. I sandbagged the lunch pail on two sides and loosely attached the commo wire to the handle on top. Mike and I backed away to our jeep and got behind it. I gently pulled on the wire and heard the top hit the sidewalk. We waited ten minutes and when nothing happened, we looked over the top of the jeep and waited another five minutes.

We went back to the device and bent over it, peering inside; we were looking at a very sophisticated IED—the bottom two-thirds of the pail contained U.S. plastic explosives, with a centered fuse from a U.S. M-33 high-explosive fragmentation grenade.

The grenade pin was pulled, and the striker held in place all the way back by a thin metal wire soldered to the side of the pail. An inch above the solder point was a small metal canister, like a CO_2 cartridge, but smaller. From a pin-sized hole in the end just above the wire, some kind of acid dripped, eating through the solder and wire holding the striker away from the fuse detonator.

Mike went to the jeep and got a pair of needle-nose pliers. When he returned, we squatted on opposite sides of the lunch pail. He told me he was going to grab the striker with the pliers and use it as a block between it and the detonator. As soon as he had the striker, he wanted me to use my side cutters to cut the wire. He grabbed the striker with the pliers, but before I could cut the wire, the acid ate through it, and the wire broke as intended. Had he grabbed it a split second later, bye-bye Mike and Stu.

We looked at each other and Mike smiled. Then he pulled the fuse out of the C-4 and pitched it down the sidewalk, needle-nose pliers and all. We hit the sidewalk quickly, knowing we had about five seconds. The fuse flew 20 yards and went off before it hit the ground.

We were far enough away that the little bit of shrapnel thrown by the blasting cap came nowhere near us. When we got back to our hooch at the Tuy Hòa Base Camp, we wrote a technical report on the device and later received a letter of commendation for our work that day.

In early June, 1969, I was on-site at Tuy Hòa, again with Mike, and we got a call from 5th Special Forces Group in Na Trang about a problem at an A-Team camp in far eastern II Corps, just west of the South China Sea. We flew in a Huey to 5th Group HQ and met with the Group Intel officer who said the A-Team at Cung Son had something very strange happening in their well; it was smoking and bubbling.

Lizak and I looked at each other and, almost simultaneously, said, "White Phosphorus." As previously noted, white phosphorus is one of the most horrible inventions of war. When exposed to air, the substance will burn through flesh and not stop until air is cut off, usually by immersion in water or cutting it out with a knife. We loaded our gear into a 5th Group chopper and, with a gunship escort, flew to the Cung Son camp of A-221. We knew nothing about the area around the camp, but the gunship escort said it all.

Flying in, we saw the camp on a hill above a village, Cung Son, I assume. The commander and team sergeant met us on the chopper pad and took us to their tactical operations center. We stored our gear and the young officer said, "We're having a problem with our well." Lizak and I looked at each other and Mike said, "Excuse me?"

"Well," said the Green Beret, "The well is smoking."

We both knew that we were talking about some kind of white phosphorus thing, but we could not imagine what it was until the commander took us to the well. Sure enough, the smoke had that unmistakable smell of WP. Mike said, "Looks like someone dropped some kind of WP round in the well, and it rusted through. The WP is floating to the surface."

Mike and I started talking about how to deal with this strange situation. Our first thought was to pack the well with C-4 and blow the crap out of it. The officer said, "Hey, that's our only fresh water source, and the villagers use it, too."

"Okay, scratch that," Mike said. "We're going to have to figure a way to get whatever it is out and then blow it."

I asked the captain, "Any way to shut off the flow of water to the well?"

He said, "We can shut down the pumps." This done, we asked him if they had a bilge pump and generator; they did. We moved the pump and small generator next to the well, and over a period of several hours, drained most of the water from it. As the water level dropped, the WP smoke got heavier and heavier as more and more chunks of this dangerous substance surfaced. It was acrid and thick, white and billowing. It burned our eyes.

With the well almost dry, Mike and I gingerly approached and peered inside. "Holy crap," I said. Through the murky water, down about fifteen feet, we saw a pile of ordnance. There were 60-mm mortars, some of which were leaking WP, and some high explosives—not a good combination. We also saw some weird looking grenades. Mike said, "We have these at the school. They're French."

We were looking at ordnance the French had dumped into the well, probably after the fall of Điện Biên Phủ in 1954. There was a lot of ammo, including linked ammo, bazooka, and recoilless rifle rounds, and several dozen artillery projectiles. Mike said, "Now we've almost dried up the well, we better get this stuff out of there before the WP cooks off and blows the well and us."

The captain got us a long fire ladder, which we dropped down the well. Then we fashioned a sling out of camouflage netting and rigged it to a length of very sturdy rappelling lines. We took turns going into the well, breathing that stinking WP smoke, loading the ordnance into buckets of water, then into the sling, and bringing it to the surface.

We kept the leakers in a box we had lined with tarp material, then covered them with water. This took about three hours to complete. We stacked all the ordnance in a pile about 200 yards outside of the camp perimeter, and Mike took a picture of me, squatting by the pile, smoking WP and all, as I added to the smoke by lighting a cigarette. This was probably not the smartest thing to do, but, hey, it was Vietnam. This was one of the black and white Polaroids I mentioned in the chapter about LZ English that had faded away over the years.

We set the pile off with C-4, and the A-Team people thought we were the greatest. Mike's knowledge, after many years at the EOD School, was what allowed us to figure out how to deal with this problem.

My last trip to Tuy Hòa, in July, 1969, gave me a chance to use a technique we had learned in school that I never thought I would get to do. We got a call from the 4th Battalion, 503rd Infantry—a 173rd Airborne Brigade unit. I was with Ron Carlton on this one.

We went to some little village about ten clicks inland from Tuy Hòa, where the unit had been in contact with the enemy the night before and called in an airstrike, almost directly on top of their position. When the enemy was inside your perimeter, it was sometimes your only chance to survive, even if you lost some of your own men.

One bomb, a dud, was sitting on the surface—a big teardrop-shaped metal egg waiting for either the enemy to grab it to make IEDs, or some villagers after the steel. It was a 250-pounder, sitting right in the middle of the village, surrounded by a platoon of infantry to keep the villagers and the enemy away. It only had a nose fuse, and most of that was missing, but the part still inside the fuse well was the bad part—what was left was the detonator.

We could not blow the bomb where it lay because it would have obliterated the center of the small town, including several shops and the school. So, Ron looked at me and said, "Let's cut this baby into pieces and haul it out of here." He wanted to use linear shape charges to cut the bomb into pieces. When this technique worked, it caused people to "ooh" and "ahh" as if we were minor gods. The trick was to do it without the nose fuse detonating the bomb.

We only had enough shape charge containers to go around the bomb once, so Ron called for a chopper and sent me back for more. I returned an hour later and we began to line the containers with C-4. We circled the bomb with four sets of the shaped charges, capped them, and hooked it into the wire roll, reeling off a couple of hundred feet, attaching it to the blasting machine after getting behind an APC. "Here goes," he said. "Boom!"

It was slick. The bomb lay in the middle of the center of the village cut into five slices. Where the C-4 had cut through the bomb's explosive center, each side of each slice was glazed from the heat of the blast. This was not a completely done deal in terms of our safety. We moved the bomb sections a safe distance from the village and destroyed them.

There was one sort of, kind of, underwater job I went on with Mike Lizak. We got a call from either the Sea Bees or the MPs at the port at Vũng Rô Bay about a mine on the side of a ship. They told us a VC sapper had been killed in the water near the ship, and they found the mine-checking ships in the harbor. We called Qui Nhơn and requested the unit call the Navy EOD Team at the Qui Nhơn harbor. They were not available. We had to handle the call.

The MPs took us down to the beach where we climbed into a Boston Whaler with a small outboard motor and cruised out to one of the oil tankers tied up to a pier jutting far out into the harbor. The MPs had dragged the body of the dead VC onto the beach with a long rope, and we would eventually have to check it for unexploded ordnance. We pulled up alongside the ship; it was good the tide was out or the mine would never have been discovered.

The mine contained twenty 1-pound TNT blocks wrapped in sandbags with a 3-foot length of time fuse and a non-electric blasting cap inside one of the explosive blocks. The time fuse had an American fuse lighter on the other end, which had been pulled, and the fuse had burned a few inches, then gone out, luckily for the crew of the ship. The mine had been stuck to the side of the ship with a putty-like substance. We never did figure out exactly what it was.

Our main concern was whether there was a secondary fuse under the mine that would blow the explosives when we removed the mine from the hull. Mike said that we needed something long, hard and thin so that we could probe the putty, so we returned to the beach and went to the Seabee metal fabrication shop. Mike got a 4-foot length of 0.5-inch steel rod and had someone in the shop grind a long, sharp point on one end.

We went back out to the tanker and used the steel rod to probe under the mine, pushing it through the putty on one side until it came out on the other side. We did this at intervals of about 1 inch all the way around the mine and were pretty well satisfied there was no secondary device. This is not the same as certainty.

I had picked up a roll of rope in the metal shop and looped it around the outside of the mine with a simple slipknot, then pulled it tight, imbedding it in the putty. The MPs backed their boat up about 100 feet then I pulled the line taut. We got down below the gunwales of the boat, and I pulled the rope as hard as I could. The mine peeled off the side of the ship and splashed into the water. We waited ten minutes, and when nothing happened, approached the mine.

Mike decided there was no need to drag the mine back onto the beach. We capped two lengths of our own time fuse and had the MPs drive their boat out into the harbor, towing the mine with the rope. When we got out a couple of hundred yards, we pulled the mine up to the boat, jammed caps into two of the TNT blocks, and pulled the fuse lighters. We drove back to the beach, docked, and about two minutes later, the mine went off throwing a plume of water high into the air.

We walked to where the dead VC sapper lay in the sand on his stomach. He wore pants cut off just below the knees and that was it. A 40-mm high-explosive grenade had blown off the top of his head and part of his brain hung out the back where the skull was missing. Mike flipped him over; we checked his pants pockets for explosives and found none.

From July 1–16, 1969, I was at Phú Hiệp with Ron Carlton. Except for the bomb in the village, it was almost a vacation since we had no other unusual calls, no fly-outs, nothing particularly dangerous. There were only sixteen calls on eight days out of the sixteen. The only complicated call was a hung 40-mm HE grenade in an M5 launcher on a Huey helicopter.

When I returned from this trip to Phú Hiệp, I had less than sixty days left on my tour. I had mixed feelings about leaving and had started thinking about extending for six months, despite everything that had happened, particularly getting wounded and the events surrounding the Qui Nhơn ammo dump.

11

Extending My Tour and Moving to An Khê

On July 28, 1969, exactly three years from the date I had enlisted, I extended my tour for another six months. This meant that instead of going home on September 2, 1969, I would not leave Vietnam until March 23, 1970.

On July 31, 1969, I was transferred to the 25th Ordnance Detachment (EOD) at An Khê. My narrow escapes with the Qui Nhơn team played a part in that transfer. There was an unwritten rule in EOD—superstitions were a fact of our lives. Too many negative events and you went to a new team.

It was another version of a cat having nine lives, and our control unit was worried I had used up several in a short period of time with the Qui Nhơn team. It turned out for the best; if not for An Khê, I would not have gone to Phu Bai and met the men from the 287th with whom I have maintained a lifelong friendship.

In June 1969, I got acid in one eye from a truck battery thought to be booby-trapped. Having been wounded twice within a week in May, I had gone back into the ammo dump when sappers blew it up again in July. Then there was the Tank Farm, the two fires in Vietnamese villages when fuel stolen from a pipeline exploded, many close calls in between, and a lot of insane shit on operations with the 173rd out of LZ English and Tuy Hòa.

Maybe I was jinxed; who can say? You started fresh when you moved, or so you believed. I was not in An Khê very long when I found myself inside another exploding, burning dump, this time full of petroleum products, not massive quantities of artillery projectiles and mortar rounds. I fail to see a distinction between dodging flying bullets, and flying 55-gallon drums of gasoline, oil, and paint thinner, surrounded by walls of flame.

The 25th was located on one of the main base camps for the 4th Infantry Division, Camp Radcliff. Elements of the 173rd Airborne Brigade were there, as well. The 7th Battalion, 15th Artillery Regiment, was also there, and manned various firebases and LZs in the Central Highlands with 8-inch and 175-mm howitzers. The 1st Battalion, 69th Armor, provided security for 4th Division and 173rd Airborne firebases and LZs, and for QL 19, as dangerous a piece of road as there ever was. It ran all the way from just north of Qui Nhơn to Duc Co—another bad place—near the Cambodian border. They are the most decorated armor battalion in Army history.

We supported these units in combat operations throughout Central and Northern II Corps and spent a lot of time in dangerous places like the Son Con and Ia Drang Valleys. Qui Nhơn is near the coast, and was flat and heavily populated. An Khê is in the mountains, surrounded by dense forests. The town of An Khê was just a large village. Moving down a trail in the mountains, if it was not pouring rain and no one was shooting at you, was reminiscent of the Blue Ridge Mountains near my home in Virginia— almost, but not quite.

The Ia Drang had been the scene of one of the bloodiest battles of the war, as depicted in Mel Gibson's movie, *We Were Soldiers*. It was no less dangerous when I was there with units of the 4th Infantry Division. I also went back to the An Loa Valley and Mountains, as when I was at LZ English, but in different Areas of Operation. It was as if I had not left Qui Nhơn; I continued to go on operations with the 173rd Airborne Brigade. In addition, the 25th had taken over the on-site team at LZ English. Only the terrain was a little different; the war stayed the same.

I was at An Khê for almost four months. My overall memories of that duty station are vague; I am not sure why. I have vivid memories of so many of the events in Qui Nhơn and Phu Bai, but very distant memories of An Khê. If not for materials recovered from the National Archives, and recent conversations with a couple of my former team members, I would not remember squat about this place.

An Khê got mortared and rocketed a lot; there were numerous ground attacks, including sapper attacks. That much I do remember. Of the three units I was in, as well as temporary duty with the 44th in the Delta, the 25th had the most spectacular bunker. That structure could have withstood a direct hit from a 122-mm rocket.

I went on some intense operations with the 25th. The one that sticks most in my mind, that I actually remember, occurred on August 11, 1969, twelve days after I joined the unit, and three before I left on extension leave. At about 11.30 p.m., VC sappers attacked the Petroleum, Oil, and Lubricants (POL) dump at the base camp. Just like the Qui Nhơn ammo dump, no one saw them cross a huge expanse of the base and set their satchel charges, then leave without being seen.

The incident report stated:

Before the detonations stopped, CPT Robinson, SFC Kidd, SSG Small and SP4 Tremain were in the area. Two satchel charges were rendered safe inside the main gate to the PA&E yard. SFC Kidd called back to the unit and requested flashlights and one more EOD man. SP4 Tremain returned to the unit and got flashlights and SP5 Steinberg. Upon returning to the PA&E yard, SP5 Steinberg went with CPT Robinson and began searching one side of the yard while SFC Kidd and SSG Small searched the other half. SP4 Tremain remained with the vehicle and the radio. At approximately 0130 hours on 12 August 1969, the EOD team returned to the unit. It should be noted that the EOD teams conducted their search while vehicles and buildings were still burning. There were several small detonations when a building containing paints exploded.

So, I was in yet another exploding pile of dangerous materials. It was like the Qui Nhơn ammo dump but seemed less deadly since there were no red-hot, flying scraps of shrapnel whizzing by my face, or bouncing off the ground at my feet, no 2.75-inch rockets flying all over the place, and no huge piles of artillery projectiles exploding. I remember a couple of 55-gallon drums—I no longer remember what was in them—exploding, watching them rise into the air at high velocity, yet, somehow, seeming like slow-motion, a trail of fire following their ascent.

Moving through the dump with Captain Robinson had that same eerie feeling as in Kubrick's *Full Metal Jacket*, when the Marines move through a bombed-out, burning building in Hue City during the Tet Offensive of 1968. You can smell things that have exploded or burned; there was a smoky pall hanging over the POL yard, an occasional flare or illumination round going off overhead. Doing our job while the war exploded all around us seemed a constant theme, sort of like trying to work in an office and get paperwork done, but the phone keeps ringing.

As I extended my tour for six months I was given a "free" thirty-day leave, with transportation from Vietnam to the States and back, which did not count against my regular annual leave of thirty days.

According to the 25th's incident logs, the last call I went on before going on leave was on August 12, 1969, the day after the POL dump event, and the next was not until September 29. The leave was only thirty days; the rest was getting from An Khê to the States, then back to Vietnam.

I had not told my parents I was extending. They were expecting me home at what would have been the end of my original tour, somewhere around September 4, 1969. I showed up at my dad's office in Washington, D.C., wearing my dress greens with all my ribbons. He was surprised. That was one of the few times I saw him cry.

I told my dad that I had extended, and that I would be going back after thirty days. He had arranged to have dinner at Trader Vic's at the Hilton to celebrate his birthday, which had been on August 11. He called the restaurant and told them he wanted to surprise my mom with my being there, and arranged to have me come through the back door to the kitchen, where they would hide me until they brought out *hors d'oeuvres*. He also asked me not to tell Mom I had extended until the next day.

When it was time to bring out the appetizers, I came up behind her with a tray of food and said, "Excuse me, ma'am, but would you like to try some of this?" It was a tearful reunion for both of us, and a very nice evening. The next day, when I told her I was going back, she got very upset. She could not understand why I would do that. I tried to explain it, but she never understood.

I cannot remember a single thing about that leave. I guess I spent time with our neighbors, Howell and Jean Farnsworth, because Howell and I had become good friends. They had three beautiful daughters, Linda, Ginny, and Pam, for whom I always had the hots. Maybe I got together with my friend that I had enlisted with who was discharged for medical reasons, but I cannot remember if this actually happened. What I do remember is going from home to Ft. Monmouth when my leave was over, then back to Vietnam.

One of our neighbors, a good friend of my dad's, was an Army lieutenant colonel, a helicopter pilot who had been to Vietnam and was now stationed at Ft. Belvoir, about 20 miles down the road. He offered to fly me to Ft. Monmouth in a Huey and I, of course, accepted.

I arrived at the replacement station at Ft. Monmouth in a set of worn jungle fatigues and jungle boots that were barely held together and had long ago lost any semblance of color. I also wore a boonie hat with a black camo EOD badge stitched to the front. I had a U.S. Army Vietnam patch on my right shoulder, signifying that I had been to Vietnam once before.

I was with several hundred soldiers going to Vietnam for the first time, the only person with a previous tour. The cadre assigned to us were a bunch of pricks who attempted to treat me like a green troop. At one point, they tried to assign me to some shit-house job, and I told them to shove it. They did not screw with me after that.

We flew from McGuire Air Force Base, New Jersey, to Alaska, then Okinawa, then Vietnam. I landed at Biên Hòa and contacted the 42nd Ordnance Detachment (EOD) who sent someone to pick me up. I spent a few days there, then caught a C-130 to Qui Nhơn and a chopper back to An Khê.

Enemy sappers hit the POL yard again on November 1, 1969. The team that went in, CPT William Eskew, Boyd Kidd, Willard Small, and Joe Tremain, all got first-and second-degree burns from exploding and burning petroleum products. Only CPT Eskew was not burned. He did, however, end up getting a Silver Star, while the others all got Bronze Stars with "V" Devices for heroism.

Joe was injured a second time that night when he was partially thrown from our jeep and then dragged before it could stop. I was at LZ English with MSG Dave Lewis, so I missed one more exploding dump.

The Mang Yang Pass, northwest of An Khê, was a brutal environmental monstrosity. On one side, the mountain wall went straight up from the roadside, and on the other, there is a high cliff. The enemy could drop grenades right on top of you from one side, and fire mortar rounds or rocket propelled grenades on you from the other.

It was near the Mang Yang Pass that the Viet Minh massacred the French Group Mobile 100 in 1954. Their white crosses were still there when I first went there. One commentator on the web site of the 7th Battalion, 15th Field Artillery Regiment, succinctly put it:

> The Mang Yang Pass itself is perhaps the worst ambush site with its steep walls thickly covered with brush. In the area of the pass, hundreds of grey, leafless tree trunks stand, casualties of the countless barrages and bombs that have hit there.

I do not how many times I made the run through the Mang Yang with a teammate from the 25th. That I survived all of them without incident says something, since many, many convoys were ambushed there, and we were called out to deal with the duds, mines, and booby traps just before, or just after—before if they were lucky enough to discover something. This happened very rarely; people were usually dead by the time we got there.

There was another perfectly fucked up mountain pass on QL 19, and I also made that run many times, going to and from An Khê to Qui Nhơn and back to get explosives, time fuse, caps, and the other tools of our trade. Turning west off QL 1 onto QL 19, the road rose into the low mountains of the Central Highlands, where potential ambush sites lay around every corner. The An Khê Pass was thirty miles east of where we lived with the 4th Division; it was as dangerous as the Mang Yang. When you made the An Khê to Qui Nhơn run, your heart was in your throat, and you were hyper-alert.

When you started into the An Khê Pass coming from An Khê, there was a hairpin turn right at the very top. Then you headed downhill to the bottom, and you hauled ass all the way down, as fast as you could without losing control and rolling the jeep. Elephant grass grew to the edge of the road; if you were shot at, there was no way to tell where it came from. You just kept on hauling ass.

On the ridges just west of the foot of the Mang Yang, on the way to Pleiku, was Firebase Blackhawk, home of the 119th Assault Helicopter Company. One of their jobs was to protect the road from Pleiku to the intersection of QL 19 and QL 1 near Qui Nhơn. Their location near the Pass subjected them to constant mortar and rocket attacks, as well as ground assaults by both the VC and the NVA. The enemy loved to mine the road, particularly for the convoys resupplying Blackhawk and Pleiku.

On November 7, 1969, we got a call about mines in the road in the Mang Yang Pass. Master Sergeant Frank Forester, SP5 Neal, and I set out from the base camp heading west on QL 19 to LZ Schueller. LZ Schueller was on QL 19 between the 4th Division base at Camp Radcliff and the Mang Yang Pass. If you could avoid driving beyond Schueller, you did. When we got to Schueller, I was amazed at the massive firepower there. I never saw anything like it anywhere else in Vietnam.

The 1st Battalion, 69th Armor, and the 2nd Battalion, 17th Field Artillery Regiment, were the residents of LZ Schueller. They supported 4th Division and 173rd Airborne Brigade operations throughout the An Khê-Pleiku corridor. They had quad-.50 caliber machine guns mounted on large trucks, tanks, 40-mm Dusters, 105-mm howitzers, 8-inch howitzers, self-propelled guns, and the always-nasty 175-mm really large cannon. When a 175-mm round went over you, it was like a freight train going by at high speed.

When we arrived at LZ Schueller, a sergeant from the 1st Battalion, 69th Armor, briefed us. He said the entire road, right in the middle of the

Mang Yang Pass, had been blocked with many large baskets. The battalion commander wanted us to fly in and find out what they were. Individual vehicles and convoys were being held at Schueller, and in An Khê and Pleiku.

A small convoy was trapped several hundred yards from the blockade just at the far west end of the pass, almost to Firebase Blackhawk. We flew out of Schueller by chopper, accompanied by gunships from the 119th Assault Helicopter Company. The gunships followed us and continued to orbit overhead, because once the chopper set us down in the road, we were on our own. We landed and began to move toward the baskets, carefully watching all around and above us for any sign of ambush.

There were ninety baskets, each about 3 feet high and 3 feet across. They were filled with dirt, and we cleared every one of them, finding no explosives or improvised explosive devices. We concluded that the blockade was meant to be just that, and the enemy intended to ambush the first convoy that got to it. Fortunately, a light observation helicopter flying low over QL 19 had seen the baskets and stopped the convoy at the other end of the pass.

I wondered, as we did our job, how the enemy managed to bring in ninety baskets, fill them with dirt, block the road, and then leave without being observed. The enemy was invisible when they wanted to be. No amount of security or observation could change that reality. I know I have said that at least a dozen time by now, but it was the one constant of the War that never changed and was always there.

After we cleared the road, just as we were about to climb back on the chopper, the pilot told us that troopers at a 1st of the 69th strong point overlooking the pass thought they had found a mine just outside their perimeter. After moving the baskets out of the way, we climbed on the chopper and flew up to the strong point. MSG Forester and I walked outside the firebase and found a Russian MUV-5 fuse sticking out of the dirt.

We carefully removed the dirt around the fuse and partially exposed a 20-pound basket mine buried just outside the perimeter in an area where ambush patrols left and returned to the small outpost. We expected secondary devices under the mine, so we borrowed a grappling line from a "Duster" crew and used it to remove the mine remotely. There were no secondary devices, so MSG Forester removed the fuse, and we took it back with us to An Khê for destruction.

Bob Leiendecker was the CO of the 85th Ordnance Detachment (EOD) at Pleiku. He is now a retired lieutenant-colonel and recently sent me incident logs from the 25th that he had at his place in Charlottesville, Virginia.

Thumbing through the daily incident logs for the 115 days I was at An Khê, I was stunned at the number of calls we handled.

From July 31, 1969, when I joined the unit, until November 14, we responded to 638 calls. During one fourteen-day period at LZ English—the 25th had taken over this on-site team from the 184th—we handled thirty-eight incidents. MSG Dave Lewis and I handled thirty-two of them. Dave has passed away since the war ended. The incident logs I got from Bob show that I went on 103 calls at the 25th from August 1 through November 14, 1969. I was on leave for five weeks during that time, so I was on 103 incidents in seventy-one days. Bob's records did not include the last nine days I was there.

At the 2007 St. Louis Reunion of the Vietnam EOD Veterans Association, I ran into Dennis Vesper, from the 25th. Dennis reminded me of an incident that, for whatever reason, I had completely forgotten. Neither of us remembered precisely what happened; only that we were out for most of three days with an infantry unit, and both of us had the sense that it was something big.

I decided to try to find out what we had been doing since it is hard to understand how you could be involved in a three-day incident and not remember jack about it. The National Archives had no daily incident logs for the 25th for that time-frame, and I was at a dead-end.

Several months later, Bob Leiendecker sent me some additional logs he had located in his files from the 25th. Going through them, I found an entry that showed that from October 8–10, 1969, Denny Vesper and I were on an operation with the 4th Infantry Division's 3rd Battalion, 8th Infantry Regiment. We had flown into LZ Hardt Times.

Where the description of the incident would have been, it said, "See Unusual Incident Report." That report, unfortunately, is still missing in action. So, I made a request to the National Archives for the Daily Staff Journals for 3/8 for October 7–11, 1969. Almost six months later, I got the reports, and I have been able to reconstruct this event.

On October 8, 1969, Dennis and I drove to LZ Schueller and caught a chopper to LZ Hard Times, a small firebase deep in the Vinh Thang Valley, just off the Song Con River. There, we went to the TOC of "B" Company, 3rd Battalion, 8th Infantry Regiment. We learned that elements of "B" Company had discovered a large cache in a cave complex, and they wanted us to clear the caves for booby traps and supervise the removal of ordnance, weapons, and ammunition. We were in the bush with this unit for almost three days. It was one of those deals that kept getting bigger and bigger after we got there.

The weather was also a problem. It was pretty warm during the days, but tended to rain later in the afternoon and evening. That cooled things way down, chilly if you were soaking wet. At night, we put our ponchos together to make a tent, and it was just short enough that our feet stuck out the end. We were wet and cold all night; it was almost impossible to sleep. We had been smart enough to bring sleeping gear strapped to our rucks and several pairs of dry socks—fat lot of good that did.

The cache of enemy ordnance and weapons was in a cave complex below a ridgeline in the mountains west of the Vinh Thanh Valley and about 8 km southeast of LZ Hard Times. The Ivy soldiers had spotted the entrance to the cave when the point man of a patrol looked up over a big rock and saw a rifle protruding from a ledge.

You could not get to these caves from below, or by crossing sideways below the ridge. The only way was to climb a tree next to the rock, jump onto the top of the large rock, and climb onto the ledge. How the enemy had managed to get everything we found in the complex up there was a feat of sheer willpower and commitment to their cause.

Taking off from LZ Hard Times in a chopper, we landed on a small LZ the patrol had cut on top of the mountain above the cave complex. It was getting dark, so we pulled into the unit's night defensive position and set up our leaky tent. That night, we dined on C-rations. I had my favorite—ham and lima beans. I was the only soldier in Vietnam, and, indeed, I think, in the United States Army, who liked them. One reason the grunts liked to see us was because we had C-4. C-4 was inert, like TNT. You could beat it with a hammer, and as long as you did not do that while it was on fire, you had no problem; hit it when it was burning, and you very much did.

Now, you might ask, why set C-4 on fire in the first place? Well, you could take an empty C-Ration can and make a little stove out of it by putting holes in the bottom and turning it upside down. Then you took a little piece of C-4, maybe an inch thick, set it on fire and put it on the ground with the empty can over it. Now, you have a stove.

You cooked your can of food—say, ham and limas—by opening it, put it on your stove and, *voila*, you have hot food no matter how bad the weather is. Sometimes, burnt to a crisp, but hot, nonetheless. As we always carried more C-4 than we would probably need, we could take a few blocks, cut them into strips, and pass them out to the grunts.

That first night, it rained; the wind blew hard enough that it would wake you as it hit the sides of the tent, if you actually slept. Fog drifted in, and in the darkness and rain, you could not see more than 10 or 20 feet to your front.

If you got up in the night to take a piss, a soldier moving by you in the mist looked ghostly, and you were startled, as if seeing an apparition. They just kind of popped out of the fog in front of you, or to the side, and scared the living crap out of you. It was amazing no one inside the perimeter shot another GI because you could not tell who you were seeing, except the average GI was taller and thicker than a VC or NVA soldier.

We were up the next morning before light, boiled some water, and made horrible instant C-ration coffee. I made a little C-4 fire and heated some canned scrambled eggs and whatever meat was in the can. You always burned this meal, no matter how hard you tried not to. You ate it just the same, wolfing it down with stale crackers and jam from a little tin.

On October 9, as soon as it was light, we made our way to the ridge above the cave, along with an infantry platoon, and moved down the trail across the mountainside until we came to a pine tree crowded against a large rock formation. The tree was big by Vietnam standards, maybe four feet around the base and probably a hundred feet tall. The rock formation jutted about twenty feet into the air.

From our position on the ground by the tree, we saw the barrel of an SKS carbine sticking out from a rock and dirt ledge above the rock that ran along the side of the mountain. An infantryman had climbed the tree and onto the rock where he was able to look over at the ledge. He saw a small cave entrance about 5 feet in diameter. The company commander asked us to clear the entrance and the surrounding area so he could send in his tunnel rats.

Denny and I climbed the tree and jumped over to the rock. It was not very steep, just slippery and craggy, and hard to keep a footing. We pulled ourselves up onto the 3-foot ledge, stopped and surveyed the scene, looking for signs of a booby trap or mine—trip wires, recently turned soil, or pressure devices sticking up from the muddy, rocky soil. Seeing nothing, we pulled ourselves up onto the ledge and gently stepped onto the ground in front of the cave entrance.

After all that work, and freezing our wet asses off the night before, we found nothing to stop the tunnel rats from entering the cave. They went in, found no enemy, and came back out, telling us and the rest of the platoon that what they had found was amazing. They were not exaggerating.

The cave was a complex on four levels, each connected by steps cut into the dirt and rock. Each level also had tunnels leading off its main room that went nowhere. After the tunnel rats came out, Denny and I crawled into the entrance, flashlights and weapons in front of us, and proceeded to check each level, and the cache of weapons and ordnance for booby traps. Finding none, we began to supervise the removal of the cache.

At 3.25 p.m., while we helped catalogue the cache, a patrol from "D" Company of the same battalion found a base camp just down the trail from where we were working. Denny and I left the cache, with a patrol from "B" Company, and went to the second location. The base camp was practically invisible from the air; you would never know it was there if you had not stumbled into it, as the "D" Company patrol had.

There were two hooches, one 10 feet × 10 feet, the other only 4 feet × 4 feet. Around the hooches were four fighting bunkers dug into the ground, each about 12 feet × 12 feet and 5 feet high, with 2 feet of each bunker below ground level. Outside of the fighting bunkers was a 10-foot wide sleeping bunker, 50 feet long, and 5 feet high, with 2 feet entrenched in the ground. The infantrymen estimated it could sleep a minimum of thirty.

Denny and I checked the area for booby traps, and then cleared the bunkers. We removed one RPG-2 rocket launcher and three RPG-2 rockets, 200 AK-47 rounds and eight Chinese hand grenades. We removed the fuses from the rockets and the grenades. In addition, we found canteens, rucksacks, NVA fatigues, small shovels, an NVA belt buckle, personal papers, a photograph of an NVA officer, and miscellaneous cooking utensils.

After one of the infantrymen photographed everything, we put the rockets and grenades inside one of the bunkers and blew them with C-4 on a short-delay time-fuse. We then moved back up the trail to the large cache. It was getting dark by this time, so we moved back to the night defensive position and settled in until the morning of the 10th. It rained, again, most of the night.

By 9.30 a.m. on the 10th, elements of "A" Company had begun to improve the LZ we had come in on so it would be big enough for a Chinook to land and lift out the bulk of the large cache. At 1.15 p.m., the Chinook lifted off with two 81-mm mortar tubes, complete with base plates and traversing mechanisms; five new Russian automatic rifles similar to the American Browning; seventy-five brand new Mauser and SKS carbines; 100 cans of AK-47 rounds with 500 rounds per can; and six cans of 82-mm mortar fuses with ten fuses per can.

At the base of the large rock below the cave entrance, we stacked up the following: 100 RPG-2 rockets; six 75-mm high-explosive recoilless rifle rounds; twenty Russian anti-tank mines; 200 rifle grenades; 400 81-mm mortar rounds; 400 82-mm mortar rounds; 2,000 feet of time fuse; and one

U.S. 81-mm mortar round. As we prepared to blow the ordnance and the cave complex, we were told that a patrol from "B" Company had found another enemy base complex within 200 yards of the one found on the 9th. As they entered the base camp area, they saw two NVA soldiers about 100 meters through the bush, opened up on them, and called in artillery.

We left the site of the big cache with a patrol and headed to the new site. Three of the infantrymen stayed behind to protect the charges we had set. The only ordnance we found at the third site were three full AK-47 magazines, fifty loose AK rounds, and one electric blasting cap from an American claymore mine. This was definitely a base camp for a sizable enemy unit.

There were three hooches, each 10 feet × 10 feet × 7 feet, a 10 feet × 20 feet × 6 feet sleeping hooch, two 8 feet × 2 feet tables, and a cave dug into the ground 30 feet deep and 10 feet high. There were also rucksacks, clothing, ponchos, a brassiere (I swear), a shovel and pick, canteens, and various documents. Just off the trail leading into this area, we found two graves with bodies reduced to bones. The infantry said that at least fifteen to twenty enemy soldiers had used the trail in and out of this third complex within the past few days.

We moved back to the big cache site. By now, it was almost 3 p.m. The extraction chopper came in, and the infantrymen headed off down a trail at high speed as we set the shot on the ordnance. We loaded a few remaining weapons and the rocket launchers on the slick, pulled the time-fuse lighter, and took off. Two minutes out as we were gaining altitude, the shot went off and presumably all of the ordnance and the cave were obliterated. The day, however, was not over.

We flew from the cave complex site to Fire Support Base Sheridan, about eight clicks south of the caves, and landed there about 4 p.m. We could not get a chopper back to LZ Schueller, where our vehicle was, so we spent the night at Sheridan. At 6.35 p.m., we started receiving incoming mortar and recoilless rifle fire just as we were getting something to eat.

The firebase started firing artillery and mortars at where the enemy fire was coming from and, at 6.55 p.m., the incoming stopped. Two minutes later, we got incoming small arms fire for about three minutes. As soon as it stopped we took another three rounds of mortar fire. At 7.05 p.m., the 4.2-inch mortar area of the firebase took more incoming rounds, and from 7.11–7.14 p.m., there was more small arms fire.

One of the artillery crew was wounded so he was medevacked, and we settled in for the night. It had been three pretty grueling days; that night at

Sheridan was the topper. We were truly grateful to get back to Schueller and then An Khê early the next morning.

The upside was that I got two of the Russian SKS Carbines from the cache, covered in Cosmoline, a sticky gray grease to keep it from rusting in storage, and wrapped in canvas. They came scoped, so I am pretty sure they were sniper rifles. They were brand new, and I brought one home with me in 1970; I traded the other one for air conditioners after I got to the 287th in Phu Bai. This mission was my last fly-out with the 25th.

Reading through the incident reports from the 25th, I remembered that sometimes calls turned funny. On August 12, 1969, Boyd Kidd and I were called out by the 3rd Provisional Rifle Company at Camp Radcliff. They had found a Vietnamese lunch pail in a suspicious location and presumed it was an improvised explosive device. It turned out to be a lunch pail with a Vietnamese beer inside. We took it back to the unit and drank it.

On October 14, 1969, Joe Tremain and I went to the 8th Battalion, 26th Artillery Regiment, to check out a box left in front of the door of a building. It was box with someone's low-quarter dress shoes in it.

Then there were the incidents when you just leaned back, squinted one eye, and said, "What the fuck?" Two days prior to the shoebox incident, we got a call from the S-2 (Intelligence) officer at the 1st Brigade, 4th Infantry Division, Tactical Operations Center, at Camp Radcliff. He said some engineers had a found a very weird looking item along a dirt road they were clearing and had brought it back to the base camp because they thought it might have intelligence value.

When CPT Eskew and I arrived at the TOC, it lay on the ground near the entrance. We could not believe what we were looking at. It was a BLU (Bomb Live Unit) 31B, apparently, a dud, because the nose fuse was smashed, and part of it had broken off on impact. This thing was 8 feet long and weighed 766 pounds, although the military called it a 750. It was an anti-vehicle demolition bomb and mine, loaded with 236 pounds of Destex. Destex is a type of TNT with the addition of aluminum powder so that when it detonates, you get an extremely fierce fireball burning at thousands of degrees.

Here is why we were thinking, "What the fuck?" The BLU-31B was used for vehicular interdiction, including tanks. It was armed with acoustic and seismic sensors, tuned to the sound and vibrations of heavy vehicles like tanks. However, once dropped, if it did not function within eighty-three hours, it was supposed to self-destruct. I cannot remember how we determined that it was safe to transport to our demo area, but we must have because we were not blown up.

There were calls that seemed to repeat themselves. The 647th Quartermaster Company provided petroleum for all units along the QL 19 corridor, from the turnoff at Highway 1 in Qui Nhơn, all the way to Pleiku and Kontum. They maintained a pipeline that ran along QL 19 and every 10–20 miles had a pump station. Their job not only included keeping the fuel flowing, but also patrolling the pipeline and maintaining security at their pump stations. Given their remote locations and the small number of soldiers stationed there, the pump stations were regular targets of enemy incoming mortars and rockets, as well as ground attacks.

Incident logs I got from Bob Leiendecker show that Pump Station 10 at the Mang Yang Pass was hit twice within four days on October 11 and 14, 1969, and had called in mortar fire on the attacking enemy. On October 11, Denny Vesper and I took care of a dud 4.2-inch HE mortar round on their perimeter; on October 14, CPT Eskew and I returned for the same thing. I noted from the log that we reported driving 40 miles, which means that we traversed QL 19 twice all the way from Camp Radcliff to the Mang Yang Pass and back. Even if we had an MP gun-jeep escort, this was a dangerous piece of road to negotiate without heavy firepower.

Just to show you how dangerous QL 19 was, this is from the 1968 Annual Report of our control unit:

[O]n 10 Apr 68, MSG Calhoon was killed and SP4 Dick was wounded near An Khê on Highway # 19. Both men were from the 25th Ord. Det. (EOD). A controlled mine had been found in the road and MSG Calhoon and SP4 Dick had been dispatched to remove it. When the mine had been removed, MSG Calhoon and SP4 Dick were walking off the road to dispose of it when they were fired upon by enemy troops lying in ambush. MSG Calhoon died as the result of bullet and fragmentation wounds. SP4 Dick received bullet wounds in his arms, legs, and jaw and was evacuated to [the United States].

This could well have been a deliberate act on the part of the VC to kill an EOD team. I recently read that the enemy in Iraq, like the enemy in Vietnam, had a bounty on EOD men.

12

Phu Bai and Northern "I" Corps

I make no bones about why I extended my tour. I loved my job and the thought of returning to a stateside assignment without the adrenalin-pump of Vietnam seemed a boring proposition. Either that, or I was freaked out that I might get another assignment like Dugway. When I left Vietnam after eighteen months, that is exactly what happened, although I was able to get out of that assignment and sent to a regular detachment.

Additionally, the camaraderie among EOD men was one of those things you get to have once or, if you are really lucky, twice in a lifetime. No matter where you went in Vietnam, if there was a local EOD team, you had a home, and guys you immediately bonded with.

It was a close-knit family, bound by the brotherhood of war. That did not exist in stateside units, and you could spend an entire tour in the States without any contact with another team. When I was at Dugway, I did not even know where the next closest team was. The same was true with the 67th at Ravenna Arsenal in Ohio, after Vietnam.

In Vietnam, every team knew where every other team was, and it was not unusual, as during the Qui Nhơn ammo dump cleanup, for members of one team to assist another team. In November–December 1968, I went to Cu Chi in the Delta when the 44th was short of men.

I do not mean to sound like the Robert Duvall character in *Apocalypse Now*, ("I love the smell of napalm in the morning"), but I think there was some of that in my reason for agreeing to try not to get blown up or shot for another half-year. I would have extended for another six months, but they told me I had to go back to the States for nuclear weapons school. I might have stayed until the end of the war, if they had let me, and I managed to survive.

My life before Vietnam had been the very definition of a suburban lifestyle. I lived in the upper middleclass suburbs. I attended suburban high schools, played no sports, and had few friends who were not outcasts, or, at least, not members of the in-crowd. I barely noticed the in-crowd, and when I did, they seemed senseless.

I am Jewish, and Jews were not exactly lining up to volunteer for Vietnam. When I went out to the country club to tell my parents I had enlisted, they freaked out. I do not think I enlisted to piss them off, but I could be wrong about that.

The jocks, the cheerleaders, and the well-dressed "collegiates" in their mahogany Bass Weeguns, Gant shirts, and khaki slacks seemed like foreigners to me; I could never understand their desire for sameness. I am sure that some of them had similar negative thoughts about me and my few friends, whom I guess you could describe as hoodlums. I had run-ins with the law on a couple of occasions for really stupid, completely un-thought-out things, and if I had not found the Army, I would probably have done some time by this point in my life.

My family life was pretty dysfunctional, as my mom and dad worked all the time, and I remember they fought a lot over finances. My dad and I never saw eye-to-eye on anything. When I joined the Army in 1966, my life had no purpose. I had no sense of family, no direction of any kind. The Army gave me all that, and more, mostly because I ate it up and was recognized, for the first time in my life, for accomplishments that were important then and, in some strange way, still have importance, today.

A few years ago, my thirty-four-year-old son asked me, "So, Dad. Now that you're retired and look back on all the things you've done, how do you see yourself?" That was a question I had never thought about. It is not like my retirement was voluntary; my disabilities from the war finally caught up with me with a vengeance in the summer of 2002 and forced me to stop working. I had to think about my son's question and the answer surprised me.

I thought about teaching and how much joy that had given me, particularly since I knew from students and supervisors that I was pretty good. I had taught at the Georgetown University Law Center for two years, then at Franklin Pierce Law Center in New Hampshire, which reinforced my belief that I knew what I was doing. Before that, I had taught high school and helped run a dorm for adolescent males at a Quaker school in rural Virginia.

Then there were seven years as a criminal defense attorney, which, although they ended disastrously, were seven good years. I took on cases no one else wanted, and I sometimes funded major criminal cases out of my own pocket because the court would not appoint me when a defendant asked for me. I took the cases anyway. Maybe that was why I was always broke during those years.

From 1989, until I retired in January 2003, I worked as a private investigator. My wife and I moved to Oregon in 1995, and I eventually hooked up with a group of lawyers and investigators known as the "Capital Defenders." We were the only lawyers and investigators allowed to work on capital murder cases, and, in Oregon, the capital sentence was either the death penalty or life in prison with no possibility of parole.

I am proud to say that I handled nine of these cases and helped save my clients' lives in eight of them. The one case I lost is still on appeal. It was not unlike the lives my teammates that I helped save in Vietnam; death was the ultimate possible outcome in both situations.

Then there are those years—1966 through 1971—when I was a soldier. In many ways, they were the best years of my life. Then, again, they were also some of the worst. I mulled over my son's question for a few minutes, thinking about all these things, and I said, "I think of myself as a soldier first; everything else is second." It could be my epitaph, and I would be happy at that. I do not say this out of gung-ho patriotism; it is just the way it is.

By extending my tour in Vietnam, I thought less experienced members of my team would die unless I was there to watch their backs. This "philosophy"— if I may call it that—extended into my professional life after I left the military, with each subsequent job a little more dangerous than the last.

The life-and-death scenario continued to be a part of my life, particularly the twenty-two years as a criminal defense attorney and a capital defense investigator. During the years 1997–2002, I was ultimately responsible for the lives of nine men charged with capital murder. Like I said, I helped save the lives of eight of them; the ninth has a good chance for a new trial after the conclusion of his post-conviction proceedings.

I finally came face-to-face with my ongoing need to save lives when my VA social worker asked me in August 2002, "When are you going to get off mission?" I could not continue to work like that without damaging my psyche beyond recovery. So, on December 24, 2002, when a jury found my last capital client not guilty of all charges, I retired from a job I loved.

Even though the VA has determined that I am totally and permanently disabled by PTSD and numerous other physical problems caused by my service in Vietnam, I still feel guilty about not helping defend all the clients I might have whose lives I might have saved.

On November 26, 1969, after being in An Khê for almost four months, our control unit was looking for a volunteer to go north and join the 287th EOD at a place called Phu Bai. All I knew about the area was that it was in Northern "I" Corps and that it was a very, very bad place.

I had heard about the infamous A Shau, Arizona, and Que Son Valleys and the battle at Hamburger Hill, where the 101st fought valiantly for ten days. They lost seventy men and killed more than 600 NVA soldiers, took the mountain, then left. Men from the 287th were in all these places.

My friend, Gary Raines, who left the 287th just before I got there, landed on Hamburger Hill on May 20, 1969, just after the 101st took the summit. Gary and I eventually ended up together after we returned to the States. My good friend, Joe Jimenez, was there, as well as Floyd Ames. Things were still so chaotic in the area that the CO, Mike Tavano, recently told me he had no contact with the team for three days.

That was the story of the War—we took ground and then immediately gave it back. Like Khe Sanh, where embattled Marines and Army soldiers held off a vastly larger NVA force for seventy-nine days between January and April 1968. Westmoreland then ordered the abandonment of the place after 402 Marines and soldiers were killed, and 2,249 were medically evacuated.

I volunteered to go to Phu Bai and left An Khê by helicopter the next day. I flew into Qui Nhơn and caught a C-130 to Da Nang, where I spent the night in a crowded, smelly terminal, then got a 101st Airborne Division chopper into Phu Bai the next day, November 27. This time I had my weapons, so I felt safer in this Chinook than the one I rode on when I first got to Viet Nam. I was not any less scared—you were always a little freaked out flying over open country, especially in Northern "I" Corps.

Here is how bad it was in Northern "I" Corps, which consisted of Quảng Trị and Thừa Thiên-Huế Provinces. The III Marine Amphibious Force, which included the 1st and 3rd Marine Divisions, was headquartered in Quảng Trị and then in Phu Bai. The other major units in Northern "I" Corps were the 5th Infantry Division (Mechanized), also based at Quảng Trị, and the 101st Airborne Division (Airmobile), with major bases at Camp Eagle, Camp Evans, Phu Bai, and LZ Sally.

I have the Coffelt Database, which is a sortable database of all soldiers killed in action in the Vietnam War. According to the database, 11,976 soldiers were killed in Quảng Trị and Thừa Thiên-Huế Provinces during the war.

The 1st Brigade, 5th Infantry Division, lost 556 men. Their units were only in Northern "I" Corps, and I mean the northern-most part, right up against that badass DMZ.

The 101st Airborne Division had 2,378 men killed in action in Northern "I" Corps; the Marines lost 6,518 men. During the four months I was in Phu Bai with the 287th, 404 soldiers were killed in Quảng Trị and Thừa Thiên-Huế Provinces. According to the Coffelt Database, 58,912 men and women lost their lives in Vietnam. That means that 20 percent of them were killed in Northern "I" Corps.

My first impression of the Phu Bai Combat Base, flying over it in the Chinook from Da Nang, was how huge it was. It dwarfed An Khê, main base camp of the 4th Infantry Division, and made the Phu Tai compound where the 184th had been located seem like a speck on a map.

Highway 1—the same road that went by the Qui Nhơn ammo dump several hundred miles to the south—ran right through the southwestern section of the base and was bordered to the east by the Song Dai Giang River, which ran from the northwest to the southeast.

The city of Hue was 13 miles to the north; Da Nang was 40 miles south; and the DMZ 40 miles north. As we flew into Phu Bai, I remember thinking there was something really screwy about building this huge base so that Highway 1 bisected it.

When I got to Phu Bai in late 1969, the major combat units in Northern "I" Corps had their rear areas there—the 101st Airborne Division (Airmobile), III Marine Amphibious Force (III MAF) and the area's major command, the Army's XXIVth Corps. Marine Air Group (MAG) 36 was there with both fixed-wing aircraft and helicopters, and the 101st had another large batch of helicopters.

The original base, much smaller, was built by Army Special Forces, and rumored to be a National Security Agency base, as well. Given the location there of an Army Security Agency unit—the 8th Radio Research Field Station—I suspect this was true, although I cannot remember having contact with NSA types, as far as I knew. There were, however, many spooks in Phu Bai, so who knows?

Phu Bai was a combat base, and everything about it made that clear. It might have had officers', NCO, and enlisted clubs, movie theaters, barbershops and a PX, but it was primarily built for war. Everywhere there were reinforced bunkers, all within the outer perimeter, guard towers, and row after row of barbed and razor wire. Outside the wire, the perimeter was heavily mined.

The size of the base and the large population of soldiers living there made the place a regular target for Viet Cong and NVA rocket and mortar attacks. They expected to hit people and damage structures no matter where their ordnance landed and, usually, they were right.

We got hit a lot at Phu Bai, but the base was so big we usually did not get crazy unless the incoming was landing within a few hundred yards. I remember being in our bar—yes, we had our own bar—and the alert siren would go off right about the same time we would hear the incoming ordnance detonating somewhere in the huge expanse of the Phu Bai base.

We would saunter, or stagger, outside to see where the incoming was landing, and sometimes, if it was out on the perimeter, we would climb onto the roof of our hooch and watch both the incoming and the massive outgoing firepower of a lot of artillery, and the M-16 and machinegun fire from the perimeter. It was our version of the Fourth of July on a regular basis. Just a little more dangerous.

Then, eventually, Army and Marine Cobra gunships would fly fast and hard, low over the perimeter, and lay down a barrage of rockets and 40-mm grenades at some spot where counter-fire radar had pinpointed the source of the incoming rounds.

The back-blast of the 2.75-mm rockets launched by Cobras was white-hot bright and seemed to linger in space long after the rockets left their tubes, heading downrange. It reminded me that Vietnam was a deadly and mysterious place, where death could come from any quarter, day or night, with little or no warning.

In its day, Phu Bai was the largest helicopter base in the world, not surprising considering the number of choppers with the Marines' MAG 36 and the Army's 101st. One of the sounds that you eventually ignored, like getting used to the heat and humidity, was the constant noises of all sizes of helicopters and fixed-wing aircraft taking off and landing virtually every minute of every day. That sound, which every modern combat solider knows, is with me today. I know they are coming before the human ear can hear them, like Radar on *M*A*S*H*.

There is nothing like taking off from a hot LZ, door guns blazing, and every passenger leaning out the open doors, firing into the jungle or trees below. The smell of burnt cordite and dense smoke permeates the chopper's interior, getting you high when you cleared the enemy fire and knew you would make it home. Those rides were silent once the shooting stopped.

When the local air life chopper flies near my home, or I hear it coming, driving in Bend, Oregon, near St. Charles Hospital, it takes me back to those flights. I see me on a Huey, cruising over some godforsaken place, door gunners at the ready, CAR-15 across my lap, finger on the trigger. My rucksack is tight on my body, full of food, clothing, and EOD gear; I feel nylon straps cutting into my sides. My eyes are closed, and the wind is a calming relief from the boiling heat, as my blood begins to pump, waiting for the gunners to alert us that we are going into whatever place, thinking, "Please, let this be okay."

When I climbed off the chopper in Phu Bai at the XXIVth Corps pad, I saw the 287th's jeep. A thin, smiling man sat behind the wheel, boonie hat hanging by its strap down his back. It was Paul Duffey, as good a man as I have ever known. No matter how bad it got—and it got bad—Paul was always able to smile. Well, at least until Fire Support Base Rifle.

After that incident, I stopped smiling, too. As I described it in Chapter One, it was a life-changer, one that fully and clearly brought home the savagery and inhumane nature of war.

The 287th had arrived in country on October 28, 1968, brought over by CPT Mike Tavano. After the Marines pulled their EOD Teams out of Northern "I" Corps, the 287th and the 59th in Quảng Trị took over all Northern "I" Corps EOD duties. They supported the 1st Cav, 101st Airborne Division, III Marine Amphibious Force, the 5th Infantry Division (Mechanized), and all the dozens, maybe hundreds, of artillery, aviation, transportation, quartermaster, MP, and armor units in "I" Corps.

The 287th, in May 1969, helped clean up after the savage battle at Hamburger Hill. Later, after I was gone, members of the team were in the siege at Firebase Ripcord in the A Shau Valley, which lasted for twenty-three days.

The 287th was family, not that the other teams I was on were not close, but there was something different about the 287th. Though I was only there four months, I got extremely close to all the team members, including the CO, CPT Andy Breland. SP5 Paul Duffey became my closest friend in Vietnam. He is one of only three people I had any contact with after the War. The others were my pals, Chuck Watson from the 287th, and Roger McCormack, from the 184th.

Other than CPT Breland, Paul Duffey and me, the 287th consisted of Master Sergeant Del Randles, the first sergeant, SSG Jim Qualls, SSG Dave Becker, SP5 Rick Lanham, SP4 Tom Miller, SP4 Chuck Watson and our clerk, Don Urquhart. Later, SFC Rod Wilkinson would replace Del Randles, and Dan Reese would replace Urquhart. Rod and I were in touch regularly until he passed away around Thanksgiving, 2009. He died from complications of diabetes caused by exposure to herbicides.

Shortly after I joined the 287th, an EOD man who had become a MACV adviser and was an ex-Green Beret, started to hang out with us and go on incidents because he was bored. His first name was John, but we called him "Tiny" Morris because he was, of course, huge. Even though he was not assigned to us, he became a part of the team and ran incidents, just like the rest of us. "Tiny" passed away after returning from Vietnam.

The 287th primarily supported the 101st Airborne Division and the III Marine Amphibious Force, including recon teams from both units. As a result, I spent a lot of time in the A Shau Valley, areas along the Laotian border, and near the DMZ, and many little villages along the coast where the Marines ran ambushes with Combined Action Platoons (CAP) who lived there with the locals.

These were dangerous places. On November 28, the day after I joined the 287th, I went on my first call with Staff Sergeant Dave Becker into a remote site on the coast where we destroyed a dud 175-mm high-explosive artillery shell for CAP Team 3-1-3.

Flying into these forward outposts, we often went in under fire. We went on many combat assaults with the 101st and the Marines, and we often landed in the first choppers, with the Pathfinders and recon units. We swept the assault LZ for mines and booby traps so the choppers could safely land.

I did these things with the 184th, the 44th, and the 25th, but the war in Northern "I" Corps seemed very different from the Central Highlands and War Zone "C". There was something dark and foreboding about it; as if a demonic black pall was draped across the landscape, even when the sun was shining and the temperature was about a gazillion degrees.

The DMZ ran along the entire Northern edge of this combat zone; there was a feeling of constant danger close to that area, or near the Laotian Border at the end of the A Shau Valley.

The NVA launched artillery and rocket attacks from inside North Vietnam across the DMZ anytime they wanted. Remote outposts just south of the demarcation line, manned by the Marines, the 5th Infantry Division (Mechanized), and the 101st Airborne Division (Airmobile) had been the site of relentless and savage attacks. Attacks continued throughout the time I was there in 1969 and 1970.

Highway 9 ran west from Hue, following the Cam Lo River to the site of the bloody siege at Khe Sanh, and the Lang Vei Special Forces camp at the far west end of the A Shau Valley at the Laotian border. On February 6, 1968, while the battle at Khe Sanh was shifting into high gear, Special Forces

Detachment A-101 fought one of the most heroic battles of the Vietnam War at Lang Vei.

Defended by twenty-four Green Berets and their 500-man Montagnard Strike Force (Civilian Irregular Defense Force—CIDG), the Lang Vei defenders were vastly outnumbered by two NVA infantry regiments who were supported by artillery and armor units. They were eventually overrun on February 7. It was the first time the NVA used tanks against an American outpost. During the battle, the defenders knocked out seven enemy tanks with recoilless rifle fire and anti-tank rockets.

Of the twenty-four Special Forces men, seven were killed, eleven wounded and three were missing in action. Some 200 of the CIDG soldiers died. Like the siege at Khe Sanh from January–April 1968, these kinds of events, although on a smaller scale, were regular occurrences in Northern "I" Corps.

Hamburger Hill was in the A Shau, as were a number of other hellholes I flew into, such as Fire Support Bases Davis, Bastogne, Vehgel, Jack, and Airborne. Parts of the Ho Chi Minh Trail ran through the western end of the A Shau Valley, fanning out from Laos like a spider web gone berserk. The A Shau Valley was a place that holds special memories, mostly bad, for anyone who was there.

The A Shau Valley was everything—and more—that you have ever heard about it. Hamburger Hill and Khe Sanh are the places that became famous. Yet there were countless firebases and LZs where battles were just as vicious and bloody. The battle at Fire Support Base Rifle was one of those.

Sorting through the 287th's incident logs, I was struck by the number of calls I went on in the 119 days I was there in 1969–1970, before returning to the states—175. That works out to about 1.4 calls each day, but there were days I was back at the unit, either manning the communications gear, or doing maintenance on our rigs, and did not go out. I actually went on those 175 incidents in only thirty-nine days.

Among those 175 calls were three combat assaults with the 101st; we flew into the bush on thirteen other occasions, and hooked up with Army and Marine infantry units already on the ground—I had 11.5 hours of combat flight time. We drove by ourselves into forward firebases like Bastogne, Tomahawk, Roy, and Sally, many times, on roads that we probably should not have traveled without gun support. There were really bad places like Firebase Destiny, at the northwest end of the A Shau Valley, only 3 miles from the Laotian border—all hellholes, every single one of them.

In the next few chapters, I will go into detail about life during my 119 days at Phu Bai with the 287th. I could have done this with my entire tour, adding hundreds of pages that would have obscured one of the major points I want to make.

The incident at Fire Support Base Rifle that I describe in Chapter One was not a large-scale battle like Khe Sanh, or the Ia Drang. However, I wanted to tell the story of at least one small battle that was just as significant to the men who fought it as were the larger more famous battles to their participants. The same is true for those who were not in the combat arms—the Infantry, the Artillery, and the Armor. Danger is danger; dead is dead. The majority of those killed in action were from the combat arms. Yet we all died, or were wounded, the same.

During the war in Vietnam, MOS 31E was field radio relay assistant or field radio repairman. Twenty were killed. Laundrymen were MOS 57E. Ten of them died. Crawler tractor operators had MOS 62E; they had 173 guys killed. Various types of men in the photo MOSs lost twenty men; they began with eighty-four. The MOSs that began with seven—the clerks, supply specialists, payroll specialists, intelligence analysts, and computer geeks—had a staggering 973 men killed during the Vietnam War. It did not matter what your job was; you were in the War just like me and my teammates.

Every day you were in Vietnam might have been your last no matter what you did, or where you were. It was no different for me. After I joined the 287th, from November 26–December 13, 1969, I only went on seventeen calls. Most of them were not unusual incidents, requiring a detailed report; they were memorialized in a daily EOD incident journal that was like entries in a receipt book.

The unit clerk went across the page from left to right, entered the incident number, followed by the Julian calendar—9332, for instance, was November 28, 1969. Then he entered the incident location, personnel dispatched, mode of travel (ground or air), miles/hours of travel, and the items encountered and remarks. If it was an "unusual incident," he noted that under "remarks," and the two men on the incident wrote a detailed report.

The first sixteen calls I went on were mostly uneventful. Like I said, my first call with the Phu Bai unit was with Dave Becker out to one of the Marine CAP teams. I cannot remember the circumstances, other than the incident journal noting that we destroyed a dud 175-mm artillery round.

Dave and I drove by ourselves, since no air flight time was noted, and it was only 12 miles in each direction from our base camp to the CAP team and back. Most of the areas outside of the Phu Bai Combat Base were enemy-held territory, even when there were firebases, landing zones, and CAP teams all over the place. Yet, as on most occasions when we were not flying to an incident, it was just me, my teammate, and the War.

If we had let the fact we could be killed just driving to and from a call enter into our thoughts, we would never have left the base without asking for an MP gun-jeep escort. We did not do that; I think it was another aspect of that EOD thing about being invincible. The job itself was inherently dangerous; everything else seemed a minor distraction.

The other fifteen calls during those first sixteen days in Phu Bai seemed benign in late 1969 when I was young and believed I was immortal. Today, I have a different view.

Four of them involved dud U.S. 40-mm high-explosive, shoulder-launched grenades, fired from the perimeters of a base camp, LZ, or fire support base, probably during a perceived enemy threat that precipitated what they called a "mad minute." That was when everyone on the perimeter fired their weapons like crazy—M-16s, machine guns, and 40-mm grenade launchers. Any artillery units fired deafening salvos. I guess they thought that if they did this enough, they would eventually kill an enemy soldier.

The belief was, well, the enemy might be out there, you cannot be sure, so why take a chance? Let's just blast the shit out of everything and see if there are any bodies there in the morning. Sometimes, this happened based on intelligence reports, though they were inaccurate much of the time. Most of the time, in my opinion, it was just a way to blow off steam.

As I have noted before, a dud 40-mm grenade is a dangerous item once fired. Even when you do not know it has been fired, you have to assume it was if it has been separated from the casing. It is another device that makes you wonder, "What kind of asshole would design something like this?"

It has an "always-acting fuse," which meant that no matter how it landed, or what it hit, once it was armed, it would detonate. At least, that was the theory. These things became ineffectual way too many times in the opinion of most EOD people. They killed at least three EOD men that I know of, and wounded a number of others.

There was a fifth incident during those first weeks at Phu Bai involving a 40-mm grenade, but this one was not a dud; it was stuck in the barrel of the launcher used to fire it. A man in a bunker on the Phu Bai perimeter had fired at suspected enemy approaching the wire; and the round jammed halfway up the tube. This incident was not uncommon. Theoretically, the 40-mm grenade had to leave the barrel and rotate so many times before arming, but we always considered it armed if it had separated from its casing.

The written and taught "rendering-safe" procedure with a device in this condition, as with any dud 40-mm grenade, was to "blow it in place" (BIP). That was also the rendering safe procedure for the mortar round that blew me up in the Qui Nhơn ammo dump and, as with that event, the book-prescribed procedure, often had no meaning in combat. In the case of the stuck grenade, we often tried to save the gun, since it was costly and not easily replaced.

On December 2, 1970, Rick Lanham and I drove out to "D" Sector on the Phu Bai perimeter and found the weapon just outside a bunker. This was my first unusual incident. The soldier who had fired it—as probably anyone except us would have done—had broken the weapon open at the breech, like a shotgun, and looked up the barrel, seeing the stuck round.

The grenade launcher lay on the ground where he dropped it. He stood with another soldier near the entrance to the bunker. I got on the ground, looking up the barrel, and saw the round about 4 inches up.

Right then, the officer in charge of that sector drove up in a jeep, got out, and came to me, saying, "I'm the one who called you about this. I hope you can do something that won't destroy the weapon; we don't have many of them."

"Don't worry, sir," I said. "I'm going to work a little EOD magic."

Having done a couple of these before, I had brought a couple of 40-mm grenades from the unit, loaded with shot. The 40-mm grenade launcher came with a number of different rounds—high explosives, flechettes (small darts), tear gas, smoke, flare, and a shotgun shell with a dozen large pellets. The shotgun round was the key to this solution. I do not remember who came up with this procedure, but it was pure genius. The ingenuity of our people was surpassed only by their willingness to take on missions that were above and beyond what they had signed up for.

I took out a shotgun round, removed the warhead, and shot, leaving only the casing and propellant charge and stuck it into the breach of the grenade launcher, which I then closed. I asked the soldiers on the bunker to bring six sandbags and propped the gun up on three of them, placing it in an upward-angle on the pile. The stock rested on the ground with the launcher angled on the pile, the end of the barrel pointing skyward. I went to our jeep and cut off 20 feet of blasting wire, which I tied around the trigger of the launcher.

I placed the other three sandbags on top of the gun, holding it in place. We got behind the jeep and I yanked on the wire, which pulled the trigger and fired the shotgun round. The HE round in the tube ejected as if it had been fired, flying 10 feet into the air, then hit the ground without detonating. We blew the round where it lay and recovered the undamaged launcher, returning it to its very impressed owners.

The other incidents during that sixteen days included investigating a suspected booby trap on the Phu Bai perimeter, which turned out to be just a couple of cans. There was a dud 155-mm high-explosive artillery projectile outside the perimeter of Firebase Bastogne, on Route 547 along the road to the A Shau Valley.

Dave Becker and I, like a couple of idiots, as with the trip to the CAP team, drove out there alone, humped to the location with some 101st grunts, blew the damn thing, humped back to Bastogne, then drove back to Phu Bai, also alone. It was a 50-mile round trip through bad-guy territory.

On another day, Tom Miller and I drove to the 45th Engineer Group supply room and picked up three M-33 fragmentation grenades. Who knows why they were in a supply room in the first place? Duffey and I then drove to the 1st Battalion, 39th Artillery Regiment HQ at Phu Bai and picked up another grenade, drove out to the perimeter, and retrieved a bad illumination grenade, then back to the 1st of the 39th for one of the 40-mm grenades I mentioned, one that was not a dud.

On December 9th, 1969, Staff Sergeant Jim Qualls and I flew out to Eagle Beach courtesy of the 101st Airborne Division Aviation Battalion, to the site of a crashed light observation helicopter ("LOH": we called them "Loaches") to check for booby traps before it was lifted out. We did not find any, but it was my first chopper ride since joining the 287th, and it was good to get that behind me.

After Jim and I returned to the unit, Rick Lanham and I went on three calls, one of which included a 40-mm grenade we picked up at the Graves Registration unit at 85th Evac Hospital. The other two involved seven hand grenades at the Air Force Aerial Port and two 60-mm high-explosive mortar rounds from the 46th Supply and Service Battalion, a 101st unit, out at Camp Eagle. It was a busy day; other team members handled eleven calls for a total of fifteen for the day.

Flying in helicopters was always more adrenalin-pumping than driving. We were up in the air, usually outside the range of enemy ground fire. There was something discomforting about flying in something that seemed to defy gravity even more than an airplane. The pilots understood how they got off the ground and stayed in the air, but I did not; it always made me nervous.

There were many reasons why a chopper could crash; mechanical failures and being shot down were the two major ones. The one Jim and I went out on had recently gone down due to a mechanical failure. That bothered me. Hitting the ground from that kind of altitude had probably messed it up.

On December 12, Rick Lanham and I drove out to Camp Eagle, the 101st main base camp, picked up a grenade, then drove back to Phu Bai to the 39th Transportation Battalion and recovered a white phosphorus grenade and another 40-mm grenade. On the 13th, Paul Duffey and I went over to "B" Sector of the Phu Bai perimeter. Some lieutenant wanted us to take eighty-four 40-mm grenades off his hands because he did not like the way the box they were in looked. I told him to run them over to the 571st Ordnance Company at the ammo dump and turn them in.

During those same sixteen days, other members of the team handled another sixty-three calls. There were eighty calls in that two-week period. On December 14, 1969, I got into my first bag of shit in Phu Bai.

13

Somewhere Near LZ Sally, The War Raged All Around Us

On December 14, 1969, three weeks after joining the 287th, I went on my first combat assault with elements of the 101st Airborne Division. Captain Breland was also on this mission. Andy Breland had been a librarian in his native Louisiana and his dad was an U.S. Congressman. He is as nice a person as you would ever want to meet and treated the enlisted members of the team as equals. Quiet and thoughtful, he took his turn on dangerous calls, just like the rest of us. He was respected by all, not something many units could say about their officers.

Near a forward firebase of the 101st Airborne Division (LZ Sally), a Chinook helicopter, on its way to an even more remote firebase of the 2nd Brigade, had taken enemy ground fire. They jettisoned a sling-load of artillery ammunition, M-33 fragmentation grenades, small arms, and machine gun ammunition—resupply for the firebase after an enemy attack the previous night.

We got the call from the 101st just before 5 a.m. and were told we would combat assault into the area with the 2nd Squadron, 17th Cavalry Regiment's Aero-Rifle Platoon. Now they would be called a "Quick Reaction Force," all volunteers and always in the shit. We flew into LZ Sally, just off QL 1 and northwest of Hue City.

After arriving at LZ Sally, we picked up gunship support and flew out to grid YD 698150. It was in the middle of nowhere and about twelve clicks SSE from Sally, halfway between Fire Support Bases Bastogne and Birmingham. We were on the ground by 6 a.m. and still 600 meters from the ammunition.

The terrain was uphill and thick with vegetation and trees. This area was controlled by the NVA. Enemy contact had been heavy for a week.

It took us more than an hour to hump from the LZ to the site where the ammo had landed. We had to cross several streams, taking the long way around to avoid known enemy trails, which were probably booby-trapped. During the hump, we were trailed by a light observation helicopter, outfitted with a forward-mounted mini-gun.

After hacking our way through dense brush, we arrived at the site where the Aero-Rifle Platoon took up defensive positions around our perimeter. CPT Breland and I began to survey the downed ammo. There were several ICM—improved conventional munitions—rounds in the ordnance the helicopter had dropped.

Despite the official nomenclature, these were unconventional munitions in that, instead of exploding, they burst open and dropped a bunch of little anti-personnel bomblets. They were unbelievable killing devices when used against an enemy attack or for interdicting enemy routes.

They were also bad because of their anti-disturbance feature; they could lie around for an indefinite period of time. We think one of these is what killed Lew Black from the 184th team in Qui Nhơn when he was on the crew that cleaned up the Marine ammo dump at Đông Hà on July 18, 1968. The device was buried in the dirt; he never saw it.

This brings up another sad, murderous legacy of the Vietnam War. In the chapter on LZ English, I wrote about the number of minefields left unmarked by the French and Vietnamese. In addition, there are still millions upon millions of these airdropped unexploded anti-disturbance bomblets and anti-personnel devices from artillery rounds like the ICMs, all over Vietnam, Laos, and Cambodia.

From 1999–2001, the Vietnamese recovered and destroyed more than 35,000 mines in Quảng Trị province, alone. The figures on the number of Vietnamese civilians killed each year by unexploded ordnance (UXO) differ wildly. Official Vietnamese media sources report sixty to seventy killed each year, less than 200 wounded. However, one non-government organization involved with the UXO problem in Vietnam estimates that at least 1,110 are killed each year and as many as 1,882 wounded.

The Brigade artillery officer, who had flown in with us, wanted to bring the ICMs back to LZ Sally because they were classified. However, after examining each one of the ICMs, we found that all had been damaged. We told the artillery officer we would not transport these rounds and would destroy them with the rest of the ammo. Ground commanders and higher-ranking officers did not argue with us; on the ground at an EOD incident site, what we said was what happened.

One day when I was in the rear, staffing the office with our clerk, Don Urquhart (the one who knocked the Marine out in our bar—there was a knock at the back door. Don got up to see what it was, since grunts or the MPs would often bring ordnance—nothing dangerous—to the office. Well, usually nothing dangerous. Don went through the door separating the two rooms in the hooch, and then came back a few seconds later. "Uh, you're the ranking man here; I think you have to deal with this."

I got up and walked into the next room, where I saw a full-bird colonel standing with a lieutenant. I noticed the colonel's Combat Infantryman badge and jump wings, as well as 101st Airborne Division patches on both shoulders. "Can I help you, sir?" I said. I did not salute; maybe this is what set the guy off.

He then snapped at me, "I'm with the 101st Inspector General, and I'm here to inspect you."

EOD teams were not assigned to units (like the 101st) except at the ammunition dumps at Qui Nhơn, Cam Ranh Bay, and Long Bình. Even then, it was only for logistical support. Our chain-of-command went from the team, to control, to U.S. Army Vietnam, to Washington. Maybe some things went to Military Assistance Command Vietnam (MACV), or 1st Logistics Command, but not many. Even the teams attached to ordnance battalions were not inspected by that unit. Only EOD Control could inspect us.

The main reason for this was that our work was classified and most of it, including our publications, was "Top Secret" and "Eyes Only"; that meant for EOD eyes only. Our offices, which contained numerous classified EOD publications, were off limits to everyone else.

My guess was that this particular colonel had learned that an Army EOD team was living at the Phu Bai Combat Base with 3rd Marines Force Recon, which was true, and he could not understand how that could be. We typically lived where we wanted and, in this case, that meant staying away from regular Army units, largely because of people like this colonel.

The colonel knew that nowhere in his various orders designating units he was responsible for did it say anything about the 287th Ordnance Detachment (EOD); yet, here the little man was, standing on my doorstep, knowing that a brawl of wills was about to occur. Urquhart stood in the doorway behind me, watching my back, I guess.

"Sir, I'm sorry, but you're not authorized to come in here." Then I explained the protocol. He began to screw up his face as I told him what the deal was.

As soon as I was done, he exploded, yelling at me, "Specialist … Steinberg"—he read my name tag—"if you don't let me in, I will call the MPs."

I pulled my EOD ID card out of my back pocket and said, "With all due respect, sir, there's a phone number on this card. If you call it, they will tell you that you cannot come in here, and a very pissed off Major is going to yell and probably curse at you."

The colonel returned to his jeep; his aide stayed on the stoop. Then, the colonel got on his radio, and I guess someone at 101st HQ patched him in to the 533rd Ordnance Detachment (EOD Control) in Saigon. I could see the colonel start to talk. The colonel almost immediately stopped talking and, for the next two minutes, just held the phone.

When the 101st colonel hung up the radio, he waved his aide to the jeep, and they left in a hurry. We never saw this person again. That is why the brigade artillery officer did not argue with us.

It took quite a while to police the ammunition since it was spread over a large area. We recovered thirty-two 105-mm high-explosive and ICM rounds, five 105-mm armor-piercing rounds, five 105-mm smoke rounds, and seven 105-mm illumination rounds. Additionally, we rounded up an entire case of M-33 HE fragmentation grenades from all over the place because their case had been obliterated when it hit the ground. The same had occurred to numerous cases of linked 7.62-mm ammo for M-60 machine guns, and thousands of rounds of 5.56-mm ammo for M-16s. More than 10,000 rounds of this ammo were all over the area; we had to police up every single one of them.

After gathering all of the damaged ammo, we set our shot using C-4, detonating cord, and non-electric caps with a short burn of time fuse, maybe ten minutes. With the enemy around us, we did not want them coming in, disarming the thing, and then using it against American troops later. At this point, the aero-rifle platoon leader sent most of his team back to secure the LZ.

Just as they were leaving, and as we were getting the shot ready, enemy small arms fire broke out. Everyone, including Captain Breland and I, returned fire in all directions, since we could not see the enemy. Bullets buzzed around us like a swarm of very pissed off bees. The LOH, which had started to move toward the LZ, turned around and its mini-gun tore up the vegetation all around the site.

Pieces of trees, dirt and plants flew everywhere; the smell of gunfire filled our nostrils, almost to the point of suffocation. The Aero-Rifle Platoon men unloaded everything they had—M-16s, 40mm grenades from shoulder-fired launchers, and M-60 machine guns. They even fired a couple of 66-mm LAW anti-tank rockets.

We saw smoke, or a flash of movement, and unloaded an entire clip at whatever, pulled another clip from a bandolier, loaded, and continued to fire. Then, just like that, the firefight ended and the infantry lieutenant sent the squad back to secure the LZ. Somewhere on that 600-meter trek, they again came under enemy fire.

Hearing this firefight as we pulled the shot, the only other people with Captain Breland and myself were the infantry lieutenant and his radio operator. We moved quickly toward the LZ and the ongoing shooting. Just before we caught up with the rest of the Aero-Rifle Platoon, the second firefight ended. We were halfway to the LZ when the shot was due to go off, so we got down behind some fallen logs and waited.

We were 200 meters from the shot when it went off; 105-mm base-plates and shrapnel shrieked overhead like angry hornets. When stuff stopped dropping around us, we hauled ass for the LZ and extraction. The LOH overflew the site and reported a clean shot. We scrambled onto Hueys and headed back to LZ Sally, then caught a bird back to Phu Bai.

The ease with which we learned to accept and deal with the violence we saw and experienced on a far too regular a basis is troubling to me, now. It was not then, and I understand why. If you let those things get to you when they were happening all around you, you would not be able to function in combat. You did not think about it, you did not talk about it, and you did not dream about it—that is what I tell myself.

Maybe that was why we drank so much, why the military was willing to supply us with unlimited beer and liquor. They even flew beer into remote firebases. It was warm, but no one cared. If I did dream about these things when I was there, I have no memory of it, and maybe that was a good thing because the actual memory is bad enough. I do, however, occasionally dream about these things today—when I am able to sleep.

You know the phrase, "Shit happens?" In Vietnam, shit happened every day. Just being there was enough to last a lifetime. Writing this is the first time I have been able to "talk" about some of these things, and I am hoping it does some good, if not for me then for those who might read it.

I recovered the "Unusual Incident Report" on this event from the National Archives. That was the only reason I can write about it because until I got that report and read it sometime in early 2004, I had no memory of it. Reading it, I was stunned, wondering how I could forget something like that. One of the things about PTSD is that we numbed ourselves to certain things, but still, when I talked to Andy Breland several months after I found the report, I asked him what he remembered about this incident. He said, "Not a fucking thing. Are you sure it was us?" He wrote the report.

14

More Phu Bai and Northern "I" Corps

Andy Breland and I spent seven hours in the air and on the ground during the LZ Sally incident. The report says we were on the ground near the incident site at 8 a.m., and we spent two hours in the air; that means we were probably back in Phu Bai between 2–3 p.m. that afternoon. That was not the end of our day, however, and this is what I mean when I say that we were on duty 24/7/365.

After Andy and I got back to Phu Bai, the daily incident journal for December 14, 1969, shows that Paul Duffey and I returned to Camp Eagle for two calls. The first was on the Eagle perimeter where we destroyed two dud 40-mm grenades. We then went to the 1st of the 39th Artillery site at the bridge at Gia Lo on a dud-fired 60-mm mortar round. Then, we returned to Phu Bai.

These calls took a total of 3.5 hours; we drove to both sites and back to Phu Bai alone. By then, it was probably about 7 p.m. The day was still not over. As soon as we got back, Captain Breland and Duffey immediately returned to Camp Eagle on what turned out to be a false alarm. That call lasted two hours, so they got back about 9–9.30 p.m. They drove to and from Eagle in the dark, by themselves.

The day was still not over because Duffey and I then went to the 8th Radio Research Field Station at Phu Bai to recover five unfired 40-mm grenades. That took an hour, so the day finally ended sometime between 11 p.m. and midnight. Now the day was over. I did get the next two days off, but on the 17th, I ran three calls with Captain Breland.

From December 15, 1969, until January 23, 1970, the day before Jim Qualls and I landed at Fire Support Base Davis, I went on sixty-three calls. During those forty days, I was at the unit—either staffing the office, doing maintenance, blowing ordnance at our demo area, or teaching classes—for eighteen days. This means that I ran the sixty-three calls over a twenty-two-day period, including the other three I ran on the fourteenth after returning from LZ Sally. Most of them were routine.

On December 20, 1969, Captain Breland and I went back to Camp Eagle. This time, we removed a dud 40-mm grenade from its launcher, then sauntered over to the 101st Aviation Battalion, and removed two stuck 2.75-inch rockets from their pod—just another day's work. On the 22nd, Jim Qualls and I blew a dud forty out on the Phu Bai Perimeter. Later that day, First Sergeant Randles and I went out to Camp Eagle and put pins back into two M26 grenades that, somehow—miraculously—had not had the spoons fly off after the pins were pulled—lucky for someone.

On December 24—Christmas Eve—Tom Miller and I were at Camp Evans at the 2nd of the 506th Infantry blowing a dud 122-mm rocket that had landed in the base during an incoming attack the previous night. After finishing this job, we jumped on a chopper and spent eight hours in the bush with the 3rd of the 187th Infantry taking care of a dud 250-pound bomb.

When we got back to Evans, we drove out to Phi Lu and blew a dud Chicom 82-mm HE mortar round that had landed in the village the night before. In between these calls, we managed to drop by the 158th Assault Helicopter Company to pick up a bad trip flare.

We also ran two calls at Evans at the 1st of the 506th Infantry and recovered seventeen one-pound blocks of Chinese TNT and twenty-two Chinese 60-mm HE Mortar rounds. We brought these back to the unit for later destruction. Including the trip from Phu Bai and back, Tom and I put in about sixteen hours that day—Merry fucking Christmas.

January 1, 1970—our New Year—the VC apparently thought it should be our Tet. We ran eight calls that day; I was on three of them with Paul Duffey. I am glad it was Paul.

Phu Bai was hectic, and in 119 days, I went on 175 incidents. For me, it was a very intense period, maybe the most intense of my entire time in Vietnam. There were days that passed without putting my life in danger, and then there were others when I went on three, four, five calls in ten hours.

Some were routine, like picking up a grenade the MPs had taken off a drunk GI. Others involved duds from an incoming attack, or a booby trap found under a truck that had been to the trash dump where lots of Vietnamese came to pick through the trash and booby trap our vehicles.

On January 20, 1970, Tom Miller and I went on what became an intellectual exercise on how not to blow up a Vietnamese village school. We actually might have won a few hearts and minds, that day.

We got a call from Battalion Advisory Team (BAT) 46 of the 3rd Battalion, 187th Infantry, 101st Airborne Division. They were located in the village of Ap Hien Luong and had found a Viet Cong mine planted in the floor of the village school. Ap Hien Luong stood between Firebase Bastogne and Firebase T-Bone, both remote 101st outposts on the way to the A Shau Valley from Phu Bai. Bastogne was at the point where you entered the mouth of the valley on Highway 547. T-Bone was an engineering marvel, built on the intersection of two extremely steep ridges; the only way in was by chopper.

We drove there from Phu Bai, just the two of us, tooling along in enemy infested territory. Bastogne and T-Bone were places that the enemy attacked frequently. This village was smack between both bases. It was one of the few villages in this area where people still lived: only because the BAT team was there. On my map, the few villages marked were all listed as "abandoned."

After arriving at the village, the BAT leader, a sergeant named Jackson, led us to the school, a low, one-story, two-room building with a flat roof. I guessed, given the materials the building was made from, that it was built by American soldiers. We entered the school and discovered an American Bouncing Betty mine in a hole in the dirt floor under a very thin wooden plank, coated with cement to make it blend into the floor. The pressure-activated fuse was secondarily fused with a pull friction device that Tom Miller discovered as we cleared the dirt from around the mine. How the mine was placed without the VC being seen was a mystery, but I surmised that one of the villagers was a VC sympathizer.

A small wire was pegged into the dirt in the side of the hole containing the mine, the other end of the wire attached to the pull-friction device on the mine fuse. The VC apparently hoped that either someone would set it off with pressure by stepping on the thin plank, or someone would find it, not see the secondary fuse device, start to pick it up, and set it off when the trip wire functioned the pull-friction device.

The Bouncing Betty was developed by the Germans (they called it the "S Mine") and used it against allied soldiers during World War II. After that, everyone—including the United States—rushed down to their local mine-builder's shop and had them made.

By the time we got to Vietnam, the French and the South Vietnamese Army (as I mentioned in the Ha Tay Special Forces Camp incident) had left them buried all over the place, and, then, not marked their minefields. The Viet Cong used the Russian model, as well as some supplied by the Chinese, to kill Americans in a particularly devastating fashion.

The cylindrical mine had a pressure fuse in the top, usually the only part sticking out of the ground. They were impossible to see unless you paid close attention to where you walked. When an unsuspecting soldier stepped on one, he knew immediately what had happened because there was a distinct clicking sound as the pressure fuse functioned, setting off a propellant charge at the base of the explosive charge.

The propellant then blew the mine out of the ground, and, at about a level between the waist and the eyes, it detonated, showering the soldier who had initiated the mine and everyone close by with steel balls traveling at a high rate of speed. A body hit by them was shredded; they had a big kill zone.

They can also be set with a trip wire, as the pressure fuse has a secondary pull friction fuse in the side. That was the deal with the one we found in the school floor. I told Miller I was concerned that if the VC went to the trouble to set it with a trip wire, there could be a secondary device under the mine. This was the kind of situation that could have been meant to kill an EOD team if they were not careful.

I had seen such a device before, with an HE grenade buried under it, pin pulled, with the mine holding the grenade striker in place. The VC were obviously very pissed off at this village because they were cooperating with U.S. forces by letting the BAT team set up there and run ambushes at night.

I decided we could not blow the device in place without damaging the small school building. I wished we had brought some shaped charge containers so we could blow a hole through the floor near the device, then tunnel up underneath it. Tom suggested that the plastic cover on one of my 40-mm HE rounds—I was carrying a grenade launcher—might do the trick.

I took the plastic cover off one of the HE rounds and fashioned a crude shaped charge by putting a thin layer of C-4 around the plastic cap. I set the shaped charge about 15 inches from the mine hole and set it off with a blasting cap and a fuse lighter as we ran into the next room and got up against the wall.

It worked like a charm, blew a hole in the dirt about 8 inches in diameter and a foot deep, cracking the cement floor right up to the hole the mine was in. Tom and I picked up the broken pieces of cement between the two holes. I used my K-Bar and a stick to burrow sideways, then up under the Bouncing

Betty. There was no secondary device, so Miller cut the trip wire, we removed the device, took out the fuse, and clipped off the blasting cap detonator.

I drew detailed diagrams of the device and how we had fabricated the shape-charge to help us get under the mine. Captain Breland sent the reports and diagrams back to our Control unit and, they sent copies to all in-country teams.

Standing there in the small school after Tom and I disarmed the device and destroyed it, I remember thinking, "What the fuck is wrong with people who would want to kill innocent children who had no part in bringing the soldiers into their village?" I would never figure that out, and it was not the only time I saw things like this. It was one of those situations where American soldiers, in trying to do the right thing, often caused the opposite. It was kind of like that expression about the cure being worse than the disease.

I could go through each of the incidents from Phu Bai, but then this chapter would be a hundred pages long. However, there were two life-altering events in Phu Bai. Fire Support Base Rifle was one of them. The other was Fire Support Base Davis.

15

Fire Support Base Davis: Once Again, I Should Have Been Dead

Like the ammo dump incident when I was blown out of the truck by the mortar round that was not a dud, Fire Support Base Davis has never been far from my thoughts. By all fair standards, and also considering the ammo dump events, I should be dead and not writing this, and would not have been at Rifle. Fire Support Base Davis was an abandoned French outpost located in mountains bordering the north end of the A Shau Valley, literally in the middle of nowhere. The only way in and out was by helicopter. It was one fucked up place.

On January 24, 1970, Jim Qualls and I were picked up by a 101st chopper at 7.30 a.m. and flown to Firebase Currahee. Currahee was located on the floor of the A Shau Valley. There, we joined "D" Company, 2nd Battalion, 506th Parachute Infantry Regiment, 101st Airborne Division; Pathfinders from the 160th Aviation Battalion; combat engineers from the 326th Engineer Battalion; and artillery from the 2nd Battalion, 319th Artillery Regiment. We were about to participate in an action that was part of Operation Randolph Glen, which ran from December 7, 1969, until February 14, 1970.

Currahee was another firebase in the A Shau where the enemy attacked at will with artillery, rockets and mortars, as well as ground attacks. It was a couple of kilometers east of Hamburger Hill and west of Fire Support Base Berchtesgaden.

Looking at all the troops, choppers, artillery pieces, and huge sling-loads of artillery projectiles waiting to be lifted into the air, I felt a little naked with all of those ready-made targets close to my body. I hoped the NVA were still having their morning tea and reading the Hanoi Post when this flying armada approached the landing zone.

After several days prepping the area with B-52 strikes and artillery, which, of course, told the enemy we were coming, the combat assault prepared to lift off. Qualls and I checked our gear and weapons one last time. Jim had an M-16; I had my CAR-15. I got it from a MACV adviser in Qui Nhơn when I was at LZ English. I traded a Browning .45 pistol for it, recovered during an arms cache removal in the An Loa Valley.

It was what they called an artillery raid. Fly in fast and hard, infantry secures the LZ, helicopters lower the big guns and ammo; they set up and shoot the shit out of everything for miles around. This was an area permeated with NVA who had their own artillery and mortars.

Jim Qualls and I were in the lead chopper with a team of Pathfinders from the 160th Aviation Battalion. Behind us in the second chopper was a team of combat engineers from "B" Company, 326th Engineers. The Pathfinders' job was to set up the lower LZ, where all the Hueys would land and drop their troops, after we had cleared it. The engineers were to blow any abandoned ordnance we found—and there was a shitload of it—left behind by the ARVN, who had occupied this hellhole after the 1st Cavalry Division.

We were in the first ships to hit the ground, at 9 a.m. The rest of the assault, dozens of Hueys, gunships from "A" Troop, 2nd Squadron, 17th Air Cavalry, and Chinooks from the 101st Aviation Group with artillery pieces slung beneath them, hovered and circled overhead as the main infantry assault hit the upper level of the LZ, between 9.04–9.08 a.m.

The artillery pieces and their ammunition started coming in at 9.10 a.m. Our task was to sweep a large area on the lower level of the LZ, which had been cleared by the air strikes. It was on a flat plain below a hill where the infantry and artillery were to set up.

Our chopper and the second chopper landed near one edge of the clearing. Qualls and I, the team of Pathfinders, and the engineers got out. Qualls told the engineers and Pathfinders to stay put while he and I swept the perimeter. We separated, and each of us went in a different direction around the perimeter. Almost as soon as we began, I called to Qualls that I had found what was called a "diamond mine marker."

This was five stones set on an ammo can top, one in each compass position with a stone in the middle. The VC and NVA used this marker to show their friends that there were four mines or booby traps around the perimeter, one generally at each compass position, and one in the middle. Sometimes, though, it was clear that the enemy did not know their compass points.

I remember thinking that it was strange that the marker would be so obvious and not even minimally camouflaged. Qualls and I decided to find the one in the center of the LZ first and began to sweep across the area about 100 feet apart. Now I think the deliberate placement of the marker was to get us to do exactly that.

As I neared a point about two-thirds of the way across the clearing, I stopped because I thought I saw something in the tree line about 70 meters in front of me. I set down my demolitions bag, removed my rucksack, and laid them on the ground after checking the immediate area. I flipped the safety off on my CAR-15, made sure that it was on full automatic, and cradled it in my hands, finger on the trigger.

As I peered into the tree line, I began to feel something moving under my left foot. I looked down and noticed that there was movement in the dirt directly under, and in front of, my foot. I called to Jim that I was standing on something and that it was moving. I pulled my knife from my hip and, bending from the waist, began to turn over the dirt directly in front of my foot. I saw a piece of black communications wire and realized that it was being slowly pulled away from me.

I grabbed the wire with one hand, pointing my rifle at the tree line, and pulled the wire toward me, getting a lot of resistance at the other end. At that moment, I saw an NVA soldier in the tree line with the wire in his hands; I think he saw me at the same time.

There was that brief moment when we looked each other dead in the eye, even from that distance. I pulled out my side cutters and cut the wire, hoping whatever was buried there did not have a collapsing circuit. I think he was so surprised when he knew I saw him, that he stopped pulling from his end.

I opened fire on the tree line and threw a red smoke grenade, alerting the assault to the enemy presence. Several Cobra gunships flew in and fired up the tree line with high-explosive and white phosphorous rounds. The Pathfinders closed in on the enemy position and killed two NVA, the second apparently there to provide cover for the man trying to kill me, Qualls, and everyone else in the vicinity.

I was standing on a 155-mm high-explosive artillery projectile rigged with a Chinese pull friction fuse, with five other blasting caps packed in C-3 (a plastic explosive) pushed inside the fuse well. The 155-mm HE round contains 14.79 pounds of TNT. The commo wire was attached to the fuse at two of the blasting caps' pull rings. The enemy soldier had been trying to detonate the booby trap while I stood directly over it.

This would have destroyed the two choppers nearby, killed both Jim Qualls and me, and injured the Pathfinders, the engineers, and chopper crews. Jim and I brushed the dirt off the mine, checked under it for secondary devices, disarmed it, and then moved on to complete our task. I received a Bronze Star with "V" Device for Heroism for this incident.

I never gave it much thought at the time, and when Qualls and I got back to the unit, I never mentioned it. I had no idea that Jim had put me in for an award until March 1971 when, stationed with the 67th EOD in Ravenna, Ohio, my CO told me I was getting some kind of award from Vietnam. Some colonel, I think from 5th Army, came to the unit with a photographer and presented me with the medal.

As I write this paragraph, it is September 4, 2007. Last week, I recovered more historical documents from the 2nd of the 506th. The National Archives sent me several issues of the 2nd of the 506th's battalion history called, *We Stand Alone*. It was apparently written by someone who occasionally "waxed poetic" about the trials and tribulations of men at war, commenting:

> Death is the handmaiden of the Infantry solider. We all must go to her sooner or later but the Infantryman walks with her constantly. How well we tread with her and how well we meet her certain destiny becomes the final measure of a man.

I always thought Death was a male figure, but what the fuck do I know?

What this history of the 2nd of the 506th for the year 1970 contains, in part, were descriptions of the artillery raid into Davis after I disarmed the mine, which I had completely put out of my mind. I suppose this is because what happened to me before in the ammo dump was traumatic enough. When Qualls and I wrote up the incident report for the Davis event, we left out everything else we did that day. I am not sure why we did that because the rest of the day was completely insane.

The documents particularly mention Captain Dwight Walhood and Delta Company. I talked to Dwight about ten years ago; his memories of that day are as clear as mine. After we cleared the LZ, the combat assault that was hovering overhead began to land. The unit history writes:

> … Delta Company, under Captain Dwight Walhood, would go far and wide searching for the enemy. Two artillery raids were planned for January

and Delta Company would make aggressive thrusts to Fire Base Shepard and Fire Base Davis … The raid to Fire Base Shepard yielded little in the way of action, but the raid to Davis was a different story. Delta Company located and destroyed enemy caches, booby traps and minefields. As the 3rd [Platoon] hovered into Davis to join the remainder of Delta Company, enemy small arms fire met the aircraft. Intense suppressive fire quickly discouraged the enemy and he fled the area.

I had forgotten about the choppers taking fire as they came in on the upper LZ, but Qualls and I were busy on the lower one. It was another one of those deals where we just tuned out the War. I particularly like the part where it said that Delta Company "located and destroyed enemy caches, booby traps and minefields."

That was the part I had forgotten until I read this document. Now my memory of this event is clearer than in more than forty-six years. Along with Jim Qualls, I "destroyed enemy caches, booby traps and mine fields," and Walhood's action reports make this clear. I am not sure where the author of the unit history got his facts, but it sure was not from anyone who was at Davis that day.

According to the Daily Staff Journal for the 2nd of the 506th about what Jim Qualls and I found during the entire operation at Davis, Captain Walhood reported to his battalion Tactical Operations Center the following:

At YD 255289, FSB Davis, D/2/506 reported [that EOD found] one modified 155 r[oun]d [with] a C-3 explosive device at its head and a Chi[nese] Com[munist] push-pull firing device rigged as a booby trap. Additionally, they found [forty-seven] 40mm M-79 [grenades that were] dud rounds, [ten] 57mm canister and HE recoilless rifle rounds, two 60mm and one-hundred 81mm rounds, fifty M15 anti-personnel mines, four M14 Thermite grenades, one M34 white phosphorus frag grenade, one M26 frag grenade, one M18A1 Claymore [anti-personnel mine] facing up the hill, and four M72 LAW [66mm anti-tank rockets].

This was what we had taken care of in approximately four hours, since Captain Walhood made this report at 1 p.m. This was all ordnance left behind from some previous incursion by South Vietnamese units that simply abandoned it because they were too lazy to take it out and did not destroy it.

How it is that the NVA never found this ordnance and used it against us is hard to understand; unless, there was originally much more of it left behind and the enemy took what they wanted as the need arose—the more likely probability.

At 1.45 p.m., sweeping the west side of the upper LZ, Jim and I discovered a triangular sign marked, "M-I-N," a South Vietnamese Army minefield warning, nailed to a tree with no clue as to where the mines actually were. Captain Walhood requested the whole area be zapped with napalm after we left. They could not do this for two more days, meaning all the ordnance and the minefield were waiting to be picked clean for that long.

At 4.45 p.m., as we cleared the area near the extraction site, we discovered two booby-trapped 81-mm high-explosive mortar rounds rigged with trip wires. According to Captain Walhood's report, "They were deactivated and destroyed." As all the old ordnance we discovered could not be immediately destroyed, we got the 326th Engineers to help us crate it up in empty artillery projectile boxes, loaded it on a Chinook, and flew it into an open area blown out by the air strikes of the previous two days. We piled everything up, set charges using C-4 and det. cord. We did not cap and fuse it until just before we flew out.

At 5.23 p.m., we lifted off with the Chinook following us, landing at Currahee at 5.30 p.m. Just before leaving Davis, we pulled the shot we had set for all of the found ordnance except the eleven cases of 57-mm recoilless rifle rounds, which we took back to Phi Bai and destroyed in our demo area the next day. Just as we were circling Currahee to land, the shot at Davis went off; you could see the plume of debris, smoke and a fireball from the blast rising into the air above the A Shau.

After Captain Walhood's 1 p.m. report, we found an additional nineteen loose 57-mm rounds and six more 60-mm mortar rounds. There was another claymore, also pointed uphill at the LZ and rigged with a trip wire. There were 1,000 30-caliber rifle rounds, 2,000 M60 machine gun rounds, three more thermite grenades, four smoke grenades, and sixteen more anti-tank rockets.

From our cursory investigation of a small section of the Vietnamese army minefield, we estimated there could have been as many as 100 booby-trapped 81-mm mortar rounds in an area about the size of a baseball diamond. This was the K-Mart of American ordnance, and the enemy was looking for the Blue Light Special. We could not attempt to disarm or destroy all the booby-trapped mortar rounds, so I hope that they did eventually napalm the place. None of the reports I recovered said this happened, so I have no reason to believe it did. All that stuff is probably still lying around where we left it.

16

Louis Caruso:
He Came to Visit and We Did
Our Best to Get Him Killed

After almost fourteen months in country, I felt I was pretty good at what I did. On February 27, 1970, a young SP5 named Louis Caruso came to the 287th from the 170th Ord. Det. (EOD). The 170th was the EOD team for the American embassy in Saigon and handled calls inside the city; they rarely went to the bush. SP5 Caruso wanted to get out of the city and see what it was like in the bush with a team constantly on combat operations. Caruso got his wish.

Early the next day, we got a call from III Marine Amphibious Force HQ that a Combined Action Platoon in a small village outside the Phu Bai Base Camp had been alerted to a minefield just outside the village in a garden. Caruso and I packed our gear and weapons. I grabbed a 40-mm grenade launcher with HE and flechette rounds as well as a vest for carrying extra rounds.

I was a short-timer and not taking any chances. I threw a couple of LAW rockets into the jeep as well. This was a single-shot, shoulder-launched anti-tank round that could blow the crap out of just about anything. It was lightweight and compact. My motto during those last weeks in Vietnam was, "You can't carry too much fucking firepower."

We grabbed an explosives bag, got in a jeep, and took off for the village. It turned out it was a little more than "outside the wire" of the base camp. It was 25 miles and it was just the two of us driving on two tracks through country totally controlled by the VC and NVA. We kept our weapons in the lockdowns on the jeep's doors. We were just two guys. If we got hit, there would be time enough to start shooting if we survived the initial ambush.

The CAP team was in a village at grid YD 775080 about 5 miles northeast of Hue toward the coast of the South China Sea. We walked out of the village and down a path bordering the small field. There was a large hole in the ground about 8 feet to the right of the path. Before I could say anything, a Marine, pointing at the hole, said, "That's how they found the minefield. One of the villagers walked through there and stepped on something. Not much left of him. When we went in to get the body, one of my people saw wire prongs sticking out of the dirt. We marked it with that stick."

Caruso and I dropped our gear, except for our weapons. I surveyed the area directly in front of me, and to the sides, then stepped off the path. The ground was a little damp and muddy. I waved Lou over. We squatted down, surveying the area to our front, looking for disturbed ground, trip wires or anything else obvious. Based on the size of the hole and the description of the "wire prongs," I guessed this would be another bunch of abandoned Bouncing Betties. I was right.

We found and destroyed nineteen Bouncing Betties. These were American mines, but I could not determine if American or South Vietnamese soldiers had planted them on some long-ago operation. They might have also been planted by local VC, who could get American ordnance on the black market.

Several years ago, Louie reminded me of something else that happened that day, a black, satanic event I had driven deeply into my subconscious. When we first arrived in the village, the CAP team leader said they wanted to show us something. We walked down a dirt road that ran through the village to a small shack of a house. An old Vietnamese woman ran out when she saw the Marines, wailing and throwing her hands in the air. A Marine took us into the small hut. In the middle of the floor of the single room was a woven mat. He pointed at it.

The old women went over and lifted the mat, motioning us to look. There was a small hole in the floor. In the hole were the remains of a baby, literally torn to shreds and very, very dead. It was sickening and, at the same time, surreal. "What the fuck happened?" I demanded.

The Marine said, "The VC came in here last night while we were out on ambush. They don't like that the villagers let us stay here, and then we go out and kill their friends. So, while they were threatening the villagers, this kid came running outside and they just cut her down with AKs." I did not know what to say. Lou was really shaken up. He had never seen anything like this around Saigon. I had never seen anything like this either.

After Lou and I had reconnected in 2004, he wrote me, telling just me how haunted he was by this event. I wished I could have consoled him. Nothing you could say about something like this would resolve anything. Like "The Day It Was Raining Dead" at Rifle, there are just some things so fucked up they are always there, lurking in the part of your brain that remembers stuff you want to forget.

The next day, March 1, we got a call to go into the A Shau Valley and hook up with a long-range reconnaissance team from the 101st Airborne Division. Doing recon after an air strike, they had run into a dud 750-pound bomb lying on the surface. I called for a chopper from the 101st. They picked us up at the XXIVth Corps pad, and we flew out to a small LZ the Recon Team had cut into the heavily forested side of a mountain.

It was raining like hell and chilly when the chopper dropped us off. As this was a very hot area, controlled by the NVA, the chopper never set down. We jumped off the skids from six feet off the ground. As soon as we hit the ground, two soldiers in tiger-stripe fatigues and painted faces came out of the trees and motioned us over to their position.

The team leader said, "Look this was as close as we could bring the chopper in. We've had contact most of the day and just found a well-used trail near where the bomb is."

I looked at the painted-up soldier and asked, "Well, just how the fuck far away are we?"

"Oh, about two clicks," he said.

I turned to Caruso and said, "Well, man, this is going to be your true baptism." We took off, midway in the well-spread-out little group. We made our way up the side of the mountain, crossing streams, cutting through thick vegetation. Whenever we hooked up with an infantry unit in the bush, they did everything they could to protect us. They knew we might be saving some grunt's life by taking care of this bomb before the VC or the NVA got hold of it and turned the explosives inside into dozens of mines, claymores, and stick grenades.

After two hours, we were in the area where the bomb was; I told the team leader I wanted one of them to take me to the bomb. I told Caruso I wanted to check things out before we made a decision on how to handle the incident. Everyone took defensive positions around the clearing made by other 750 and 1,000-pound bombs that had been dropped. One of the Recon men and I moved to the bomb, about 100 yards away. As we approached, I saw that the bomb had done something we learned about at school, but that I had yet to see in almost eighteen months in Vietnam.

The bomb had porpoised—it had actually penetrated the ground, gone in, hit something and then reversed itself, popping out of the ground 3 feet from the entry hole. I stopped when we got about 5 feet away because I did not like the look of the fuse in the nose of the bomb. It was one of those very dangerous Navy fuses and heavily damaged. We went back to the group. I told Caruso to drop his ruck and bring his M-16 and the C-4 he carried. "Look," I said, "We are not going to touch this thing, because we're not getting near that fuse."

Caruso and I went back to the bomb. Between us, we had twelve sticks of C-4, 10 feet of det. cord, time fuse, fuse igniters, and non-electric caps. We put five sticks on each side of the bomb, about 6 inches out from the sides. Two sticks were just to the sides of the damaged fuse. I tied it together with det. cord and blasting caps, set twenty minutes of fuse on a non-electric cap, shoved it into the C-4, pulled the fuse lighter, and we hauled ass.

We made our way back through the heavy growth and down the side of the mountain. It was raining as it only rains in Southeast Asia; we were making very bad time because we were having a hard time maintaining our footing. I suddenly thought to look at my watch. "Jesus Christ," I yelled. "Get behind something because this thing is gonna blow in about ten seconds." We hit the dirt behind a huge pile of trees the air strike had uprooted.

The shot went. We were about 300 yards away when the bomb detonated and shrapnel and dirt flew all around us. I heard the base plate take off and go flying into outer space. At that exact moment, one of the Recon men stood up. Before I could grab his dumb ass, I heard the base coming back down through the atmosphere, sounding like a freight train, moving at incredible velocity.

The thing landed three feet in front of him with a huge crash; it threw dirt, rocks, and tree debris all over us. The LRRP turned and looked at me, his eyes the size of the base plate, and said, "Shit, man, why didn't you tell us that might happen?"

"Frankly," I said, "I was only thinking about getting the hell out of here."

We returned to the LZ, and the radio operator called for our extraction. However, the weather had turned really foul and nothing was flying. We put up a perimeter around the LZ, and Caruso and I found ourselves in the infantry. We stayed in the heavy bush for almost four hours, rain soaked and very cold, before a chopper was finally able to get in and pick us up.

Louie reminded me when we saw each other in 2007 that he had gone into a tree with the team's sniper when we got to the extraction point. After a few minutes, the expert shooter handed his rifle to Louie and said, "Here, look through the scope over on that ridge."

Looking through the scope, he plainly saw five or six NVA moving down a trail. They were probably looking for us after the bomb went off. When we landed back at Phu Bai, Caruso turned to me and said, "I can't say I'll be unhappy to get back to Saigon."

During the four days SP5 Caruso was with us, he went on eleven incidents. In addition to going with me on the mines in the village and into the A Shau Valley, he went on incidents involving a dud LAW rocket—a very dangerous item—and another with me to destroy a dud French 105-mm artillery shell left over from lord knows when. Then, he assisted Captain Breland in destroying a bunch of VC mines in a field where an MP gun truck had gotten trapped; he went with Tom Miller to Firebase Bastogne (a very heavy place on the way to the A Shau) to deal with a dud 90-mm HEAT round. On his next-to-last call, he went back to Camp Eagle for another dud LAW rocket.

Caruso finished off his time with us when he went on a call with Master Sergeant Randles and Paul Duffey. The VC had mined the railroad tracks somewhere out in the bush and the 1st Bn., 327th Inf., 101st Airborne Division, had surprised the VC and killed them. The device that Caruso helped dismantle and destroy contained 32.5 pounds of Chinese TNT tied together with blasting caps, a pull friction device, and a buried wire that went to a VC spider hole.

17

My Final Days in Phu Bai

The rest of the time in Phu Bai—other than catastrophic incidents like setting the shot on the downed load of artillery with Captain Breland, FSB Davis with Jim Qualls, and, of course, FSB Rifle with Paul Duffey—was just as dangerous, but without a firefight going on in the middle of our work, yet before that, a little levity.

One of the big problems in Vietnam were the rats—big, ugly, snaggle-toothed rats. They were everywhere, and I swear, the VC and the NVA had exposed them to something that made them huge—as big as cocker spaniels; maybe they had mutated from herbicides. One night, after we had gotten loaded in our bar, I went back to my hooch and crashed in my bed. Later, the other guys went to bed, and all the lights were turned out.

I was getting one of my few good nights' sleep when something went "thud" right in the middle of my chest. I woke immediately, and thought, "Oh, Lord, please don't let this be a grenade," thinking the VC had somehow crossed a mile of the base to attack us. When nothing exploded, I slowly opened my eyes and adjusted to the darkness. There was still a weight on my chest. I felt it move a little. I raised my head slightly and saw two red, beady eyes staring at me. I grabbed my flashlight and turned it on the biggest, ugliest, snaggle-toothed rat ever, at least a foot long, crouched in the middle of my chest.

I leaped, screaming, and flipped on the lights. Everyone else woke and yelled stuff like, "What the fuck? Are we under attack?" I grabbed my .45 and chased the rat down the middle of the hooch.

Duffey and Watson started laughing hysterically. The rat went through a hole in the floor before I could get a shot off. Apparently, it had gotten in through the hole and was slinking across the exposed two-by-fours above my bed when it fell. I nailed a board over the hole that morning.

We had two pets in Phu Bai. The dog, "Philo Kvetch"—named after a Soupy Sales character—was the First Sergeant's great love. He had brought her back from a village as a puppy, to prevent her becoming a main course for the villagers. We also had a white domesticated duck that Duffey says I grabbed from some guy in a village when it was a duckling, so it would not end up as dinner. I think I paid about $5 in military scrip. I have always thought that ducks were the coolest things going and had always wanted one. We named it, "Bolivar P. Shagnasty," after a Red Buttons character.

Bolivar was our "guard duck" and took his job very seriously. We do not know how or why he started patrolling around the hooch, because who knows what a duck is thinking? Our hooch had a moat under it to catch rainwater and help the areas flood less than otherwise. Over the moat on both sides of the hooch was steel grate with half-inch square holes.

Bolivar patrolled the hooch at night, which never ceased to crack us up. We would be in the hooch, playing cards or reading, and Bolivar would be doing his thing. He quacked the entire time. The quacking got louder as he came abreast of where we were, and fainter as he marched away, circling the hooch. One morning we found both Philo and Bolivar dead, apparently from eating rat poison.

On December 23, 1969, ten days after the incident near LZ Sally with Captain Breland, I went on my second combat assault with the Phu Bai team and a unit from the 101st.

Tom Miller and I flew out of the XXIVth Corps pad at our base and went into a heavily wooded area near the village of Ap Thanh Tan, about 10 kilometers SSW of Camp Evans. We were called out by a recon team from the 3rd Battalion, 187th Parachute Infantry Regiment, 101st Airborne Division (Airmobile), who had been in contact with the NVA most of the night.

During a firefight, they called in air support, which blanketed the area beyond their night defensive position with 250-pound high-explosive bombs. We went in with an aero-rifle platoon at first light, me thinking of the last time I went into an LZ with one of these units—the event ten days earlier with Breland. I was hoping this mission would be different and that we would not have to shoot our way out again.

At first light, the infantry unit had sent out a three-man patrol looking for enemy bodies, or blood trails, and found a dud 250-pound about 10 meters beyond their perimeter. They were lucky it was a dud. The bomb was a low-drag, or dumb bomb, with Snake Eye fins and about 117 pounds of high explosives.

The low-drag fins allowed for a low-level, high-precision attack while avoiding bomb-fragment damage to the delivery aircraft. The fuse protruded from the nose and was supposed to detonate on impact. When it did not, it could be a very nasty device to work on. The bomb the recon guys found had skidded in and severely damaged the nose fuse.

In fact, the 250-pound bomb actually weighed 260 pounds. I have no idea why the military misnamed it, unless they just like numbers divisible by fifty. Bombs were 250-, 500-, 750-, 1,000-, 2,000-pounders, though all of them actually weighed more than the advertised weight. They were the aircraft-dropped ordnance that blew up most of South and North Vietnam, Laos, and Cambodia.

The Ho Chi Minh Trail was saturated on a daily basis. Many of the bombs were duds and are still being found and destroyed by civilian contract EOD personnel. As I previously mentioned, all the dud ordnance we left, as well as hundreds of thousands of anti-personnel bomblets and mines, are still killing the Vietnamese today.

The main reason the infantry called us in on these things, instead of just walking away, was that when the VC or NVA found these duds, they would saw them into pieces, get the explosives out, and use them against us. They made land mines, claymores, stick grenades, and satchel charges from the explosives. Also, they might leave it but booby trap it with a secondary device underneath, or on the approach. One of my VA clients was blown through the roof of a 10-ton tractor-trailer when a dud 500-pound bomb was command detonated under a bridge he was driving over.

We never just walked in on a device like this. We would get to within, say, 100 feet or so, then carefully survey the scene, looking for obvious signs of booby traps, or the enemy waiting in the tree line to ambush us. If it seemed safe—you could never be completely sure—the senior man (in this case, me) went in to check the ordnance and make a decision about how to handle it. The second EOD man always watched from a distance, in case something bad happened; that person had to make the report.

I took one of the paratroopers with me and moved carefully across the clearing toward the bomb, checking every couple of feet for mines and trip wires. At the bomb, I saw that the nose fuse had been flattened on impact and smashed down into the hole the fuse was screwed into. I had to assume that the firing pin was engaged with the detonator, therefore, any slight movement of the bomb could result in the pin withdrawing, setting it off and killing us all.

I got down on my knees about 3 feet from the bomb and crawled all the way around it, keeping my rifle in front of me, stopping every ten seconds, or so, to survey the tree line, while I checked for booby traps under the bomb and any mines that might be in the ground near it. When finished, I stood up and returned to Tom's location where the grunts had set up a perimeter.

We made C-4 charges, moved back to the bomb, and set them close to the sides and the nose fuse. We tied each charge together with det. cord and I cut two lengths of time fuse for a five-minute burn, crimped on non-electric blasting caps, and put pull-friction fuse lighters on the ends of the fuse. This done, I sent Miller back to the perimeter with the infantrymen and pulled the lighters.

I ran back to join the others, and we all took off, running through the dense vegetation. I kept checking my watch. At thirty seconds to detonation, I told everyone to get behind a tree and hunker down. No sooner had we done that, the bomb went off, sending shrapnel through the trees around us. As soon as stuff stopped falling from the sky, we took off at high-speed for the extraction LZ, arriving just as our chopper was landing. We jumped aboard and were airborne in a matter of seconds—another day, another dollar, or so we thought.

We had been on the job for eight hours, but, again, our day was not done. It was getting dark as we got off the chopper. A soldier from the 101st Tactical Operations Center ran up and said we were wanted at the TOC.

We followed him there, where we were met by a major from Brigade HQ. He told us a patrol from the 2nd Battalion, 327th Infantry, had been mortared near the village of Phu Lu, that there was a dud mortar round inside the perimeter our troops put up when the enemy followed their mortar barrage with a ground assault that they had repelled.

It was raining hard, and their choppers were grounded. I said, "If you can loan us a jeep, we'll drive out there and take care of it." He did, and we took off in the black of the Vietnam night, soaked by an increasingly hard rain. We went by ourselves, which, I think now, was pretty stupid.

We went south on Highway 1 about 5 miles, then 5 miles northeast on Route 554, toward the coast and the South China Sea. These were lowlands, subject to a lot of rain, full of swamps and many rice fields. This was the monsoon season, which ran from September to January. Areas near the coast received torrential rainfall. That was what we drove through all the way from Evans to Phu Lu.

We could have easily driven off the road into a swamp. It was raining so hard that we could barely see the front of the jeep; the headlights gave about as much light as a flashlight with low batteries.

By the time we found the 2nd of the 327th soldiers, we were soaking wet and thoroughly chilled. The troopers had holed up in small huts on the outskirts of the village. Their listening posts were just inside a tree line about 50 yards away. A trooper pointed out the hut where the platoon leader—a very young first lieutenant—sat by a small fire in a hole in the dirt floor. We huddled over the fire with him and tried to get warm, which was impossible.

I asked the LT where the mortar round was. He said, "It's sticking up in the mud between this hut and that one over there." He pointed at it through the open door, maybe 10 yards out. I lit a smoke, trying to dry out a little before going back into the cold, wet night—fat chance.

Twenty minutes later, Tom and I moved out and walked carefully toward the mortar round, shining our flashlights on the ground. We saw the tail fins of a Chinese 82-mm mortar round sticking up in the mud with the entire round buried in the wet dirt. These rounds had a point-detonating fuse, and as with any such fuse, you had to consider that the firing pin was impinged in the detonator, so any slight movement might set it off.

Getting rid of this item in the middle of the village was going to be tricky since we did not want to throw shrapnel all over the place, possibly injuring or killing civilians in huts close to the dud.

We went back to the infantry hut with the nice, warm fire and got some C-4, caps, time fuse, and a fuse lighter from our bag. I told Tom to cut the block of C-4 into quarters, and put two of them back in the bag. I cut two pieces of time fuse that would burn about two minutes, crimped on the caps and put the fuse lighters on the other end. Just outside the door of the hut, I had noticed an empty U.S. wood ammo box that had held 81-mm mortar rounds. I asked the LT if he had an entrenching tool—a small, fold-up shovel—and he handed me his.

Tom asked me what I had in mind. I just waved him out the door. He carried the charges; I picked up the box. We moved back to the round, and I told Miller to place the two charges about 2 inches from opposite sides of the mortar round. Then, I took the wooden box and placed it over the round, with the two time fuses and their lighters sticking out from under the sides of the box.

I took the small shovel and began to carefully cover the box with wet mud, surrounding it until there were 2 feet of it on top of the box and 1 foot around the sides. It was like building a small mud hut. Then we dragged over some very wet sandbags and piled them on top.

I had finished my mud-work, pulled the fuses and yelled, "Fire in the hole." Tom and I ran back to the hut with the LT and some of his men. We all got down on the floor. A minute later, we heard a muffled "wump", then pieces of wood, sandbag, and mud pelted our hut and other village structures in close proximity. When we walked back outside, there was a small crater where the box had been; the round had fully detonated.

Several villagers had come up to look at our handiwork. It was obvious from their grins and rapid chatter that they were very happy we had taken care of this thing without destroying anything or hurting anyone. It was a feel-good job. Then, we got back in the jeep and hauled ass back to Evans. We reported to the Brigade officer and he had a chopper for us within minutes, thanking us for taking care of business. By the time we got back to Phu Bai, it was almost midnight.

The new year—1970—began like all the others. On New Year's Eve, we had a huge party in our new bar and basically got completely shitfaced. This was after we had run the eight incidents I mentioned previously. We invited our friends from 3rd Marines Force Recon, with whom we shared space in a remote part of the Phu Bai Combat Base.

The bar was made of wholly scrounged materials, including an air conditioner. It was covered on the sides and along the rail with rolled and pleated Naugahyde. I have no idea where that came from, but I am sure we traded something really good for it.

As we could fix enemy explosive devices, stick grenades, mortar rounds and the like so the round and the fuse were inert, soldiers could take them home as souvenirs. We were not supposed to do this, but oh well; this got us access to all the materials we needed to build the bar.

As previously noted, one of the reasons people liked our bar was because we did not allow fights and made rowdy soldiers leave. There was a Recon man named Jim Dorr. He and his good friend, another Recon Marine, were going on R&R together. The night before they were supposed to leave, they got into fight at the enlisted men's club and Dorr—I swear to God—bit the guy's ear off.

The evening of the day Dorr got out of the brig, he came to our bar. He got staggering drunk and into an argument with our linebacker-sized Wisconsin farm boy clerk, Don Urquhart. When Dorr started to get off his bar stool, Don immediately hit him in the jaw, knocked him to floor, jumped on his chest, and began to beat the shit out of him, screaming, "You are not going to bite my fucking ear off!"

We woke up on New Year's Day badly hung over, hoping it would be a slow day, meaning no calls; this was not to be. The unit had four incidents that day. Tom Miller and I blew a dud French 50-mm mortar round that the Navy Support Activity Da Nang (NASD) had found in the ground near their Phu Bai area while digging a hole for a new latrine.

Jim Qualls and Rick Lanham did three jobs that day, including two fly-outs into the mountains above the floor of the A Shau Valley. One of them, involving a dud 500-pound bomb, kept them in the bush for fifteen hours. When they landed back at the 101st base at Camp Evans, they took care of a dud 81-mm illumination mortar round.

On January 2, there were five calls, three of which Paul Duffey and I handled. For the first, we drove to Camp Evans and a dud 81-mm HE mortar round that had landed in the perimeter wire while firing in support of a patrol outside the wire. Then we drove to the 101st's forward base at LZ Sally to investigate a crater at the "Play Pen," the base's chopper pad. This turned out to be from a Russian 107-mm rocket that landed there during an incoming attack.

While we were at Sally, Paul and I were called into the 2nd Brigade TOC and told that a patrol from "L" Company, 75th Rangers, had run into a dud 500-pound bomb while doing an air strike assessment. So, we jumped on a 101st Aviation Battalion chopper and flew to the site at coordinates YC 710050, deep in a mountainous area south of the A Shau Valley. We were on the ground for five hours, blew the bomb, and were extracted. First Sergeant Randles, Jim Qualls, Captain Breland, and Dave Becker handled the other two incidents; it was another typical day.

Here are the other calls I went on (other than those already discussed) during the last ten weeks of my tour in Phu Bai from January 5–March 27, 1970:

January 7—I drove with Dave Becker to Marine Combined Action Platoon 3-3-5 in a small village and blew a dud 500-pound bomb that had landed just outside of the village.

January 13—This call was with Paul Duffey and Chuck Watson. Chuck had been in-country only a few days and these were his first incidents. We handled four calls that day, including a dud 8-inch HE artillery projectile, a dud 40-mm HE grenade and two dud 500-pound bombs that had landed outside the perimeter of Camp Evans during an airstrike. When we blew them, the cloud and fireball that shot up into the air looked like a small nuke.

The fourth call was bad for Chuck. We went to the Phu Bai Graves Registration morgue to remove ordnance from two dead bodies. When they opened the first body bag, the stench was overwhelming. Paul and I were used to it, but Chuck turned green, not just because of the smell, but also because of the remains—the body was, essentially, missing all of the flesh from below the neck to just above the groin, exposing what was left of the man's organs and ribcage. I have to admit, even I was somewhat taken aback because when you looked at the man's face, it just seemed like he was sleeping.

January 14—Two calls with Tom Miller. First, we blew a dud 81-mm HE mortar round at Camp Evans. Then we drove north on QL 1 just east of the bridge near the village of Ap Uu Phuong, where we hooked up with a company of the 3rd Battalion, 187th Infantry Regiment, doing pacification work in this area.

This was another job that could have gotten either or both of us killed, since it was a small, unmarked French minefield of very old, rusted, Bouncing Betties. We identified and destroyed twenty-seven mines.

February 4—Tom Miller and I went to the village of Phú Lộc where a Marine CAP team was located and destroyed two LAW Rockets that had misfired and were stuck in the launchers.

February 5–7—The Tet Offensive of 1970. In three days, we ran twenty-seven calls—ten on the 5th, six on the 6th, and eleven on the 7th. These included the following:

Investigating an incoming round that exploded in an 8th Radio Research site at Phu Bai and started a fire—me, Captain Breland, and Chuck Watson.

Phú Lộc District Headquarters; booby traps—MSG Randles and Jim Qualls.

YD 621277—near the village of Ao Lai Bang, 15 km NW of Hue in the middle of nowhere; dud 155-mm HE artillery projectile—Dave Becker and Paul Duffey.

Back to 8th Radio Research with CID; clear building from fire for explosive ordnance—me and Watson

Fire Support Base Roy—25 miles south of Phu Bai on Highway 1, 5 miles south into the mountains—by jeep, booby-trapped truck—Qualls and Tom Miller.

Village of Phú Lộc —again south on Highway 1, about 20 miles this time; two misfired LAW 66mm anti-tank rockets—me and Miller.

Back to Roy—tanker truck with possible booby traps; negative—Captain Breland and Miller.

Camp Eagle, 101st; dud 40-mm HE grenade—Qualls and Watson.

YD 533260—outside the perimeter of Camp Evans, 101st; dud 250-pound bomb from airstrike—Becker and Duffey.

1st Battalion, 39th Field Artillery Regiment, Phu Bai Combat Base— another dud 40-mm HE grenade—me and Andy Breland.

Several years ago, I found a February 16, 1970, *Time Magazine* article entitled, "Inoffensive Tet." I was insulted when I saw this. The media believed that the Tet Offensive of 1968 was the Tet of all Tets, which is an ignorant and false belief. Anyone who was there, or who has read the archival materials, knows that the Tet of 1969 was much worse in terms of enemy attacks on U.S. and allied bases.

According to this article, the 1970 Tet was a "mini offensive," because the enemy had only attacked "70 cities and bases" that "were shelled or mortared [on the 5th] …" and only forty-four on the 6th. I do not know what war they covered during those three days, but it was not the one that many others, including my teammates and I, lived through (or not) from February 5–7, 1970.

During those three days, fifty-eight men from forty-three different units were killed in action from the DMZ to the Delta. That was not as bad as 1968 in terms of those KIA (464) or 1969 (364 dead), but to marginalize those fifty-eight men killed in the 1970 Offensive and to claim that only 114 attacks on cities and U.S. bases was somehow trivial really pisses me off.

February 8—Three calls that day, two with Tom Miller, one with Captain Breland. Tom and I drove out to a small spit of land sticking into the South China Sea just north of Da Nang. A Marine patrol had found dozens of abandoned 55-gallon drums filled with oil. No one knew how they got there, or who left them. We had to check each for booby traps, as well as the surrounding area. We found nothing, which was fine with us.

Then we drove to FSB Tomahawk, a 101st base, about 30 miles south of Phu Bai on Highway 1, located at the north end of the Hải Vân Pass. An 81-mm mortar round had landed short, just outside their perimeter and had become ineffectual. This was the same round— armed with the same fuse—that had exploded and almost killed me in the Qui Nhơn ammo dump nine months earlier; it was in the same shape, with the fuse plunger depressed and the firing pin impinged in the detonator.

I said nothing about this to Miller. Like the ammo dump dud, we moved it remotely with a lasso of commo wire we draped around the outside of the round, without touching it, and jerked the crap out of it. When it did not detonate, we placed a charge near it and blew it where it lay.

When we got back to Phu Bai, I had many drinks at our bar then told Miller what happened my last time with this particular piece of ordnance. Duffey and Watson were listening to my story, which no one at Phu Bai knew about, and their jaws hung open. They thought I was the luckiest person they had ever met. I think they were right. However, later, when Paul, Rod Wilkinson, Bobby Lynch, Andy Breland, and Chuck survived the Battle of Firebase Ripcord, we shared that experience equally.

February 9—Once, again, Captain Breland and I went on a combat assault with the Aero-Rifle Platoon from LZ Sally to reinforce a 1st of the 506th unit that had been hit the night before, and called in an airstrike near their perimeter. At first light, they found a dud 500-pound bomb 100 yards out. If it had detonated the night before, we would have been checking bodies for booby traps.

We flew into an area about 10 miles southeast of Camp Evans along the bank of the Song Bo River, northeast of the southern end of the A Shau Valley, an area of dense vegetation and forest. During the sixteen hours this incident lasted, and before we could destroy the bomb, incoming 60-mm mortars and automatic weapons fire hit us. After we blew the bomb, the same thing happened all over again. Both times, we were there with the grunts, returning fire at targets we could not see. It was another madhouse of bullets, grenades, and rocket propelled grenades.

It was LZ Sally all over again. Not only was I with Andy Breland, but I had no memory of it until I read the report. This "amnesia" has been a theme as I wrote this book and reviewed documents from the National Archives. Even now, reading these things, I ask myself, "Did this really happen?"

Our extraction chopper backed off and returned to LZ Sally; then, two Cobra gunships came in hard, fast and low, and shot the shit out of the area around our perimeter with 2.75-inch HE and WP rockets, mini-guns, and 40-mm HE grenades fired by a chopper-borne launcher mounted in the nose side-by-side with the mini-gun. At 10 p.m., we were finally extracted and, as we lifted off, the shooting started again. Our chopper made it out without being hit.

After Breland and I returned to Phu Bai, we drove straight to Sector "E" of the Base perimeter and blew a dud 40-mm grenade illumination round. We were finally done, that day, around midnight.

February 18—There were five incidents that day; Captain Breland and I handled them all. I had five weeks left in country. The first one, also in the bush SE of Camp Evans—jeez, would we ever get out of this AO—was to destroy a Cobra gunship that had gone down with HE, WP and armored piercing 2.75-inch rockets still in the pods, which had separated from the ship on impact.

We flew in, set many charges on the two pods, blew them, and flew back out. Then we returned to Camp Evans, and, before we could leave, handled four calls there. These included two dud 40-mm HE grenades in the perimeter wire and a dud Chinese grenade with a twenty-minute chemical-delay fuse that was about ten feet from the forty mills.

February 27—Wilkinson, Tom Miller and I drove out to an area near a small bridge on an unmarked road 5 miles southeast of Phu Bai to the crash site of an OV-1 aircraft. The Mohawk was a surveillance plane and had several types of radar for close-in observation and targeting for strike aircraft, naval gunfire, and helicopter gunships. They were also armed with 2.75-inch rockets and a .50-caliber machine gun mounted in a forward pod. This one was shot down; we were called in to check for booby traps, deal with the rockets and .50-caliber ammo flung all over the place in the crash.

On December 5, 2012, Tom Miller reminded me that when we arrived on the scene, the Vietnamese firefighters would not get near the fire because they were afraid that the rockets might detonate, or that the .50 ammo might start going off, which could have happened. Wilkie, Tom, and I took the fire hoses and put out the fire before checking and policing up the rockets and the ammunition.

After that incident, we returned to the base camp. Later, Wilkinson and I were called out to the Phu Bai Base perimeter to destroy two dud 40-mm HE grenades fired at enemy soldiers probing the wire the night before.

February 28—Paul and I drove way the hell out into nowhere to a Marine CAP Team to blow another dud 40-mm found after a fire fight with local VC.

March 3—Breland and I drive to the village of Ap Hien to disarm a dud VC satchel charge from an attack the night before.

March 7—Rod Wilkinson and I flew a combat assault with the 1st of the 501st, 101st Airborne, to YD 551034, dead bang into the mountains bordering the east end of the A Shau Valley, to blow a dud 500-pound bomb.

March 8—Watson and I responded to three calls, including a dud 40-mm and a misfired LAW rocket.

March 10—I took a call from a Marine CAP team. Captain Breland told me he did not want me in the bush during my last two weeks in country. I told him it was my decision and that I intended to do my share until I left. It was like when I came back from Okinawa instead of going home when the Tet of 1969 broke out.

Rod Wilkinson had reported to the unit four days earlier; this was his first serious event, though we had gone on a call into the A Shau three days earlier. The incident with Wilkinson was a bad one; it was really bad, one of the worst, most senseless during my tour. We drove to the Marine CAP team near the village of Thôn Khê Xa, about 15 miles northeast of Phu Bai, almost to the South China Sea.

When we arrived, a Marine staff sergeant told us they had a situation that was "fucked up beyond belief" and led us to a reinforced bunker in the middle of the village. He said, "If you go in there, be prepared to see something fucked up. We had a guy kill himself last night and … well, you'll see."

Rod and I entered the bunker, which was divided in half by plywood and reinforced by sandbags. A doorway on the left side of the wall led into the second room. Entering the room, we saw the Marine sitting in a chair, slumped over, with his back to us. Looking around, I saw blood and brains all over the place—the walls, the ceiling, the floor, everywhere.

Walking around the chair, I saw what had happened. It was all I could do not to puke, and I has seen plenty of really bad shit. Between his legs was an M-79 grenade launcher he had put under his chin and pulled the trigger, firing a HE round through his lower jaw. Here is the worst part—the round had failed to detonate, passed through his head and was sticking out of the top of his skull. Brain matter and skull fragments were everywhere.

We walked back outside. Wilkinson did not look good. I thought he was going to be sick. This was his first dead person since getting to the unit four days earlier; it could not have been a worse situation for your first serious incident. The Marine sergeant said, "What are you going to do?"

"I'm going to try and get that thing out of his head without killing myself and blowing the body all to hell." I had no idea how I was going to accomplish this.

Then, I walked to the jeep and got a 50-foot rope. I told Wilkinson to follow me back inside. We walked into the room with the dead Marine. I handed one end of the rope to Rod and looped the other end around the legs of the chair. I told Rod to pull the rope through the door and into the other room. I followed him. When we got around the corner of the wall dividing the two rooms, I pulled in the slack and told Wilkinson to get up against the wall.

I took a breath and jerked the rope as hard as I could. We heard the chair scratch across the floor. It went over with a crash, the body making a dull thud as it landed on top of the chair. We waited ten minutes to make sure the 40-mm round was not going to detonate, even though there was very little chance that it had armed in the distance between the end of the barrel and the top of the kid's head.

Rod and I walked back into room. When the Marine's body hit the floor, the 40-mm round had dislodged from his head and rolled across the bunker floor, coming to rest in a corner. I called for the CAP team's sergeant and asked him to remove the dead man's body, so I could destroy the round. After they took the body out, Rod and I placed a small charge of C-4 near the round with two minutes of time fuse and piled sandbags around it. I pulled the fuse lighter, and we left the bunker. The small "whump" told us the job was done.

Standing outside with the rest of the Marine platoon, lighting a cigarette, I thought, "This is a hell of a fucking way to end my tour." Maybe I should have listened to Captain Breland and not gone on missions those last two weeks. I tried to say something to the CAP team members who stood around looking at the body bag they had placed their friend in. What could I say? Realizing there was nothing to say, Wilkinson and I climbed in our jeep and headed back to Phu Bai. Neither of us spoke a word all the way back to the unit.

When Rod and I saw each other for the first time after thirty-four years in Florida in 2004, he said to my wife, "When I first got in country, your husband took good care of me." I am sure he was talking about the A Shau Valley and the CAP team event. This was a flattering statement from a guy who had been a grunt in the Marines in Korea and in EOD for fifteen years by the time we met in Vietnam.

March 11—I was down to thirteen days before I got to go home. Breland told me again that he did not want me going to the bush anymore. Everyone else was out on calls; the 101st called about a dud 40-mm grenade inside the perimeter of a patrol at the Phu Lu Bridge, north of Phu Bai on Highway 1. Breland looked at me and shrugged his shoulders; we handled the call. Duffey and Watson flew to another remote 101st site, deep in the A Shau, to blow a dud 8-inch HE artillery projectile found by a patrol while assessing an artillery raid at a nearby temporary LZ.

This time, I began to seriously arm myself, especially going to someplace unsafe, which was just about everywhere. I had my CAR-15 with two bandoliers of .223 ammo. I think there were seven pockets in each bandolier, so that was fourteen magazines (263 rounds). The magazine I always carried in the gun was a thirty-rounder I had gotten from a MACV adviser in Bong Son.

Plus, I was toting an M-79 grenade launcher and wore a waist belt with six HE grenades and three or four flechette rounds; those are the little darts they used at LZ Rifle to mow down the enemy. If I was going into the bush carrying a rucksack, I grabbed a LAW anti-tank rocket and strapped it to the top of my ruck frame. I was taking no fucking chances. I wanted to make sure I got out of there alive and not FUBAR in the process.

March 12—Dave Becker and I drove to a spot on a dirt road near the village of Thôn Khê Xa, about 10 miles NNE of Phu Bai, where the 27th Engineers had run into my old nemesis from the Qui Nhơn dump—an 81-mm HE mortar round with an M524 fuse; we destroyed it on the spot.

March 13—Watson and I went on two calls to the 101st's main base, Camp Eagle. The first was routine; we did a frag analysis of the incoming attack the night before and determined that at least three 122-mm rockets had impacted inside the perimeter and somehow did not kill anyone. The second incident was another 40-mm round stuck in the launcher; we were able to successfully remove it.

March 14—Watson and I drove to Camp Eagle and headed for the division Base Defense shop. The previous night, Eagle had been hit with about a dozen 122-mm rockets and they believed there were two duds. We went to the TOC of the 101st Aviation Battalion where we were informed that they thought they and the 4th Battalion, 77th Aerial Rocket Artillery—I talked about this unit's gunship firepower at the battle at Fire Support Base Rifle—had been hit with ten to twelve of the 122-mm rockets.

Chuck and I checked a bunch of the craters and recovered fragments of 122 casings that had Russian and Czechoslovakian markings. Then we moved on to the area of the suspected duds. The first crater was behind the 4/77th's officer's club and we found that the round had detonated. The second crater was behind the fire station and the chopper pad of the 377th Artillery Battalion. We determined that the incoming rocket had hit an engineer stake, "shearing off the top part of the DKZ-B nose fuze," which we found on the ground. It appeared that the rocket warhead and motor assembly had penetrated the ground, leaving a hole of entry about three feet deep and a foot across.

We got shovels from the 377th Artillery and dug a hole another 3 feet deep and 4 feet across. We had found nothing to show that the rocket had detonated, so we got a front-end loader from the 377th and a mine detector from 101st Division Artillery. We swept the area with the mine detector and got a positive reading about 12 feet down.

We cleared the area and briefed the driver of the front-end-loader on the hazards of the 122—it still contained the base-detonating, graze-sensitive fuse. He asked a few questions and then began to move the dirt. After three more hours, and having moved 10 square yards by 5 feet deeper, nothing was found and the mine detector was giving us negative results. We decided that no further work with the front-end-loader was going to accomplish anything and we released the driver. We went back to the 101st Artillery and they called 27th Engineers and laid on a bulldozer for 8 a.m. the next day. Chuck and I returned to Phu Bai.

The next morning, Chuck and I, with the addition of Tom Miller, returned to Eagle. The bulldozer was loaded on a lowboy and we proceeded to the site. We got negative results with the mine detector, so the dozer operator went to work. After three hours, and enlarging the hole to 25 feet in depth, I halted the operation. We made one last sweep with the mine detector and then had the hole filled in. Could the round have gone in deeper? Sure. Since we found no frag, or the rocket motor, it could well have been a dud. If it was, I figured it was highly unlikely it was ever going to detonate.

The daily incident log shows that we spent twenty-eight man-hours on this job, not including the drive time from Phu Bai and back over the two days. I decided to go into detail on this event to show how much effort an EOD team would go to in order to make sure our fellow soldiers were going to be safe.

Later on March 14, after Chuck and I returned from Eagle, CPT Breland and Watson went to the 2nd of the 501st area at Phu Bai and it was another 40-mm grenade launcher with the round stuck in the barrel. It was the same result as the day before, and that was not the end of the 40-mm thing.

March 20—So, Watson and I got a call from the Phu Bai Base Defense to come to a bunker on the eastern perimeter of the base. It was another 40-mm grenade launcher with a round stuck in the tube. I was beginning to wonder if the rounds were somehow causing this problem, like maybe they were misshapen. Anyway, it was a different day, but the same shit.

March 21—Two days left in country. Watson and I drove ten miles up Highway 1 to a bridge where a patrol of the 1st of the 327th had run into some ordnance in a trench 20 feet off the road in dense brush. Apparently, an ARVN unit that used to guard the bridge had left behind a bunch of ammo they were too lazy to cart off.

What we found and destroyed could have provided dozens of landmines, satchel charges and grenades for the enemy. There were three HE 81-mm mortar rounds, fourteen 105-mm HE artillery projectiles, and one variable time fuse. We piled it all up and set our charges. The grunts walked down the road quite a distance in each direction, shut down Highway 1, and we blew the whole pile.

March 22—One day to go. Rod Wilkinson and I flew out, way the hell out, into the dense mountains southeast of Phu Bai and about 25 miles SSE from Camp Eagle. This would be very close to Rifle. There, we joined up with a company of the 1st of the 502nd which had been in heavy contact with the NVA the night before.

In the middle of their defensive position was an 81-mm mortar tube. I was afraid to ask what was wrong. Sure enough, there was an HE round stuck in the tube; this was the fourth time in ten months. It was armed with an M-524 fuse, as in the famous Qui Nhơn ammo dump mortar round.

Unlike the other two, this fuse still had the bore-riding pin in it so, theoretically, it was not armed—theoretically. The mortarmen had apparently forgotten to remove the pin, which is probably why it was stuck in the tube. I told the grunts we could save the tube. We took the tube and placed it on a 60-degree angle, launch end down on a pile of sandbags we piled in a pyramid. I knew that what I was about to do would amaze Wilkinson, who had only been in country about a month at that point, because I was going to use a trick I had learned from Dave Becker when he removed a stuck round from a 105-mm howitzer tube.

I asked the infantry guys to bring me several canteens of water and they did. Then I poured the water down the high end of the tube until it was full of water behind the round. I took a no. 10 electric blasting cap, unrolled the wires, and stuck it in the center of the tube with about a quarter-inch of the cap out of the water. I told Wilkinson to get me some electrical tape from the bag, which he did. I wrapped tape around the cap, then pulled the ends over and down the side of the mortar tube, solidly suspending the cap in the water.

We ran out the wires from the cap and attached them to a small roll of blasting wire, rolled it out, then got behind a nearby tree. I told everyone to get behind something, yelled, "Fire in the hole!", and cranked the handle of the blasting machine. There was a little pop, water went flying everywhere and the round slid out of the barrel and lay on the ground. The troopers in the mortar unit were amazed; they thought we were gods because we had saved their gun. We blew the round and went back to Phu Bai.

March 23—Last day in Phu Bai. Jim Qualls and I went on two calls to the MPs and to the 85th Evac Hospital for a roll of detonating cord and 410 rounds of M-16 ammo. This was a good way to call it quits—nothing dangerous, just a typical day at the ranch.

At noon, I said my goodbyes, which were very difficult, gave Paul, Tom, and Chuck big hugs, got on my chopper, and I was gone. As it lifted off from the pad, I glanced down at the Phu Bai Combat Base with very mixed feelings.

Part of me was glad, even grateful, to be getting out of there alive; part of me felt guilty. I was abandoning my friends. I had a momentary thought of asking the pilot to turn back and drop me off; I would go down to personnel, extend my tour again, and screw nuclear weapons school.

I had this feeling that if I stayed there, none of my teammates would be hurt or killed. At the same time, I knew this was nonsense. There was nothing I could do, or control, that would stop these things from happening if they were destined to happen. After I left, thank God, no one was killed, though most of those men were wounded at Fire Support Base Ripcord in July, 1970, during a twenty-three-day siege.

The 287th was the only Army EOD team in Vietnam that never lost a man killed in action. I do not know if that means we were all really good at what we did, or were just plain lucky. We were at Fire Support Base Rifle, Fire Support Base Davis, Hamburger Hill, and the Siege of Fire Support Base Ripcord; it is a pretty amazing statistic that we all survived.

Some might say that God was watching out for us, but I choose not to believe that. One thing I left Vietnam with was the thought that if there was a God, how could the things I saw have happened? How could a benevolent God, who is supposed to hear our prayers, have abandoned us in so many ways?

I looked back one more time, then Phu Bai was a distant place, in the physical sense. Even today, it is never that far from my thoughts. The time I spent there looms as large as any time I have spent in my life. Though it was only four months out of sixty-nine years, that is how it seems to me. There are times I feel I can reach out and touch what I had there. I still see the hooches, the sidewalks, the bunkers, the dusty streets; I can smell the stench of burning shit.

The feel of climbing on a chopper, lifting off, heading for some hellhole in the A Shau Valley, or a firebase in the plains along the coast that no one except us who were there remembers, is still with me, with the sound of the chopper's blades thunking as background noise, while those inside sit silently lost in our own thoughts, wondering if this mission would be our last.

18

Going Home and Afterward

March 23, 1970—eighteen months in Vietnam and I was going home. During 119 days with the 287th, I went on 175 incidents, had 14.5 hours of combat flight time, and went on four combat assaults. The team handled a total of 714 incidents during the same 119 days, making an average of six per day

My chopper flew me to Da Nang, where I caught a C-130 to Biên Hòa. Friends in the EOD unit there picked me up, and we went out and got staggeringly drunk, largely because our friend, Bob Whitted, had recently been killed by a booby trap on the base perimeter. It had been planted by U.S. soldiers to protect their drug stash. Bob had come to Qui Nhơn on a temporary duty assignment to help clean up the ammo dump; everyone liked the guy.

The next morning, they took me to Tân Sơn Nhất where I boarded a plane with several hundred other soldiers. I did not stop at the Tân Sơn Nhất drive-in, as when I first landed. I did not feel much like a burger and fries. I did not feel much of anything.

The flight home was very different from the one coming over in 1968. Tom Allen and I had flown out of Oakland with a bunch of infantry types; on my flight back, I was not paying that much attention—they could have all been cooks, for all I cared. Going over was like a party; everyone was laughing, talking about the girl back home and the cows down on the farm.

I sat by myself and did not talk to anyone. I was glad that one of the few vacant seats was the one next to me. It was not like a party. It was palpably different, and painful. There was little conversation, just kind of a buzz, as people talked about leaving that shithole. Everyone was in a daze, or like they were just waking up after being asleep for a year, or, like me, longer.

When the plane lifted off and began to climb, a loud cheer and clapping broke out for about thirty seconds. I did not cheer or clap. I was just glad to be leaving alive and relatively intact unlike many others. After that, it was pretty much dead silence all the way to Oakland; at least that is how I remember it.

I was lost in my own world, not sure I was ready to go back to the States.

I felt that guilt again, for not having stayed longer. I wondered what my teammates were doing—were they okay, did they miss me as much as I missed them? I wondered if they were safe, if they would stay that way. That was a stretch.

While I was in Vietnam, from September 4, 1968, through March 23, 1970, 16,820 soldiers died there. I have no idea how many tens of thousands more were wounded.

After I got back, they gave me two Bronze Stars, one for meritorious achievement in ground operations against hostile forces, the other with a "V" Device for heroism for the Fire Support Base Davis event.

People ask how I was able to live with what went on all around me every day, sometimes every hour. Sometimes, every second of every minute. This is what I tell them.

One day, about a month before I left Vietnam, Paul Duffey and I went to a small village several clicks outside the Phu Bai wire. A Marine CAP team stationed there had found something, I do not remember what, probably another booby trap or old, rusty French Bouncing Betties in the rice fields.

Whatever it was, Paul and I did our thing and headed back to base camp in the jeep. It had gotten to the point that, despite the danger of ambush, we left our rifles and a 40-mm grenade launcher in their racks. We were driving along the two-track road from the village, when we came to a bluff overlooking the Phu Bai base camp.

The sun was going down and the camp looked peaceful, almost like any town back home. Vehicles moved down the streets, lights on, returning to their "homes" or leaving for their "night jobs." There was the soft glow of streetlights and people walked from one place to another—going to eat, going to have a drink, or going to the movies, even though most of them carried weapons.

I stopped the jeep and pulled out a cigarette. Paul and I smoked as we watched the sun go down. I said, "You know, we're on our way home from work. It's just like the States."

Paul looked at me as if I was nuts and said, "What the fuck are you talking about?"

I turned and pointed down at the base camp and said, "Look, if we were home in the States, we'd get up in the morning, have breakfast, pack our briefcase and drive to work. When work was done, we'd drive home, maybe stop for a drink, get home, have dinner, shoot the shit, play some cards, maybe go to the club, come home and go to bed."

Paul was still looking at me as if I was babbling, and maybe I was. Then I said, "Paul, this is no different. We get up in the morning and have breakfast. Instead of packing a briefcase, we pack our explosives bags and ruck sacks, pick up our rifles and a shitload of ammo and either drive or fly off to work. Most days, we do our job, drive or fly home, get home, have a few drinks, eat dinner, go to bed. It is the same. Shit, the only difference is that, over here, people are trying to kill us."

As I already said, the most amazing thing about the 287th is the fact that it was the only Army EOD team in Vietnam that never had a man killed. Many of my teammates were wounded, some seriously. Paul Duffey, Chuck Watson, Bobby Lynch, Captain Breland, and Rod Wilkinson survived the siege at Firebase Ripcord in July 1970. I feel guilty that I was not there with them.

Rod and Chuck were blown up when a 120-mm mortar round hit the tactical operations center. Chuck was pulled from the wreckage fairly quickly, but Rod was buried under tons of debris. The 101st called the unit and told the team that Rod had been KIA. Several hours later, they found him, still alive, as they dug through the debris searching for the body of the hill commander, Lt-Col. Andre C. Lucas, who eventually was awarded the Medal of Honor.

As Chuck Watson carried Rod to the med-evac chopper, he tossed him on board and tried to return to the area under fire to get something. Just as the chopper was lifting off, Rod grabbed Chuck by the belt and pulled him into the chopper. Right after that, an 82-mm mortar round detonated on the exact spot where Chuck had been standing.

Both of them, along with Paul Duffey, Bobby Lynch and the CO, Andy Breland, were decorated for their heroic actions during the siege. Lynch was wounded three times in one day. Many of the team's actions during the siege are recounted in Keith Nolan's great book, *Ripcord: Screaming Eagles Under Siege, Vietnam 1970.*

Wilkinson was eventually medevacked when he re-injured his ankle after Ripcord. I recounted all of this in the last chapter, but my love for these people compels me to say it all again, because I am so grateful they all made it home.

The EOD training facility and our memorial are now located at Eglin Air Force Base in Ft. Walton Beach, Florida. In May 2004, eight former members of the 287th reunited at Eglin for the formal inaugural ceremonies of the memorial.

Later, in September 2004, we got together again at Chuck Watson's place in Valparaiso, Indiana. This time, Rick Lanham and Craig Harmon joined us. I am sad to say that Craig passed away in August 2013. After getting together at Chuck's, Rod Wilkinson and I went on to the National EOD Association convention in Colorado Springs where we got together with Andy Breland, our former commanding officer.

Joe Jimenez started an organization called "Vietnam EOD Veterans Association," and we had a reunion in August 2007, in St. Louis. Eighty Vietnam EOD men from all over the country came. It was a joyous time, seeing men I thought I would never see again after Vietnam. Tony Jordan, an Australian EOD man who hung out with the 287th for a few weeks, came from the Outback to spend five days with us, sick as a dog the entire time. It is a fraternity like few others.

A couple of months before the reunion, I told Joe that I did not think I would be able to make it because of financial considerations. We just could not afford it. Two hours after we had talked, I got a call from Rod Wilkinson.

He said, "What the hell is this that you won't be in St. Louis?" I explained the situation, and he said, "You have to come. If it were not for you, none of this would be happening. If you hadn't tracked all of us down, Joe wouldn't have gone to the next level. There would be no organization, and we wouldn't be going to St. Louis." I understood all of that, but there really was not much I could do about it. We chatted a little longer and then hung up.

Two hours later, Rod's wife, Karen, called and asked, "Where is the nearest airport to where you live?" I did not think about why she was asking and told her that it was Redmond, Oregon. An hour later, she called again. "Check your email," she said. I did and found an email from Northwest Airlines. Karen and Rod had bought my ticket so I could go to the reunion. I started crying. That is one of the most wonderful things anyone has ever done for me. Joe got a hotel room at a huge discount for me and Paul Duffey. Whatever was not covered, Paul paid for. It was a truly humbling experience.

During the ceremonies at Eglin in May 2004, six names—all Army—were added to the bronze plaques at our memorial. They were killed doing their job in the Iraq War. Three other names had been previously added in 2003 for

Army EOD men killed in Afghanistan. One name added in 2004 was that of the first female EOD specialist killed in combat.

Since then, many more names have been added, and as of 2016, we have lost approximately 150 EOD personnel in Iraq, Afghanistan, and the Horn of Africa, in little more than fifteen years. That is 108 more than we lost during the ten years of our war.

Since World War II, we have had more than 150 Army people killed, most of them in combat. EOD is a small field. We lost our first woman in Iraq, SSG Kimberly Voelz, in December 2003. Every loss is personal, and even if you did not know the person, you feel like you did. This is still true for those of us who have been out of EOD for more than forty years when we read about another loss.

The first woman EOD tech killed was SSG Nancy Oszakewski, along with two EOD men, in August 1980. They were killed trying to dispose of illegal fireworks seized by the Border Patrol on the Mexican Border near San Diego. In Vietnam, between May 1965 and January 1973, we lost forty-two men. Recently, the Air Force also lost a woman tech in Iraq, and another one had her arms blown off.

During "The War," all branches of the service had EOD teams in country. The Army teams were like the ones I was on. The Air Force men handled incidents in and around their bases; the Navy handled the underwater jobs. The Marines were like us, supporting their own combat units and ammo dumps.

The Air Force lost the first four EOD men in Vietnam when a B-57 waiting to take off, exploded at Biên Hòa during a mortar attack on May 16, 1965, and caused a chain of secondary explosions. They were killed trying to disarm a 500-pound bomb. The Air Force also lost the last man in the War on January 16, 1973.

Among the eight 287th men who met in May 2004 in Florida, half of us had the Purple Heart. Rod Wilkinson had two. Paul Duffey and Tom Miller got the Soldier's Medal for non-combat heroism. They cleared a road and building full of damaged and burning ordnance from helicopters that had been hit during an incoming attack on the flight line at a 101st base so that fire trucks could get into the area. There were more than 1,000 rockets in the burning building. How that was non-combat is beyond me, and them.

Every single one of us has multiple decorations for heroism, valor, gallantry, or meritorious achievement during either ground or air combat operations.

When I look back, at sixty-nine years old, my time with the men of the 287th was the best 119 days I could have asked for.

I do not mean to say that the year I spent in Qui Nhơn was not great as far as teammates go, but with the exception of Arnie Neiderhofer, Doug Rhodes, and Roger McCormack, I had lost contact with the rest of those men I served with. Recently, I have been back in touch with two of the men from the 184th, Jim Young and Jerry Culp.

Mike Lizak, Lee Miller, Larry Brooks, Roy Judkins, Bill Petersen, Tom Nutter, and Ron Carlton are dead. I saw Doug at the St. Louis reunion, as previously mentioned, and it was like the first time I saw the 287th men; it was as if we had just been together the previous week. We spent five days together in Alabama at the National EOD Association/Vietnam EOD Veterans Association convention in 2007. I shot the worst round of golf in the history of the world with Doug and Roger.

Also, in St. Louis, Dave Becker, who had been with us at Phu Bai, showed up with his lovely wife, Nita. Dave spent a year in Iraq in 2003–2004 with a civilian EOD contractor blowing up Saddam Hussein's ammo dumps. He was in his late sixties when he went there. Arnie Neiderhofer had done the same thing, and he was almost seventy.

Joe Tremain, Boyd Kidd, Dennis Vesper, and Merrill Prange, men I had been with at the 25th in An Khê, managed to make it to St. Louis as well; it was wonderful to see all of them. Prange lost a foot to a mine explosion. In fact, I met about fifty guys I had never known—all of whom served with EOD teams in Vietnam—and within five minutes of meeting each of them, it was as if I had known them all these past forty-plus years. Prange had never gotten his Purple Heart. I was able to track down the medical records and had his military record corrected to show the award.

Thirty years ago, I tracked down Roger McCormack from the 184th in London, where he was still married to Christina, the British woman he had met while on embassy EOD duty at the British Embassy in Turkey. He was running a small theater, something I found hard to believe. Plus, he had an actual British accent. Now, he is back in the States. He came to Alabama for the 2007 convention; it was fantastic to see him and we talk, now, almost every week. He came out and spent a week with me just before I went to Afghanistan in 2009.

I became the *de facto* gatherer of names as we continued to organize the Vietnam EOD Veterans Associations. Thanks to several other Vietnam EOD men, I have access to unit documents with names, some with Social Security numbers. So far, I have collected almost 791 names and have located 221 of the men who served with Army EOD teams in Vietnam.

Sad to say, I have also learned that 200 of the names are now deceased, almost 40 percent of those who were alive when the War ended. Maybe that statistic is not significant. The average age of these 200 men when they died is sixty years. Several died from Agent Orange-related diseases; at least two committed suicide. I would like to know how many more died from exposure to herbicides, but will probably never be able to find out.

My friend, John Claffy, suggested that there may be other reasons why so many of us have died so young. We were not only exposed to herbicides, but our occupation brought us into regular contact with many toxic agents. In my own case, as with many others, there was continuous exposure to chemical and biological warfare agents for months, sometimes years, at a time. Then, there were those who were regularly around nuclear weapons or other radioactive materials.

Plastic explosives, our primary tool in Vietnam and other locations around the world where EOD teams do their work, also present hazards. C-4 was the primary explosive used in Vietnam to destroy ordnance, like the hundreds of tons from the Qui Nhơn ammo dump, as well as duds and IEDs we handled in the field.

The main ingredient of C-4 is an explosive called RDX (cyclonite or cyclotrimethylenetrinitramine). The plasticizer is diethylhexyl or dioctyl sebacate; the binder usually is polyisobutylene. The names of these compounds should tell you something, mainly that you know you would not deliberately ingest them.

The Carcinogen and Pesticide Branch of the OSHA Analytical Laboratory had this to say about the toxicity of RDX:

> The clinical manifestations referable to the central nervous system of nausea, vomiting, convulsions and unconsciousness seen in the workers paralleled those previously reported in animals by von Oettingen and Sunderman … Human illness results from repeated exposures via the respiratory and gastrointestinal tracts and by skin absorption.

When all is said and done, this has been my story. I am not sure what I accomplished with all this, but I feel better putting it down, trying to get across what Vietnam means to me and, I am sure, to many of my brothers and sisters who served.

Like I told my son, I see myself primarily as a soldier. Most people will probably not understand that; some might even think it a ridiculous thing to say, since those days were more than forty years ago. Yet if you served, and particularly if you served in combat, you understand what I am talking about.

Epilogue

It is funny—when I started writing this book, I thought it was about one thing. I had started an earlier version in 2004 and deleted it; it was not what I wanted to say.

Now, after writing this version, I realize that what I wrote at the beginning does not accurately describe what I ended up saying. After writing this, and taking a careful look at myself while in my addictions treatment program, I now see that it is about something altogether different.

As I have previously mentioned, one of my VA counselors had asked me in 2002 when I was "going to get off mission." I thought I knew what he meant. Only recently did I understand the true meaning of this question. It was not giving up adrenalin-pumping jobs that helped me maintain the rush that any combat soldier will tell you exists when you are up to your ass in shit and people are trying to kill you.

It actually means getting off the real mission—the War itself. That has been my mission these past forty-seven-plus-years; I was staying in the War, not being willing to move beyond it.

By saying that the War was not the problem, and that it was the drugs, the alcohol, or both, I was denying that it was me that was the problem. This was what kept me on the offensive. I saw people trying to help me as the enemy; my job was to save myself from them. If I could disarm them with bullshit, I could ignore them and move on to the next mission.

I am doing my best to show my son how to live, not that he is doing a bad job of it because he is not. He is doing a much better job at thirty-four than I did at that age. He might not think so right now, but he is. I have been places and done things he has not. I have seen things that I hope to God he never will. I think I still have some things to teach him and hope, despite my shortcomings when he was young, that he will be willing to listen. Moving past the War, I hope, will give me the ability to do this.

Remembering all the names, where they were, what happened to me and others I never knew has become something I want to do. One reason I decided to track down the 287th guys was to see how each of us had turned out after spending those miserable, but life-defining months in that God-forsaken war. It is the same reason Joe Jimenez and I decided to set up the reunion in St. Louis.

All of us have been professionally successful in our lives. Many continued to serve and retired from the military. Others went into civilian EOD work for private contractors who did work for the government, and many of the retired military men were doing the same thing. Those of us that went into non-EOD related fields have done well for ourselves.

Writing this has been painful at times, a joy at others. I am not sure that it has given me any real sense of closure, but it has helped. Getting all of this organized, putting down my thoughts, has allowed me to look at the events in a way that finally seems nonthreatening. At first, I thought that maybe this was not a good idea; that it would stir up more issues I really did not need affecting my life. That has not been the case.

The War will always be a mystery to me. Unlike the cases I worked on as an investigator, this is one mystery I do not intend to solve. I hear people say things, and I read things others have written, about how we could have won, why we did not win and on and on. Others claim we actually did win. My response? Win what? What did we win? In the end, who really gives a fuck besides those of us who were there?

At the end of the movie *Hamburger Hill*, they roll a poem, of sorts, written by Major Michael Davis O'Donnell. He was a pilot with the 170th Aviation Company who, on March 24, 1970, was killed trying to rescue a Special Forces reconnaissance team. He died on the same day I left Vietnam.

If you are able,
save them a place
inside of you
and save one backward glance
when you are leaving

for the places they can
no longer go.
Be not ashamed to say
you loved them,
though you may
or may not have always.
Take what they have left
and what they have taught you
with their dying
and keep it with your own.
And in that time
when men decide and feel safe
to call the war insane,
take one moment to embrace
those gentle heroes
you left behind.

That says it all about what is important to most of us who survived. If you are reading this, I hope it had as much meaning for you as it did for me as I wrote it. Peace.

In Memoriam

Name	Rank	Date
Austin, James Earl "Duke"	MSG	2/18/71
Baker II, Charles Oakes	SFC	6/15/68
Barnwell, Jackie Wayne	MSG	2/19/71
Beck, John Robert	SSG	8/30/68
Berry, Ralph Thomas	SSG	1/31/68
Black, Lewis David	SP6	7/18/68
Brosius, Donald Edward	MSG	7/19/68
Bowman, Paul Barkley	CPT	1/31/70
Bunch, Claude Marvin	TSGT	5/15/65
Calhoun, Donald Eugene	SGM	4/10/68
Condon, Robert Eugene	LCDR	1/18/68
Cook, Jr., Marvin	CPT	1/26/69
Corkern, Jerry Wayne	SP4	11/26/66
Farmer, James Dale	TSGT	1/16/73
Fetty, Clarence Edward	SSG	3/10/69
Fidiam, Jr., Aaron Gregory	TSGT	5/16/65
Fischer, George Arthur	CPT	4/1/68
Hubbard, Jr., David Lee	SSG	5/16/65
Izard, Jr., Biddle Carrol "BC"	SFC	6/19/68
Johndro, Rodney George	SSG	8/6/70
Jones, James Walter	CPT	8/30/68

Age	Unit
39	3rd Ord. Bn. (EOD Section)
34	85th Ord. Det. (EOD)
36	59th Ord. Det. (EOD)
24	H&MS-17, 1st MAW (EOD)
37	7th AF, 303rd MMS (EOD)
33	184th Ord. Bn. (EOD Section)
39	25th Ord. Det. (EOD)
26	HQ&HQ Co., 25t Inf. Div.
45	13th AF, 34th AB Sqdn. (EOD)
37	25th Ord. Det. (EOD)
33	USNAVFORV, UDT-12, TF 116
38	III MAF, Prov. Serv. Bn. (EOD)
21	133rd Ord. Det. (EOD)
38	7th AF, AF Mobile EOD
25	III MAF, Sup Bn, Ammo Co. (EOD)
30	13th AF, 34th AB Sqdn (EOD)
30	3rd Ord. Bn. (EOD Section)
27	13th AF, 34th AB Sqdn (EOD)
47	MACV CMEC
26	269th Ord. Det. (EOD)
48	H&MS-17, 1st MAW (EOD)

Kekel, Jerry Edward	SSG	11/29/69
McFayden, Bruce Searight	LTJG	1/17/69
McFeron, Ernest	CPT	5/16/65
McKinley, Paul Blount	SP6	8/6/70
McWhinney, Jr., Harry DeWitt	SP5	1-/25/71
Melady, Richard Raphael	TM1	1/17/69
Metcalf, Edward Walter	MSG	5/22/71
Milton, Richard Dwayne	TSGT	4/7/72
Moore, Melbern Dean	SP5	11/22/67
Morrison, Gene Francis	SSGT	6/3/68
Nelson, Leon Grover	SP6	7/1/67
Payne, Sr., Louis "Lou"	SSG	1/9/71
Peterson, James William	CPT	5/22/71
Robbins, Charles Lester	MSG	2/15/67
Sicilia, Briggs Kinney "Joe"	CPT	1/1/69
Smith, Frederick Phillip	CPT	2/13/71
Spillane, Cornelius Vincent	MSG	8/16/68
Vasquez, Jesus Roberto	SGT	1/30/68
Vick, William Leon	CWO4	8/30/68
Winningham, Jerry Lynn	PR1	2/25/68
Whitted, Sr., Robert Albin	SSG	2/7/70

25	42nd Ord. Det. (EOD)
26	USNAVPAC, EODT 33
30	13th AF, 33rd AB Sqdn (EOD)
28	269th Ord. Det. (EOD)
21	170th Ord. Det. (EOD)
30	USNAVPAC, EODT 33
39	44th Ord. Det. (EOD)
41	7th AF, 432nd MMS (EOD)
35	191st Ord. Bn. (EOD Section)
29	III MAF, Sup Bn, Ammo Co. (EOD)
30	3rd Ord. Bn. (EOD Section)
44	184th Ord. Bn. (EOD Section)
24	44th Ord. Det. (EOD)
31	85th Ord. Det. (EOD)
31	170th Ord. Det. (EOD)
34	HQ & HQ Co., 1st Cav. Div.
44	Army Spt Cd Da Nang, 1st Log.
20	III MAF, Sup Bn, Ammo Co. (EOD)
44	H & MS 17, 1st MAW (EOD)
30	USNAVPAC, EODT 15
21	42nd Ord. Det. (EOD)